Evo Morales and the
Movimiento al Socialismo
in Bolivia:
The First Term in Context,
2006–2010

Edited by Adrian J. Pearce

INSTITUTE FOR THE STUDY OF THE
A M E R I C A S

UNIVERSITY OF LONDON · SCHOOL OF ADVANCED STUDY

British Library Cataloguing-in-Publication Data
A catalogue record for this book is available from the British Library

ISBN 978 1 900039 99 4

INSTITUTE FOR THE STUDY OF THE
A M E R I C A S
UNIVERSITY OF LONDON · SCHOOL OF ADVANCED STUDY

Institute for the Study of the Americas
School of Advanced Study
University of London
Senate House
London WC1E 7HU

Telephone: 020 7862 8870
Fax: 020 7862 8886

Email: americas@sas.ac.uk
Web: www.americas.sas.ac.uk

For Willem Assies

21 July 1954–22 May 2010

Contents

Bolivia: main political and geographical features

List of Figures, Map and Tables

Acronyms and Abbreviations

ACFO   Asociación de Conjuntos del Folklore de Oruro (Association of Folklore Troupes of Oruro)

ADN   Acción Democrática Nacionalista (Nationalist Democratic Action)

ALBA   Alternativa Bolivariana para América Latina y el Caribe (Bolivarian Alternative for Latin America and the Caribbean — Alianza Bolivariana para los Pueblos de Nuestra América since June 2009)

ASP   Asamblea por la Soberanía de los Pueblos (Assembly for the Sovereignty of the Peoples)

ATPDEA   Andean Trade Promotion and Drug Eradication Act

CCSF   Comité de Coordinación de las Seis Federaciones (Coordinating Committee of the Six Federations)

CNE   Corte Nacional Electoral (National Electoral Court)

COB   Central Obrera Boliviana (Bolivian Labour Central)

CONALDE   Comité Nacional de Defensa de la Democracia (National Committee for the Defence of Democracy)

CONDEPA   Consciencia de Patria (Consciousness or Conscience of the Fatherland)

COMIBOL   Corporación Minera de Bolivia (Bolivian Mining Corporation)

CPE   Constitucíon Política del Estado (National Political Constitution)

CPN   Comisión Política Nacional (National Political Commission)

CSUTCB   Confederación Sindical Unica de Trabajadores Campesinos de Bolivia (Unified Syndical Confederation of Peasant Workers of Bolivia)

GDP   Gross Domestic Product

FARC   Fuerzas Armadas Revolucionarias de Colombia (Revolutionary Armed Forces of Colombia)

FCT   Federación de Cocaleros del Trópico (Federation of Coca-Growers of the Tropics [of Cochabamba])

FSB   Falange Socialista Boliviana (Bolivian Socialist Falange)

FTAA	Free Trade Area of the Americas
IMF	International Monetary Fund
IPSP	Instrumento Político por la Soberanía de los Pueblos (Political Instrument for the Sovereignty of the Peoples)
IU	Izquierda Unida (United Left)
LPP	Ley de Participación Popular (Law of Popular Participation)
MAS	Movimiento al Socialismo (Movement Towards Socialism)
MIP	Movimiento Indígena Pachakuti (Pachakuti Indigenous Movement)
MIR	Movimiento de Izquierda Revolucionaria (Movement of the Revolutionary Left)
MNR	Movimiento Nacionalista Revolucionario (Nationalist Revolutionary Movement)
MRTK	Movimiento Revolucionario Túpaq Katari (Túpaq Katari Revolutionary Movement)
MSM	Movimiento Sin Miedo (Without Fear Movement)
NFR	Nueva Fuerza Republicana (New Republican Force)
PCB	Partido Comunista Boliviano (Bolivian Communist Party)
PODEMOS	Poder Democrático y Social (Social and Democratic Power)
PPB	Plan Progreso para Bolivia (Progress Plan for Bolivia)
TCO	Tierras Comunitarias de Origen (Originary Community Lands)
UDP	Unidad Democrática Popular (Democratic Popular Unity)
UN	Unidad Nacional (National Unity)
UMOPAR	Unidad Móvil de Patrullaje Rural (Rural Patrol Mobile Unit)
UNASUR	Unión de Naciones Suramericanas (Union of South American Nations)
UNDP	United Nations Development Programme
USAID	United States Agency for International Development
WOLA	Washington Office on Latin America
YPFB	Yacimientos Petrolíferos Fiscales Bolivianos (Bolivian State Oilfields)

Notes on Contributors

Willem Assies was a senior researcher at the Wageningen University Department of Environmental Sciences in the Netherlands. Between 2005 and 2008 he co-ordinated the project, *The Mystery of Legal Failure? A critical, comparative examination of the potential of legalization of land assets in developing countries for achieving real legal certainty*, at the Van Vollenhoven Institute of Leiden University. Previously, he was a lecturer-researcher at El Colegio de Michoacán in Zamora, Michoacán, Mexico, and also a researcher at the Department of Sociology and Anthropology of Law, University of Amsterdam, and at Amsterdam's Center for Study and Documentation of Latin America (CEDLA). He also gave guest lectures at various academic institutions throughout Latin America and Europe and was author or co-author of a dozen books and more than 50 essays in edited collections and articles in international journals. Willem Assies died on 22 May 2010.

John Crabtree is a research associate of the Latin American Centre, Oxford University. His main area of expertise is in the contemporary politics of the Andean region. His most recent books include: *Unresolved Tensions: Bolivia Past and Present* (Pittsburgh University Press, 2008, co-edited with Laurence Whitehead) and *Making Institutions Work in Peru: Democracy Development and Inequality since 1980* (Institute for the Study of the Americas, London, 2006). In 2005, he published *Patterns of Protest: Politics and Social Movements in Bolivia* (Latin America Bureau). He holds a master's degree from Liverpool University and a doctorate from Oxford Brookes University.

James Dunkerley is a professor of politics at Queen Mary University of London. He served as Director of the University of London's Institute of Latin American Studies from 1998 to 2004, and of the Institute for the Study of the Americas from 2004–8. In 2009 he was Andrés Bello Professor at New York University's King Juan Carlos I Center. Amongst his books are: *Rebellion in the Veins. Political Struggle in Bolivia, 1952–82 (1984)*; *Power in the Isthmus. A Political History of Modern Central America* (1988); *Political Suicide in Latin America* (1992); *Americana. The Americas in the World around 1850* (2000); *Orígenes del poder militar. Bolivia 1879–1935* (2003); and *Bolivia. Revolution and the Power of*

History in the Present (2007). James Dunkerley is currently working on Bolivian politics since 1982, as well as preparing a study of the politico-intellectual world of the North Atlantic in the early 19th century.

Sven Harten has followed Bolivian politics for the past ten years and his PhD at the London School of Economics was on Evo Morales and the MAS. He has done extensive fieldwork in the country, which included living for several months among the coca producers in the Tropic of Cochabamba and in-depth interviews with all senior MAS leaders, including Evo Morales and Alvaro García Linera. His book, *The Rise of Evo Morales and the MAS*, is due to be published by Zed Books shortly. After several years of conducting evaluations of development cooperation, including for the European Commission, he is currently working as Evaluation Officer for the World Bank-IFC in Lima, Peru.

Herbert S. Klein is the Gouverneur Morris professor emeritus, Columbia University, and Director of the Center for Latin American Studies at Stanford University. He is author of five books and numerous articles on Bolivian history. These include: *Parties and Political Change in Bolivia, 1880–1952* (Cambridge, 1969; reprinted 2009); *Bolívia: do período pré-incaico à independência* (São Paulo, 1991); *Haciendas and Ayllus: Rural Society in the Bolivian Andes in the 18th and 19th centuries* (Stanford 1993); and, most recently, *A Concise History of Bolivia* (Cambridge, 2002); second edition forthcoming (2011); Spanish edition, *Historia de Bolivia,* third edition (La Paz, 2002) — this is an updated version of *Bolivia: Evolution of a Multi-Ethnic Society* (Oxford, 1982). He is also co-author, with Jonathan Kelley, of *Revolution and the Rebirth of Inequality: A Theory Applied to the Bolivian National Revolution* (Berkeley, 1981). Other work related to Bolivia is his *The American Finances of the Spanish Empire, 1680–1809* (Albuquerque, 1998).

Adrian Pearce is a scholar of Latin America with particular interests in political, social and economic history. His research has focused on Spanish rule in the late-colonial Andes, on which he has published articles in the *Hispanic American Historical Review* and the *Latin American Research Review*, and on British commercial relations, on which he published *British Trade with Spanish America, 1763–1808* (Liverpool, 2007) and a number of journal articles. With Paul Heggarty, he is editing a collection of essays entitled *History and Language in the Andes* (forthcoming with Palgrave in the 'Studies of the Americas' series). Adrian Pearce was a member of the Institute for the Study of the Americas from 2008–10, and now teaches in the Departments of History and of Spanish, Portuguese, and Latin American Studies at King's College London.

Martín Sivak, who was born in Buenos Aires in 1975, is the author of four books about contemporary Bolivia, including a biography of Hugo Banzer (*El dictador elegido. Biografía no autorizada de Hugo Banzer Suárez*, 2001) and a portrait of Evo Morales (*Jefazo: Retrato íntimo de Evo Morales*, 2008), published in English with Palgrave as *Evo Morales: The extraordinary rise of the first indigenous president of Bolivia* (2010). He holds a Master's degree from the Institute for the Study of the Americas (University of London) and is currently completing a doctorate in Latin American History at New York University.

Acknowledgements

I wish to thank the Bolivia Information Forum, and particularly Alex Tilley, for proposing the symposium, held at the Institute for the Study of the Americas on 20 November 2009, from which this book arose. Neither the symposium nor the book would have come about in the absence of BIF's stirling efforts. Alex Tilley also sourced and sought permission to use the cover image and paid for production of the map. I thank all the authors for sending their papers and for collaborating promptly and collegially during the editing process. Herbert Klein did not attend the symposium, but nevertheless was willing to write an essay for the volume, as too was James Dunkerley. Professor Dunkerley also put me in touch with Martín Sivak, who subsequently sent his own essay. Pilar Domingo participated in the ISA symposium and met with me subsequently to discuss matters relating to the volume. Maxine Molyneux, Director of the Institute for the Study of the Americas, threw her support behind both the symposium and the publication of this book in the Institute's own excellent series. Valerie Hall and Kerry Whitston, of School of Advanced Study Publications, handled the typescript both expertly and expeditiously. Olga Jimenez helped organise the symposium with her accustomed efficiency and style. Miles Irving, an expert freelance cartographer (www.milesmap. co.uk), drew the map. My thanks and love also to my wife Concepción Zayas.

Gemma van der Haar kindly and courageously located revised drafts of Willem Assies' essay after his sudden death on 22 May 2010. This volume is dedicated to Willem, a fine scholar of Latin America and an influential Bolivianist.

INTRODUCTION

Adrian J. Pearce

This book arose from a symposium held at the Institute for the Study of the Americas (ISA) in London in late November 2009. A group of scholars took the occasion of then-imminent presidential elections in Bolivia to reflect on the experience of the first administration of Evo Morales and his party, the *Movimiento al Socialismo* (MAS), then rapidly approaching its close.

Bolivian politics and society under the MAS since 2006 — in fact, since the major upheavals of the early 2000s — have attracted close attention both from academic circles and beyond. Morales is fixed in the global imagination, indeed, as a key member of the 'pink tide' or club of new left leaders in Latin America, alongside Venezuela's Hugo Chávez or Brazil's Lula da Silva. He has attracted attention as the head of an ostensibly unambiguous 'movement towards socialism', an attention sharpened from 2006 with the initiation of a programme of nationalisation of economic resources on a scale rarely seen in the region. Perhaps still more influential in his international profile, Morales is widely touted as the first indigenous leader of a South American country since the European Conquest, and is closely identified with Bolivia's large native population (particularly with by far the most important groups in numeric terms, the Aymara and Quechua). The political process in Bolivia since the early 2000s, in which the MAS has played both a key and an increasing role, has thus provoked some (quite heated) debate as to its 'revolutionary' character; a character that might be defined in ethnic as well as political terms, and in any case may to some commentators represent that rarest of phenomena, a genuine social revolution.[1]

The papers presented at the ISA symposium addressed a range of critical issues in the Bolivian affairs of the previous four years, and were then complemented by additional essays commissioned from further contributors.

---

1   Forrest Hylton and Sinclair Thomson, *Revolutionary Horizons: Past and Present in Bolivian Politics* (London and New York: Verso, 2007); for a more cautious view, see James Dunkerley, 'Evo Morales, Alvaro García Linera and the Third Bolivian Revolution', in same author, *Bolivia: Revolution and the Power of History in the Present* (London: Institute for the Study of the Americas, 2007), pp. 1–56.

All the chapters are broadly political in focus, and taken as a whole, the (modest) aim of the resulting volume is to present an early assessment of the experience in government of Morales and the MAS from the standpoint of the end of the first term. The latter moment represented a landmark not least since there seemed grounds at times to doubt that the MAS would be able to complete its term in untroubled fashion. That Morales not only did so, but won re-election to a second term in December 2009, with a substantially increased majority, is testimony to his and the MAS's exceptional electoral appeal. Indeed, the nature, as well as the possible fragility, of this appeal forms one of the key themes of this book. Taken as a whole, the collection offers a multi-angled perspective on the MAS's first term and some of its major outcomes, with successive papers discussing a number of key aspects of Morales' policy-making or of MAS operations. These include: internal change within the party, designed to institutionalise its structures and reform its relationship with the party base, but which may have had the effect of distancing the MAS to some extent from the social movements that created it; the new 'plurinational' Constitution of 2009, widely regarded as a key document in Morales' ostentatious 'refoundation' of the modern republic; analysis of the MAS's electoral success and of the basis of the party's support during a period of extremely lively electoral activity; and Morales' foreign policy during his first administration, specifically with regard to the United States.

It may be helpful to summarise briefly the themes of each of the essays, as well as to indicate what might be regarded as their major contributions. In an extensive and wide-ranging opening discussion, **Herbert Klein** sets the historical context to the rise of the MAS throughout the period since the National Revolution of 1952. Klein's essay demonstrates how sweeping processes of social and economic change since the mid-20th century came together to make the success of the MAS and Morales possible. The National Revolution itself initiated or quickened within Bolivia processes common throughout much of the globe during this period, including explosive population growth in the context of better health, rising levels of education and literacy, extremely rapid urbanisation, and greatly increased mobility of the rural poor, all within a context of the persistence of extreme poverty in both the rural and urban milieux. From the 1980s, these processes developed within the context of the dismantling of the 'revolutionary' state and economy, with policies of neo-liberal shock which ended price controls, drastically reduced public spending, and dismantled the state-owned mining sector, with many thousands of miners laid off. In the 1990s a wave of privatisations followed, most controversially that of the state-owned oil company *Yacimientos Petrolíferos Fiscales Bolivianos*, on dubious terms and with further loss of jobs. The rise of a booming coca economy, US-backed eradication campaigns from the early 1980s notwithstanding, and of massive exports of natural gas and strong growth in non-traditional agricultural exports, provided only partial compensation.

Central to the period since the 1950s was the growth of indigenous and *mestizo* identity and political activism. Klein first discusses the revolutionary land reforms which destroyed much of the rural white elite and made way for a new *mestizo* class, a class he defines as 'indigenous who entered the labour market, adopted urban norms and bilingualism, and moved into small towns and cities throughout the nation'. The enfranchisement of indigenous people and peasants by the elimination of literacy requirements for voting also had profound implications over the long term. The growing strength and visibility of indigenous peoples and *mestizos* found physical expression in the rise of El Alto, 'a quintessential *mestizo* town', in just a few decades to second city of the republic. But the *political* activism of this sector proceeded apace only from the 1970s, in the context first of military dictatorship, and then of neo-liberal shock and economic trauma. In the 1970s, the *Túpaq Katari* movement was founded and seized control of major labour organisations, while in the 1980s, Morales himself emerged as leader of the newly influential coca producers of Cochabamba. Klein identifies the elections of 1989 as the first at which these indigenous and *mestizo* groups demonstrated mass electoral potential, and after 1993 Bolivia witnessed both its first indigenous Vice-President and a constitutional reform declaring the country 'multiethnic and pluricultural'. Decentralising reforms of the 1990s then led to a massive expansion of elected local officials, of whom two-thirds would be peasant or indigenous. Finally, an ongoing series of protests and large-scale mobilisations began in 2000, based partly on the defence of natural and national resources, and partly on broader concerns arguably ultimately related to national identity itself. It was, then, this combination of sweeping social change since the 1950s, and political developments from the 1970s, that created the conditions in which the MAS was founded and finally took power in 2006.

With the historical context established, the discussion moves towards Morales and the MAS in power and continues with perhaps the most theoretically sophisticated of the contributions. **Sven Harten**'s essay focuses first and foremost on arguably the single most important question regarding the MAS and its operation as a party: its relationship with the social movements from which it emerged. The MAS was founded by the coca growers of Cochabamba in the late 1990s explicitly as their 'political instrument': a tool for pursuing and promoting their goals on the national stage. Other social movements also became influential later on but, as Harten demonstrates, their relationship with the MAS remained little altered until 2004. Thus,

the MAS candidates for elections prior to 2004 were chosen by the coca
producers' base, which played a particularly important role in defining
ideological and programmatic priorities. It also took part in the decisions
of the party, for example relating to the electoral campaign.

The MAS still features in much of the scholarly literature, and a still greater
proportion of popular writing on the country, as in effect the creature of the
social movements — unsurprisingly, when this impression is encouraged
by its own leadership.[2] Indeed, the perception of the party as responding
faithfully to the dictates of its social base has been central to the assessments
made of it, whether positive or otherwise. And yet Harten's essay focuses on
internal reforms in the party, made *prior* to its seizure of power in 2006, which
significantly reduced the influence of the social movements over decision-
making. These reforms were intended to institutionalise the party structures,
and consisted firstly of the radical opening of the party lists to new candidates,
and secondly of a formal reduction in the influence of social movements in
decision-making. Thus,

> instead of being able to decide the affairs of the party directly ... after
> 2004 [the coca growers] were relegated to having a representative on
> the National Political Commission (CPN). And while beforehand the
> base exercised direct influence over decision-making ... from 2005 they
> had to be content with being represented by the *Executive* of one of the
> Federations, Julio Salazar, who was nominated by Evo Morales rather than
> being elected by the base.

Harten is unambiguous as to the implications of these reforms: 'the coca
growers lost much of their structural representation in the crucial period
between mid-2004 and late 2005', and 'no steps were taken at the time to
safeguard against the neglect of the demands of the party's founders' —
whatever the public discourse of the leadership. He is at pains to emphasise
that the social movements have in practice continued to exercise considerable
influence, through *informal* channels. As President, Evo Morales has made
sustained efforts to remain engaged with the social movements and particularly
with the coca growers. Nevertheless, Harten's essay provides a much-needed

---

2   'The aim here is to achieve "the wholehearted self-representation of those social movements".
     In this way, Bolivia will become "a unique example world-wide of social movements
     managing to take control of the state"'; Franz Xavier Barrios Suvelza, 'The Weakness of
     Excess: The Bolivian State in an Unbounded Democracy', in John Crabtree and Laurence
     Whitehead (eds.), *Unresolved Tensions: Bolivia Past and Present* (Pittsburgh: University of
     Pittsburgh Press, 2008), pp. 125–39, see p. 131, quoting Vice-President Alvaro García
     Linera.

corrective to acritical accounts of relations between movements and party, and should prompt closer attention to this key aspect.

I also wish to highlight here Harten's demonstration of ways in which the work of the Argentine political theorist Ernesto Laclau can be applied to the Bolivian case. One aspect of the opening of the MAS prior to the 2005 elections consisted of a 'discursive opening or broadening', in what Laclau would term a 'chain of equivalence' — that is to say, the party 'managed to broaden its discourse so as to incorporate the demands of the protest movements' which proliferated after 2000 and especially after 2003. For the MAS, the 'logic of equivalence' lay in representing the protest movements and presenting them as '*similar in their opposition to the status quo*' (my emphasis). This logic then proved crucial to the electoral success of the party and to its victory in 2005. But the opening also implied the entry of new members, from beyond the traditional party constituency and with diverse (and insufficiently scrutinised) interests. New individuals joined the party with origins and interests often quite distant from those of the social movements, of whom many of the most prominent were professionals or urban intellectuals. These individuals then 'argued for a more vertical hierarchy within the demands articulated by the MAS' — in Laclau's terms, an articulatory 'logic of difference' quite distinct to that which had developed prior to the elections and which brought the MAS success. Harten acknowledges that this 'logic of difference' is better suited to the realities of government and of the party in power, but he also points to clear pitfalls. The chief one is that, once more, 'the links with the social movements have been weakened', through the breaking of the 'chain of equivalence uniting various demands without clear leadership'; that is to say, 'without any futile attempt at leadership of the protest movements' on the part of the MAS. In short, the party may be less able to generate a broad front of social support for fundamental change to the established order than it was in 2005. (Notwithstanding all this, I should note that Harten nevertheless insists that the MAS has maintained 'the spirit of an open and participatory movement', and remains far from a 'traditional party' in Bolivian terms.) Beyond its implications for our understanding of the MAS in power, then, I think Harten's work demonstrates the increasingly urgent need for, and the potential gains by, research on the MAS itself as a political party, as opposed to its leadership and Morales in particular.

The third essay, by the late **Willem Assies**, discusses the origins and characteristics of the new Constitution for Bolivia introduced in 2009. The Constitution is already regarded as a landmark achievement of the MAS administration during its first term, and is widely celebrated for defining the country as 'plurinational' and granting its native peoples a more prominent place in national life. Assies here contextualises the Constitution and its development in two major ways, inserting it into both the historical and regional frameworks. In exploring the recent history of Constitution-making in Bolivia, he discusses the documents promulgated in the 20th century and particularly the constitutional reforms of the early 1990s that, as we have already seen, first defined the country as multicultural and pluri-ethnic. In placing the 2009 document in regional context, he draws on the work of Raquel Yrigoyen in discussing three cycles of constitutional reform in Latin America since the 1980s (thus confirming that since the 1990s, Bolivia joined a regional 'trend toward the recognition of indigenous peoples' rights and the "pluri-multi" composition of their populations'). In terms of its provisions, Assies highlights the strengthening of rights for indigenous peoples, as well as the broader recognition of indigenous forms of justice in the new Constitution, while noting curbs on these aspects in the final document with respect to earlier drafts. He emphasises the greater role of the state in an economy in which hydrocarbons are set to win growing significance,[3] through greater control over the exploitation of natural resources, but he also underlines the guarantees offered to private as well as communal and state property (perhaps to be 'construed as a transitory phase towards a socialist-communitarian economy'). Lastly, he notes the provision made in the Constitution for the introduction of autonomies at the regional, municipal, and indigenous levels. With regard to the latter aspect, however, Assies further remarks that 'relations between these different autonomy regimes will remain controversial'. And indeed, while cautious in advancing any 'final word' on the Constitution of 2009, he concludes that whatever its other consequences, 'it will provide a framework for further political struggle' in the country.

John Crabtree's chapter, which follows Assies' essay, discusses a further question central to the story of the MAS: its rapid rise through electoral validation from obscurity to unprecedented political dominance. The first part of Crabtree's essay traces this rise by analysing the results of the surprising number of electoral contests held in Bolivia between 1999 and 2010, with more than a dozen rounds of presidential, departmental, and municipal elections and referenda. The data from these elections have been available since shortly after they were held, but they are presented here with an exemplary clarity, which only underscores both the MAS's near-stranglehold over politics in recent years and the remaining flaws in its electoral success. Shares of the national vote of 54 per cent in the presidential elections in 2005, and of 64 per cent in those of 2009, represent a degree of electoral support which is little short of staggering in an open democracy. And, among a number of striking trends Crabtree identifies in his first section, the rise of the MAS vote in the

---

3   For an excellent sense of this significance, see Carlos Miranda, 'Gas and its Importance to the Bolivian Economy', in Crabtree and Whitehead (eds.), *Unresolved Tensions*, pp. 177–93.

ostensibly hostile eastern departments of the *Media Luna* region — Santa Cruz, Tarija, Beni and Pando — in elections since 2005 for the presidency and prefects or governors stands out. For even in these departments, the party won an average 43 per cent support in the departmental elections of April 2010 (41 per cent if small and underpopulated Pando, where the MAS vote was higher, is excluded). Indeed, Crabtree emphasises the significance of electoral politics in dampening — at least for the time being — the political antagonism of the eastern departments, with the August 2008 recall referendum on MAS policies producing 'a round endorsement' and 'a turning point in Morales' embattled relations with the opposition'. The sole level at which the MAS remains far from dominant is that of the municipalities: in 2004, it failed to win the mayoralties in any of the major cities of the country, and even in 2010 it did so only in El Alto, Cochabamba and tiny Cobija (in Pando). The urban setting to these elections, together with insufficient care in the selection of candidates, has continued to hold the MAS vote back.

The value of this analysis of electoral data notwithstanding, it seems likely that the second part of Crabtree's essay, devoted to the *causes* of the MAS's success, will most draw the attention of specialists. Five major themes are discussed here: Evo Morales and leadership; the capacity to fill the vacuum left by the exhaustion of previous political models and parties; the role of indigenous politics and social movements; economic policy and social gains; and the tackling of the right. Crabtree is unequivocal as to the importance of Morales to the MAS project, and situates him (perhaps uniquely) as a 'man of the people' capable simultaneously of bridging Aymara and Quechua, and *indigenista* and *sindicalista*, political constituencies. Nevertheless, the rise of the MAS grew not simply from personalist politics, but reflected the success of an ideological project based around 'a sense of rejection and protest towards the status quo', symbolised by the discredit of traditional parties and politics. Within this project, Crabtree particularly emphasises the role of economic nationalism in providing 'the political glue' which held the diverse groups supporting the MAS together. But beyond this, the party's 'broad church', committed to *indigenismo* as well as to the politics of the left, has confirmed its stance in favour of 'those long marginalised in the process of the nation's development, especially its indigenous majority'. Crabtree notes that indigenous concerns became central to the party's identity only from 2005, but that it has proved capable of appealing to diverse ethnic groups of the highlands and lowlands alike, while retaining a strong class-based body of support. It has been assisted in doing so by quite a strongly favourable economic environment, particularly of international demand for Bolivian exports. Growth in raw materials exports and revenues, the latter arising partly from nationalisations in the hydrocarbon sector, has yielded government funds for reinvestment in social programmes, including conditional cash transfer programmes, which have proved highly popular among Bolivian voters. Finally, after September 2008 the immediate threat of right-wing and regionalist opposition receded, and rival parties have remained divided and lacking a charismatic leadership capable of generating national support.

In the fifth essay, **Martín Sivak** turns to the key aspect of Bolivian foreign policy in recent decades: diplomatic relations with the US. In his opening historical section, he traces the course of these relations since the Revolution of 1952, a period that he argues witnessed the 'Americanisation' of bilateral relations, primarily by means of the imposition of grand narratives established by Washington: successively the War against Communism, War on Drugs and War on Terror. Although resented by many sectors of Bolivian society, these narratives and this Americanisation became hegemonic and were internalised by most governments prior to 2006. This section thus prepares the way for Sivak's key argument: that the Morales administration since 2006 has witnessed a transformative 'Bolivianisation' of foreign policy, evident specifically with regard to relations with the US. In an early draft of this chapter, Sivak noted that to an extent, this Bolivianisation of foreign policy 'lacks an official blue-print' and it might thus prove difficult to define in precise terms. But as he argues persuasively here, it consists clearly enough of a wresting of control and a rejection of narratives of relations derived from outside the country's borders. Sivak identifies seven main points in this agenda, from rejection of aid from the IMF or the World Bank and refusal to join the Free Trade Area of the Americas, to a regional alliance with Cuba and Venezuela. There has also been overt rejection of US influence within the country, whether in attempts to eradicate coca plantations or to influence the selection of government ministers. Most dramatically, in September 2008 the US ambassador himself was summarily expelled on charges of interference in domestic politics. And on occasions, the shift in foreign policy is explicitly cast in terms evocative of Bolivian (in fact, indigenous) culture, as with the appeal to Andean principles of reciprocity in the demand for visas for US visitors to match those demanded of Bolivians travelling to the US.

A further element of Sivak's argument, and a further important dimension to the Bolivianisation of bilateral relations with the US he describes, lies in the tense and occasionally violent relations between the eastern departments and the government in La Paz. Sivak discusses Bolivian suspicions of US collusion with the eastern elites in their opposition to Morales, as well as evidence to support these suspicions in documents declassified by the State Department. The more direct accusations of conspiracy are difficult to verify, though they ultimately lay behind the expulsion of ambassador Philip Goldberg in 2008. But more broadly, Sivak argues that the 'regionalisation of Bolivian politics' (the conflict with the east, particularly acute in late 2008), as the central theme of the MAS years, further Bolivianised relations with the US by obliging Washington to engage with a conflict that was entirely Bolivian in origin. 'For the first time, then, it was an internal and deeply-rooted conflict in Bolivia that gave leverage to US actions', rather than the succession of global wars pursued by Washington since the 1950s. Sivak thus ends with a reflection on the leitmotif of war in relations with the US, casting Morales himself in striking terms as a survivor of 'the three main wars the US has waged on Bolivian soil since the 1950s': against Communism, drugs, and terrorism (with all of which he has been associated, as 'left-wing radical, a partner of narco-traffickers, and a terrorist'). That it was the conflict with the eastern departments, itself part-product of the 'wars' over water or gas reserves in 2000–3, that helped determine US policy towards Bolivia during the first MAS administration, Sivak concludes, 'illustrates the inability of the US to generate new narrative agencies after the failed attempt to capitalise on the War on Terror'.

The final essay in the collection, by **James Dunkerley**, differs in form as well as function from the other contributions. Under the short title '*Pachakuti* in Bolivia, 2008–10', it is written as a diary, with 16 entries covering the 24 months from 3 February 2008 to 13 February 2010 (though the first two entries skip outside the strict chronological order). The diary presents its author's response to key events and episodes during the period of intense conflict surrounding the preparation of the new Constitution and the question of regional autonomy. These include the referendum on autonomy in Santa Cruz in 2008, the promulgation of the Constitution in 2009, violence in Sucre and Pando and Evo Morales' second presidential electoral victory. But in addition, it ranges widely across both Bolivian and Bolivianist affairs to embrace topics as seemingly disparate as carnival, the James Bond film *Quantum of Solace*, the arrest of a Mexican beauty queen, the Icelandic financial crisis that began in 2008, and the deaths within 48 hours in April 2009 of the Bolivian scholar and politician José Luis Roca and the British anthropologist and historian Olivia Harris. Dunkerley has described the piece as 'deliberately non-traditional', with a style 'calibrated towards reflective reportage in order to enable a more accessible application of theory, particularly with respect to understanding time and the syncretic nature of national politics'. He further comments that 'the overall aim of the chapter is to free up some associational space that is often missed by mainstream social science prose'.[4] As a whole, the piece reflects on the central theme of continuity and change in contemporary Bolivian affairs, referring to the Andean concept of *Pachakuti*, which is understood as 'not just about backwards and forwards, but both these understood as *cycle*, albeit one of unpredictable and indeterminate qualities'.

4   From the abstract to Dunkerley's paper included upon its submission.

Dunkerley has been an eloquent scholar of Bolivia for more than a quarter of a century, and the diary presents its author's original, sometimes unusual, opinions on the MAS administration and indeed on the broad sweep of Bolivian politics in recent decades. Thus, for example, we find a balanced, perhaps even generous, account of the labours of widely vilified former President Gonzalo Sánchez de Lozada (1993–7 and 2002–3), or identification of a 'willingness to be goaded' as the 'single greatest miscalculation' of the MAS since taking office in 2006. Dunkerley points to the 'other great unspoken story' of the December 2009 elections as being 'the total *volte face*' of the Bolivian electorate on the issue of departmental autonomy. This *volte face* makes it unlikely that 'localism pursued in the guise of "autonomy"' will retain its potency as a vehicle of political opposition to Morales into his second term. Not the least benefit of the diary format is that Dunkerley's views are expressed with a trifle less scholarly restraint than elsewhere, so that 'what passes for an oligarchy in Santa Cruz' here consists of 'provincial *caudillos*, caballing Croats, and outright chancers'. Evo Morales himself is 'not sure-footed tactically and has a short fuse', and 'oscillates between hubris and pragmatism', although he is seen to play hardball deftly with the US over the issue of coca production. The essay complements others in the collection adroitly, for example in Dunkerley's (approving) response to Morales' expulsion of ambassador Goldberg and indeed to his policy towards the US at large. Finally, in the immediacy of the diary's response to the political life of these years, Dunkerley reminds us just 'how difficult it is to keep pace with Bolivia, even from quite close up' and from the perspective of long-standing and close engagement with the country.

In conclusion, these essays describe a MAS deeply engaged with the relationship with its original party base, while facing questions as to the future nature of that relationship and its implications; a party nevertheless capable thus far of winning ever-greater electoral support, even in the ostensibly hostile departments of the *Media Luna* and across quite a wide social spectrum; and a movement evincing both continuity and some radical change in policy both domestic and foreign. As for the future, most of the essays collected here point to questions or potential problems for the MAS and Bolivian politics in the short to medium term. Perhaps most recurrent in these pages is the question of the eventual political succession of Evo Morales, which both Sven Harten and John Crabtree see as potentially problematic in the absence of candidates of comparable stature and charisma, or of full institutionalisation of the party structures. James Dunkerley goes so far as to question whether Morales' commitment not to stand for a third term as President in 2013 — a commitment crucial to the breaking of the deadlock around the new Constitution in 2008 — might not be 'overtaken' by the sheer scale of his victory in December 2009. Dunkerley also agrees with his fellow contributors that 'nobody in or around

MAS looks remotely like a plausible successor' to Evo, while warning that 'the very looseness of the movement strongly suggests a future of factionalism'. Crabtree further observes that in the key pending political challenge for the country, the opposition in the eastern lowland departments 'will be looking for an opportunity to flex their muscles once again', while 'new areas of tension are bound to emerge' in implementing the new Constitution and responding to the demands of the social movements — points made in similar terms by Willem Assies. Crabtree further questions the capacity for sustained growth, or to reduce poverty on a sustainable basis, of the economic model pursued by the MAS. Lastly, Martin Sivak demonstrates the difficulties as well as the virtues of the more independent foreign policy developed under the MAS, with the loss of US support to the country manifest in its 'decertification' for alleged failure to collaborate in the war on drugs, the virtual elimination of subsidies to the military, and (most seriously) the loss of Andean Trade Promotion and Drug Eradication Act preferential tariffs on Bolivian goods entering the US.

Nevertheless, as Crabtree concludes, the immediate prospects for the MAS to retain impressive levels of political support throughout almost the whole of Bolivia seem strong as the party embarks upon its second term. The sheer pace of change in Bolivia in recent times described by Herbert Klein, and the difficulty of keeping pace with events in the country emphasised by James Dunkerley's essay, make predictions hazardous. But if its impact and lasting influence remain uncertain, the party surely seems set to continue to dominate Bolivian politics for the foreseeable future.

1

THE HISTORICAL BACKGROUND TO THE RISE OF THE MAS, 1952–2005

Herbert S. Klein

Introduction

The origins of MAS and the new style *mestizo* and peasant dominated government which has emerged in Bolivia after December 2005 can be traced to the 1952 revolution and the full integration of indigenous groups into national politics for the first time in republican history. This is not to say that there was not a significant amount of political activity of these groups before then. There were constant conflicts over land and self-government which went back to the colonial period, and the indigenous *ayllus* (or communal governments) had in one way or another made their weight felt in national politics both peacefully and through violence in the 19th and first half of the 20th century. But until 1952 they could not vote or participate actively in national elections. With agrarian reform in 1953 and two subsequent periods of hyper inflation, much of the traditional rural elite were eliminated in the more densely settled highland areas. This opened up a space for community expansion and the rise of a *mestizo* middle class, which in turn was aided by the massive urbanisation which occurred in this period. From 1952 until the late 1970s the rural populations of Bolivia were fundamental for maintaining governing parties in power. Both the *Movimiento Nacionalista Revolucionario* and the subsequent military regimes after 1964 essentially relied on passive peasant and *mestizo* support in return for the delivery of land titles, education and other government services to the rural communities.

The elimination of a rural white elite in this period, combined with the extraordinary growth of mass education, and the progressive migration of the rural population to the cities, all created what can be called a *mestizo* working and lower middle class with close ties to the rural indigenous peasant mass, with which it identified even as it adopted Spanish and entered the modern labour market. In turn the rural needs became more complex with the end of major land reform in the late 1970s, with demands for more sophisticated support that not all governments were willing to provide. Thus the popular articulation of demands and their nature slowly changed over the two generations that came of age in the period since 1952. The political participation of these indigenous groups also became far more active. First came the rise of small indigenista parties in the 1970s. This was followed by the impact of federalist political reform policies in the 1990s which gave economic and political power to the communities and brought *mestizo* and peasant leaders into government positions on a significant scale for the first time in republican history. Finally the rise of El Alto, the quintessential *mestizo* and peasant city, to its position as the second largest metropolis in the nation, provided an enormous base from which these new political leaders could challenge national policies. All these factors helped shape the rise of a mass political party which directly represented these new groups and absorbed many of their members into leadership positions.

Revolution and society, 1952–82

Looking at these developments over time, we can see how profound the changes in Bolivia have been since 1952. In 1950 Bolivia produced its first modern census which provides a baseline from which to examine Bolivian society prior to the National Revolution which occurred two years later. In 1950 only a minority of the people of Bolivia lived in towns or cities with over 5,000 inhabitants. There were only six cities with over 20,000 residents and these represented a fifth of the country's total population. La Paz, the largest city, contained only 12 per cent of the national total of 2.7 million. Fully three-quarters of the population was rural.[1]

Thus Bolivians were primarily illiterate farmers living in rural areas, the majority of whom did not speak Spanish. At the time of the National Revolution most of the population spoke Quechua and Aymara, while only 36per cent were Spanish speaking.[2] Over two-thirds of Bolivians were

---

1   Dirección General de Estadística y Censos (hereafter, DGEC), *Censo demográfico 1950* (La Paz: 1955), cuadro 5, pp. 12–45. The very broad definition of urban still only included 26% of the population. Instituto Nacional de Estadística de Bolivia (hereafter, INEB), cuadro 2.01.11, 'Bolivia: población por censos según departamento, área geográfica y sexo, censos de 1950–1976–992–2001', at www.ine.gov.bo/indice/visualizador.aspx?ah=PC20111. HTM. INEB cuadro numbering on their current website does not match the numbers and tables which appear in the latest statistical annual (2008) published by the Instituto. Thus the source of all the latest tables (whether online or in the Anuario Estadístico) is clearly delineated in the following notes.

2   DGEC, *Censo demográfico 1950*, cuadro 34 p. 103. In 1900 only 13% of the population were primarily Spanish speaking; fully 51% were listed as speaking an Indian language:

illiterate.[3] The poverty and illiteracy were well reflected in the demographic statistics. In this period Bolivia had among the highest mortality rates in the Americas. Infant mortality was estimated at 176 deaths per thousand live births in 1953,[4] and average life expectancy in the early 1950s was 38 years for men and 42 years for women,[5] a rate probably little different from late-19th century life expectancy levels. Yet, at the same time, Bolivians had among the highest fertility rates in the hemisphere, with a Total Fertility Rate of 6.7 children registered in 1953.[6] The impact of these high fertility rates on the potential growth of the population was, of course, reduced by the particularly high levels of mortality which caused the population to grow at a slow pace. Between 1831 and 1900 the population grew at just 0.5 per cent per annum. After 1900, with the beginnings of modern sanitation and inoculation, mortality rates slowly began to decline resulting in a more rapid growth rate of 1.1per cent per annum from 1900 to 1950, though this faster growth was still at a low rate given the exceptionally high fertility.[7] These high birth and death rates defined Bolivia at the time of the National Revolution as a classic pre-modern population (see graph 1 below). This coincided with Bolivia having a young population with 40 per cent of both males and females under the age of 15, and a mean age of 19 years.[8]

The Revolution of 1952

There is little question that the National Revolution of 1952 had a profound impact on this population in both its intended and unintended consequences.

Oficina Nacional de Inmigración y Propaganda Geográfica, *Censo general de la Población de la República de Bolivia ... 1900* 2nd edn. 2 vols. (Cochabamba: 1973), vol. 2, p. 41.

3   Although the level of literacy and the number of children attending school had steadily increased in the first half of the 20th century, literates in the period from 1900 to 1950 rose from only 13% to just 31% of the population: DGEC, *Censo demográfico 1950*, cuadro 37, p. 112; Oficina Nacional de Inmigración y Propaganda Geográfica, *Censo general ... 1900*, vol. 2, p. 43.

4   INEB and El Centro Latinoamericano y Caribeño de Demografía (hereafter, CELADE), *Bolivia. Estimaciones y proyecciones de la población 1950–2050* (La Paz: 1995), cuadro 2, p. 5.

5   United Nations, *Demographic Yearbook, Historical supplement [1948/1997]* (New York: 2000), table 9, at http://unstats.un.org/unsd/demographic/products/dyb/dybhist.htm

6   Ibid., table 4.

7   Calculated from the estimated trend in mid-year populations given in Asthenio Averanga Mollinedo, *Aspectos generales de la población Boliviana* 3rd. edn. (La Paz: 1998), pp. 30–33 in cuadro 3.

8   UN, *Demographic Yearbook, Historical Supplement*, table 3; and INEB and CELADE, *Bolivia. Estimaciones y proyecciones*, cuadro 10, p. 24.

Clearly the two most important acts of the new regime were land reform and the enfranchisement of all adult voters regardless of literacy for the first time in republican history. The August 1953 land reform decree effectively confiscated all highland *hacienda* lands, granting them to their indigenous workers through the *sindicatos* and *comunidades* to which they belonged, with the proviso that such lands could not be individually sold. In the highland indigenous areas, almost all the lands were granted to the local communities, but in the relatively unpopulated Santa Cruz region, such medium-sized *hacienda* valleys as Monteagudo, and the small-holding vineyards of the Cinti region, no land reform was practised. Everywhere else, the *hacienda* was abolished, the *hacendado* class destroyed, and land now shifted predominately into the hands of the Indian peasants. By 1993 some 831,000 land titles had been issued for 44 million hectares — or some 40 per cent of the total land area of Bolivia — to some 626,998 persons.[9] On top of this land reform sharp periods of hyperinflation occurred in the mid-1950s and again in the early 1980s, weakening and in many cases destroying the traditional rural white elites that had ruled over the small villages and rural communities. These elites were replaced everywhere by a new *mestizo* class — that is, indigenous, who entered the labour market, adopted urban norms and bilingualism, and moved into small towns and cities throughout the nation. *Mestizos* now became the middlemen between the rural and metropolitan worlds evolving in Bolivia.[10]

Crucial as well was the enfranchisement of the indigenous population. One of the first acts of the new MNR regime of 1952 was to establish universal suffrage by eliminating the literacy requirements. In one stroke, the Indian peasant masses were enfranchised, and the voting population jumped from 126,000 in 1951 to 955,000 in 1956 and reached 1.3 million voters in the 1964 election.[11] Though the indigenous masses would take several generations to find their independent political voice, every successive government, whether

9   Ministerio de Desarrollo Económico, Secretaría Nacional de Agricultura y Ganadería, *El Agro Boliviano: Estadísticas agropecuarios 1990–1995* (La Paz: 1996), pp. 262–3. On the latest revisions of the agrarian reform law and the attempt to rationalise and legitimate land titles in Santa Cruz and the Beni, see Jorge A. Muñoz and Isabel Lavadenz, 'Reforming the Agrarian Reform in Bolivia', Development Discussion Paper no. 589 (Cambridge MA: Harvard Institute for International Development, Harvard University, June 1997).

10   For a fascinating analysis of the decline of a traditional small-town white elite in the post-revolutionary period, see Libbet Crandon-Malamud, *From the Fat of our Souls: Social Change, Political Process, and Medical Pluralism in Bolivia* (Berkeley: University of California Press, 1991).

11   Rossana Barragán, 'Ciudadanía y elecciones, convenciones y debates', in Rossana Barragán and José Luis Rica, *Regiones y poder constituyente en Bolivia* (La Paz: Programa de las Naciones Unidas para el Desarrollo, 2005), cuadro 2, pp. 299–300.

military or civilian, was required to make some gesture to satisfy their demands for schools, housing, electricity, sanitation and general economic support. While the government was less than efficient in delivering this support, and the group's demands often shifted over time, the change to national life was profound.

Equally important, the Agrarian Reform of 1953 freed all indigenous peasants from the personal servitude (*pongueaje* and *colonato*) which had tied them to the land. Abolishing these ties led to far greater mobility for the poor than ever before in national history. Migration to ever more rapidly expanding urban centres provided new opportunities for education, employment and well being.[12] At the same time, the establishment of a viable road network and the opening up of rural areas to national markets brought in new wealth to the rural area. Syndical and communal organisations guaranteed support for common projects and an ability to make effective demands for better health and educational delivery. These organisations were so important, in fact, that they became the norm in the new lands being opened up to highland migration in the Eastern lowlands districts.[13]

Demographic change and health

With a new commitment to the health and welfare of its citizens, the MNR government established or deepened important earlier initiatives in health

12 Between 1950 and 2001, Bolivia's seven largest urban centres were growing at a rate of 4% per annum. These cities also enjoyed far better delivery of services than most of the rural *municipios* of the country. See Lykke E. Andersen, 'Migración Rural-Urbana en Bolivia: Ventajas y Desventajas', Documento de Trabajo no. 12/02 (La Paz: Instituto de Investigaciones Socio-Económicas, Universidad Católica Boliviana, 2002), cuadros 1 and 2, pp. 4, 6. Moreover, as Andersen argues here, this migration had a major impact on improving migrants' economic and social conditions, despite the usual socio-economic problems associated with dense urban populations.

13 For an account of the especially high level of rural and urban popular mobilisation and participation in areas known as *'organizaciones territoriales'*, i.e. *'Sindicatos Campesinos'* and *'Juntas de Vecinos'*, and their demand for services, see the important study by Godofredo Sandoval *et al.*, *Organizaciones de Base y Desarrollo Local en Bolivia: Estudio de los municipios de Tiahuanaco, Mizque, Villa Serrano y Charagua* (Washington DC: World Bank, Local Level Institutions, Working Paper No. 4, 1998). In an interesting essay, Fernando Calderón calls attention to the important process of *'recampesinización'* ('repeasantisation') in the new colonisation zones such as Chapare (Cochabamba) and Yapacaní (Santa Cruz) — the former being the home base of Evo Morales. Fernando Calderón G., 'Oportunidad histórica: cambio politico y Nuevo orden sociocultural', Nueva Sociedad 209 (May–June 2007), pp. 35–6.

and education, which eventually had a major social and demographic impact. While earlier efforts in sanitation and health delivery had begun to lower overall mortality, the major investments in health carried out by the government led to a rapid decline in infant and child mortality and a significant increase in life expectancy. By the time of the first post-Revolution census of 1976, average life expectancy had increased by over ten years for both men and women (reaching 48 and 52 years respectively), and the infant mortality had dropped to the 130s — still an extraordinarily high rate, but a major advance over those of 1950.[14] As the 1976 census revealed, Bolivia had finally begun to experience the effects of the arrival of modern medicine and education.

In contrast to the significant drop in mortality rates after 1952, the traditional high levels of fertility declined more slowly. These two factors guaranteed an explosive growth in population. From 1950 to 1960 the population grew at over 2.1 per cent per annum, and rose again to 2.3 per cent per annum in the following decade. By the late 1990s it had climbed to 2.7 per cent per annum natural growth, meaning that the population would double in 26 years.[15] From the census of 1950 to that of 1976 the total population increased by 1.6 million. By 1992 it had grown by 1.7 million and by 2001 by a further 1.8 million — 2.7 times higher than the pre-revolutionary population. This high fertility and declining mortality meant that the median age of the population actually decreased by almost a year, from 19 to 18 years of age by the census of 1976, the period just before the fall in fertility rates.[16] By the late 1970s, however, Bolivians had finally begun to respond in the classic way to the ever increasing survival rates, the number of births declined from these historic highs and Bolivia at last experienced the universal demographic transition.[17] Birth rates now fell at an ever increasing rate, reaching just 3.7 children per fertile woman in the period 2005–10 (see graph 1).[18]

14   INEB and CELADE, *Bolivia. Estimaciones y proyecciones de la población 1950–2050*, cuadro 10, pp. 24–5.

15   Comisión Económica para América Latina (hereafter, CEPAL)/CELADE — División de Población, 'Bolivia: Estimaciones y proyecciones de la población de ambos sexos ... 1950–2050', *Boletín demográfico* no. 66 (July 2000). Using their current population projections, I calculate that the Bolivian population grew at 2.13% in the 1950s decade, rising to 2.43% per annum by the 1970s.

16   For median ages see INEB, cuadro 2.01.18, 'Bolivia: Indicadores Demográficos por Sexo según Quinquenios, 1950–2050', at www.ine.gov.bo/indice/visualizador.aspx?ah=PC20118. HTM

17   The 1976 census thus captured the beginnings of the fertility decline, with the Total Fertility rate dropping one full child to 5.8 children per woman of childbearing age: INEB, *Bolivia. Estimaciones y proyecciones 1950–2050*, p. 25, cuadro 10.

18   INEB, 'Bolivia — Indicadores Demográficos', at www.ine.gov.bo/indice/indicadores.aspx

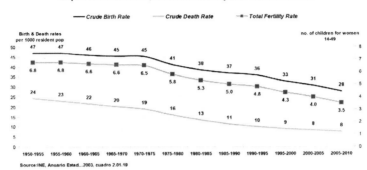

Graph 1: Bolivia: Crude Birth, Death and Total Fertility Rates 1950-55 to 2005-2010

Source:INE, Anuario Estad...2003, cuadro 2.01.19

This declining fertility and increasing life expectancy had an impact on the median age of the population, which slowly began to increase, reaching 21.9 years by 2010.[19] A look at the age distributions by sex shows a significant reshaping of the classic pyramid shape and the beginnings of a more jar-like structure typical of advanced industrial societies, with lower birth and death rates between 1950 and 2010 (see graphs 2 and 3).[20]

Graph 2: Age Pyramid of Bolivian Population in 1950
(2.7 million)

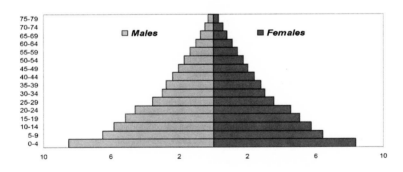

CEPAL / CELADE - División de Población. Boletín demográfico No. 66 de Julio de 2000 "Bolivia"

19   For median ages see INEB, cuadro 2.01.18, Bolivia: Indicadores Demograficos por Sexo segun Quinquenios, 1950–2050,' at www.ine.gov.bo/indice/visualizador.aspx?ah=PC20118. HTM

20   Data for the 1950 census age and sex breakdown comes from the UN, *Demographic Yearbook, Historical supplement*, Table 3, 'Population by age, sex, and urban/rural residence, each census: 1948–1997', at http://unstats.un.org/unsd/demographic/products/dyb/dybhist.htm The 2010 report is a recent projection given in INEB, cuadro 2.01.01 'Bolivia: Población total proyectada, por años calendario y sexo, según edades simples, 2005–2010', at www.ine.gov.bo/indice/visualizador.aspx?ah=PC20410.HTM

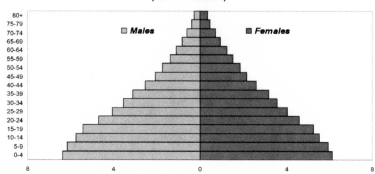

Graph 3: Age Pyramid of Bolivian Population in 2010 (est. 10.4 million)

Source: INE, cuadro 2.01.01 "Bolivia: población total proyectada...2005-2010"accessed March 2010

The economic crises and relative stagnation of the 1980s and early 1990s were not matched by any stagnation in the demographic indices. Not only did fertility decline, but mortality dropped even more quickly (see graph 1 above). Much of this more rapid decline in recent years was due to a series of acts and decisions made in the 1990s. In the 1994 Popular Participation Law some 6 per cent of monies devolved to the communities went to develop a Basic Health Care Program, which was supplemented by a specific fund to support free access to medical care for childbirth.[21] By 2005 infant mortality reached 61 deaths per 1,000 live births, and maternal mortality which was as high as 547 deaths per 100,000 live births in 1980, declined to 180 deaths in 2008.[22] Although these rates are still high by world and even Latin American standards,[23] they represent a profound and long lasting change in Bolivia.

---

21 Marjorie A. Koblinsky (ed.), *Reducing Maternal Mortality: Learning from Bolivia, China, Egypt, Honduras, Indonesia, Jamaica, and Zimbabwe* (Washington: World Bank, 2003), p. 84.

22 Margaret C. Hogan, Kyle J. Foreman, Mohsen Naghavi, Stephanie Y. Ahn, Mengru Wang, Susanna M. Makela, Alan D. Lopez, Rafael Lozano, and Christopher J. L. Murray, 'Maternal mortality for 181 countries, 1980–2008: a systematic analysis of progress towards Millennium Development Goal', *The Lancet* 12 April 2010, p. 8. For infant mortality see INEB, 'Resumen de Indicadores por mes publicados anteriormente — Indicadores Demográficos — Marzo 2010', at www.ine.gov.bo/indice/indicadores.aspx

23 For comparative world rates on infant and maternal mortality in 2005, see Marian F. MacDorman and T. J. Mathews, *Behind International Rankings of Infant Mortality: How the United States Compares with Europe* (Hyattsville, MD: Centers for Disease Control and Prevention National Center for Health Statistics, DATA Brief, no. 23, Nov. 2009); and World Health Organisation, *Maternal mortality in 2005: estimates developed by WHO,*

With this decline in births, the average natural growth rate of the population dropped to 2 per cent in 2000–5, and finally fell below 2 per cent in 2009.[24] It also meant that life expectancy rose even more dramatically from 1950. By 2010 life expectancy had increased an extraordinary 26 years on average in this 60-year period for both sexes, and reached 66.3 years of age (64.2 years for men and 68.5 years for women).[25]

The decline of mortality, especially among children and infants, was exclusively due to government health programmes, particularly the massive increase in the immunisation of children. As late as 1980, only 10–15 per cent of children under three years of age had been protected. By 2008, over 80–95 per cent of infants were inoculated with all the major vaccines, including BCG, DPT-1, DPT-3, POL-3, MCV and, since 2000, HepB3 and Hib3.[26] Moreover, the differences between urban and rural rates of vaccination declined. Thus in 2000 some 92 per cent of children under three years of age received the polio vaccination in urban areas and 86 per cent of rural children.[27] There has also been a slow but steady increase in prenatal medical consultations and assistance at births,[28] all of which effectively helped to bring down infant and maternal mortality. Finally, the increasing availability of potable water and sewerage in Bolivian homes clearly brought down the high rates of intestinal disorders which were the biggest killer of children. Whereas two thirds of all Bolivian homes in 1976 had no potable water, this had declined to just over a third of the homes in this condition by 2003.[29] Rates of intestinal disorder and malnutrition among infants and children have also declined significantly.

UNICEF, UNFPA, and the World Bank (Paris: World Health Organisation, 2007). Today, both infant mortality and maternal death rates in the advanced industrial world are below 10 deaths per 1,000 births.

24 INEB, 'Resumen de indicadores por mes publicados anteriormente — Indicadores Demográficos — Marzo 2010', and INEB, *Anuario Estadístico 2008* (La Paz: 2009), cuadro 2.01.22, p. 171.

25 INEB, *Anuario Estadístico 2008*, cuadro 2.01.22, p. 171; INEB and CELADE, *Bolivia: Estimaciones y Proyecciones 1950–2050*, p. 25, cuadro 10; and INEB, 'Bolivia — Indicadores Demográficos'.

26 World Health Organisation/UNICEF, *Review of National Immunization Coverage 1980– 2008*, Bolivia (July, 2009), at www.who.int/immunization_monitoring/data/bol.pdf

27 INEB, *Anuario Estadístico 2000* (La Paz: 2001), cuadro 3.03.14, p. 149.

28 INEB, *Encuesta Nacional de Demografía y Salud 2003*, cuadro 3.01.23, at www.ine.gov.bo/ indice/visualizador.aspx?ah=PC30123.HTM

29 INEB, *Censo Nacional de Población y Vivienda 1992, Resultados Finales* (La Paz: 1993), p. 69; INEB, *Anuario Estadístico 2000*, cuadro 3.02.04, p. 133; and INEB, 'Resumen de Indicadores por mes publicados anteriormente — Indicadores Sociales', at www.ine.gov.bo/ indice/indicadores.aspx

By the last decade of the 20th century, cases of malnutrition had dropped to just 10 per cent of the children under five years of age treated in health centres, though diarrhoea and respiratory diseases — classic indices of poverty — still remained the biggest killers of children.[30]

Although there have been important differences in mortality and fertility by region, class, and ethnicity,[31] there is little question that the direction of the secular trends in all regions and among all groups is the same. The question then arises as to how many of these changes are accounted for by the political impact of the National Revolution and how much by general hemispheric changes. In some ways, both influences can be seen in comparable world demographic statistics. Despite these impressive gains in health, Bolivia has not changed its rank position — among the worst in the Americas — in terms of mortality or life expectancy compared to all the other nations of the hemisphere, though the gap between the healthiest and the higher mortality populations has declined consistently over time.

Literacy and education

Bolivia has, however, exceeded its past ranking in literacy and education, to such an extent that it is no longer among the poorest nations of the hemisphere in terms of these factors, both so important in the creation of human capital. Although it has been suggested that increasing investments in education and rising student enrollments preceded the National Revolution,[32] there is little question that the most rapid changes in education and literacy have occurred in the past 50 years. From among the lowest indices of an educated population in the hemisphere in 1950, Bolivia by 2010 had finally achieved a level close

30 Malnutrition in 2003 was estimated to be affecting 7.5% of children aged under five; INEB, 'Resumen de Indicadores por Mes publicados anteriormente — Indicadores Sociales'.

31 CELADE, Fondo Indigena, Sistema de Indicadores Sociodemográficos de Poblaciones y Pueblos Indígenas, currently (March 2010) estimates that the indigenous ratio of infant mortality is 74 deaths per thousand live births, and 54 deaths for the non-indigenous population. The same is the case for child mortality (under five years) which is 96 deaths for the indigenous population and 67 for the non-indigenous. Moreover, the urban rates for both groups are consistently lower than for the rural ones; see http://celade.cepal.org/redatam/PRYESP/SISPPI/

32 See Manuel Contreras, 'Reformas y desafiós de la Educación', in Fernando Campero Prudencio (ed.), *Bolivia en el siglo XX. La formación de la Bolivia Contemporánea* (La Paz: 1999); and his essay, 'A comparative perspective of education reforms in Bolivia: 1950–2000', in Merilee Grindle and Pilar Domingo (eds.), *Proclaiming Revolution: Bolivia in Comparative Perspective* (London and Cambridge MA: Institute of Latin American Studies/ David Rockefeller Center for Latin American Studies, 2003), pp. 259–86.

to that of all its neighbours and well ahead of most of the Central American republics and Haiti. In fact the evolution of its educational and literacy indices compares favourably with that achieved by neighbouring Brazil during this period.

By the end of the century the government was spending more of its GDP on education, approximately 8 per cent, than most countries in the region.[33] In 1950 the country was still only educating a quarter of its children in primary schools, but this net matriculation ratio had risen to 84 per cent by 2007.[34] Bolivia does less well at secondary school level, educating just 47 per cent of boys and girls in this age group in 2007— rates that would place it below most Latin American countries. In this same year there were 1.9 million students in primary and kindergarten schools and another 537,000 in secondary grades.[35] The gross rates of enrollment, however, show that there are often more students attending than the age group at risk, which suggests significant levels of retention and failure. But these rates have been slowly declining and both the retention and drop-out rates have fallen to under 10 per cent in recent years for both primary and secondary school students.[36] But whatever the current problems with the system, the trend is towards universal coverage, at least for the primary grades, and ever-increasing rates of net enrollment in secondary schools. This has meant that the average number of years of schooling has also climbed steadily in this period, from four years to nine years, and that the ratio of those who have had no education who are aged 19 or older in 2006 has fallen to 12 per cent (7 per cent for men and 17 per cent for women).[37] As

---

33 UN, CEPAL, *Statistical Yearbook, 2001* (Santiago de Chile: 2002), table 41, p. 49.

34 Manuel Contreras, 'Reformas y desafiós de la Educación', p. 484; and for 2003, INEB, 'Resumen de Indicadores por Mes publicados anteriormente — Indicadores Sociales — Marzo 2010'. Though this extraordinary high rate of enrolment has been challenged, all recent studies suggest that these statistics are correct; see Miguel Urquiola, 'Educación primaria universal', in *Remontando la pobreza. Ocho cimas a la vez* (La Paz: EDOBOL, 2000).

35 INEB, *Anuario Estadístico, 2000*, cuadro 3.04.01, p. 171.

36 The dropout rate was 4% for primary schools and 7% for secondary schools in 2007. The repeating of grades was 7% and 8% respectively. In that year net enrolment rates were 92% for primary education and 57% for secondary schools: Ministerio de la Presidencia, Unidad de Análisis de Políticas Sociales y Económicas (hereafter, UDAPE), cuadro 7.3.2, 'Indicadores de educación por nivel según departamento: 1997–2002', at www.udape.gov. bo/

37 INEB, cuadro 3.02.01.04, 'Bolivia: Nivel de instrucción alcanzado por la población de 19 años y más de edad, por sexo, según área geográfica, 2002–2006', at www.ine.gov.bo/indice/ visualizador.aspx?ah=PC3020104.HTM

might be expected, the more recent generations have much higher completed schooling years than the older generations and the national average.

Unlike most other social and economic indicators, which consistently show that the non-indigenous part of the Bolivian population is richer and healthier than the indigenous sector, in primary education attendance, there is virtually no difference between the two groups. As of this century, 93 per cent of children aged six to 11 in both these groups attend school (with only the rural rates showing a slight difference in favour of the non-indigenous — that is 90 per cent attendance rate versus 87 per cent). As might be expected, given the greater poverty of the indigenous sector, the rates shift at secondary school level, revealing that only 79 per cent as opposed to 83 per cent of the non-indigenous group attend schools for 12–16 year-olds. Equally, in completion rates for secondary school for teens aged 15–19, non-indigenous students have an 85 per cent — compared to 75 per cent — rate of completion. Obviously, education attainment at the advanced level is not equal between the two groups, or even between boys and girls. Nevertheless, the government of Bolivia has gone a long way towards providing access to education for the entire population, and secular trends indicate an ever-increasing movement of all students into secondary education.[38]

These developments in education had a direct impact on literacy. Given Bolivia's extraordinary language complexity, the nation's rapid reduction of illiteracy is truly impressive. Only 31 per cent of the population aged over 15 was considered literate in 1950, but by 1976 the figure had climbed to 67 per cent, and by 2003 grew to 87 per cent. In fact, Bolivia moved during this period from 13th place in terms of literacy to the eighth highest literacy rate in Latin America, better than neighbouring Brazil.[39] By world standards, this places Bolivia at the same level as those countries listed as Lower-Middle Income.[40]

---

38 Surprisingly, the same proportion — 18% — of the indigenous and non-indigenous population attends tertiary institutions of learning according to data generated by CELADE, Fondo Indígena, Sistema de Indicadores Sociodemográficos de Poblaciones y Pueblos Indígenas (March 2010) at http://celade.cepal.org/redatam/PRYESP/SISPPI/

39 UN, CEPAL, *Statistical Yearbook, 2001*, table 33, p. 42, and (for 2003) INEB, 'Resumen de Indicadores por Mes publicados anteriormente — Indicadores Sociales'.

40 Somewhat impressively Bolivia ranks 43 in the world in gross enrolment rates at primary school level and 67 in terms of literacy, even as it ranks 113 out of 183 countries in the overall Human Development Index of the UN for 2009. See UN Development Programme, *Human Development Report 2009 Bolivia* at http://hdrstats.undp.org/en/countries/country_fact_sheets/cty_fs_BOL.html

Indigenous languages and indigeneity

That Bolivia now educates almost all of its children at primary level has had a profound impact on all aspects of society, but especially on the national languages spoken. Spanish did not become the dominant language until the 1976 census. As of this date, although 62 per cent of the total population were still listed as Amerindians, more than 83 per cent over the age of six now spoke Spanish, though only 42 per cent of the population were monolingual in that language.[41] This means that, through education, most of the indigenous population has become bilingual and literate in the dominant national language. In the census of 2001, some 74 per cent of 3.7 million speakers of native languages were bilingual in Spanish. It is worth noting that Aymara speakers are considerably more bilingual than Quechua speakers, a fact which may help explain their greater militancy. Among the 1.3 million speakers of Aymara, some 80 per cent were bilingual; in contrast, among the 2 million Quechua speakers, the proportion was 69 per cent. At the same time, monolingual Spanish speakers of whatever identity now made up 53 per cent of the 2001 population.[42] This would seem to suggest a continual movement from monolingualism in an indigenous language to bilingualism was the norm until the early 1990s and by the new century there was a shift from bilingualism to monolingualism in Spanish. Nevertheless, the large proportion of the population that knows and speaks an indigenous language is still quite impressive. The more rapid population growth among the indigenous peoples meant that those speaking a local language went from an estimated 1.8 million in 1950, to 4 million in 1992. But this number declined to 3.7 million in the 2001 census. The number of monolingual native language speakers, despite the growth of the rural population at unprecedented rates, nevertheless continued to decline. Quechua monolinguals had fallen to 632,000 and Aymara monolingual speakers to 263,000 by 2001. Moreover, by 2001 they were all essentially rural dwellers, the majority of whom lived dispersed in the countryside (only 10 per cent and 17 per cent respectively of these groups lived in towns or cities of over 2,000 persons).[43] At the same time, the number of bilinguals has slowly begun to decline as more indigenous people drop their native language, despite the introduction of bilingual education in the 1990s. The majority position

41   INEB, *Censo Nacional … 1992*, cuadro PP-12, p. 131; see also Raul Prada Alcoreza, *Análisis sociodemográico Poblaciones nativas* (La Paz: Instituto Nacional de Estadística de Bolivia, 1997).

42   Ramiro Molina B. and Xavier Albó (eds.), *Gama étnica y lingüística de la población boliviana* (La Paz: Programa de las Naciones Unidas para el Desarrollo, 2006), cuadros 5.2 and 5.5, pp. 106, 115.

43   DGEC, *Censo demográfico 1950*, cuadro 33 p. 102, for the 1950 data.

achieved by Spanish as of 1976 was proof of the impact of the schools on the rural areas. Not only had the *mestizo* population expanded enormously, as these figures imply, but even more importantly, rural indigenous peasants were now using Spanish on a large scale along with their traditional native languages.

Despite the loss of native languages, the number of persons who self identified as indigenous in fact remained somewhat high. Although only 45 per cent of the total population in 2001 were either monolingual or bilingual speakers of a native language, it has been estimated that 5.4 million people (or two thirds of the national population) were in reality indigenous.[44] Of this population among those aged 15 years or more, some 4.4 per cent who spoke a native language were not identified as indigenous, whereas 14 per cent who did not speak a local language were identified as such.[45] In a national household survey of 2005 it was reported that 53 per cent of the population identified itself as indigenous, but only 42 per cent spoke a native language.[46] While some transition occurs to non-indigenous status of indigenous peoples, identity still remains strong for the majority, despite the decline of both monolingual and bilingual speakers of native languages. Moreover, those who identify as being either Quechuas or Aymaras are in fact largely urban, even though few monolingual speakers live in the urban areas.[47] Finally, it was estimated in the national household survey of 2007 that 79 per cent of the population who were native speakers were literate. In the urban area the figure for this group was 87 per cent literate and in the rural areas it was 73 per cent.[48] The fact that self-identified indigenous peoples are primarily Spanish speakers and primarily literate, even if they speak an indigenous language both in the urban and rural areas, suggests an indigenous population highly integrated into the national society and polity despite its high levels of poverty.

44 Molina and Albó, *Gama étnica y lingüística de la población boliviana*, cuadro 2.4, p. 40.

45 Ibid., cuadro 2.3, p. 40.

46 In this case 8% who spoke an indigenous language did not self-identify as indigenous persons. See Milenka B. Figueroa Cárdenas, '¿Son sensibles los retornos a la educación según la clasificación étnico lingüística de la población que se utilice?', UDAPE, *Revista de Análisis Económico*, 22 (2007), see cuadros 2 and 3.

47 INEB, cuadro no. 2.01.13, 'Bolivia: autoidentificación con pueblos originarios o indígenas de la población de 15 años o más de edad segun sexo, área geografica y grupo de edad, Censo 2001', at www.ine.gov.bo/indice/visualizador.aspx?ah=PC20112.HTM; and INEB cuadro no. 2.01.14, 'Bolivia: población de 6 años o más de edad por idioma o lengua que habla segun sexo, área geografica y grupo de edad, Censo 2001', at www.ine.gov.bo/indice/visualizador.aspx?ah=PC20114.HTM

48 INEB, *Anuario Estadistico 2008*, cuadro 3.08.03, 'Bolivia: Tasa de alfabetismo de la población de 15 años y más, por idioma materno, según área y sexo Encuesta de Hogares 2007', p. 378.

Urbanisation and poverty

Increasing urbanisation of society had a profound effect on language and literacy. From being a primarily rural society, the nation moved towards a predominantly urban one in the 58-year period since the National Revolution. In 1950, only 20 per cent of people lived in towns with a population of over 20,000, while by the census of 2001 the figure had risen to over half. The two cities of La Paz-El Alto and Santa Cruz alone, which in 1950 held just 364,000 persons and accounted for just 12 per cent of the national population, in the 2001 census numbered 2.6 million persons and by 2010 climbed to 3.4 million, or a third of the estimated 10.4 million Bolivians.[49] This urbanisation of the national population also brought with it an increasing standard of living. Every index of health, welfare and education shows a consistently better situation for the urban populations than the rural ones.

That said, rates of poverty, however defined, have declined very slowly in the past few decades in Bolivia, especially in the urban areas. Although poverty levels have fallen rather sharply within the rural population, urban poverty has remained fairly constant through income transfers and other government measures. Extreme poverty between 1999 and 2007 dropped from 59 per cent to 48 per cent in rural areas, but remained at the same 21–22 per cent level in the urban zones.[50] Moreover, overall national poverty levels (extreme and normal poor) remained at roughly 60 per cent for this entire period, with a corresponding Gini index of inequality at an especially high reading in the upper 50s and lower 60s — among the worst in the world, though as we shall see this has a great deal to do with under-registration of income in a highly informal economy.[51] Although urban conditions were better than rural ones, poverty was still the norm for the majority of Bolivians. In the same year when Bolivia had 31 per cent of the population listed as being in extreme poverty (usually defined as having insufficient food intake), only Honduras, Nicaragua and Paraguay had the same or great levels of indigence.[52] Moreover, by the definition of the government, some 60 per cent of Bolivian homes in 2007

---

49 Ibid., cuadro 2.01.12, 'Bolivia: Población total proyectada, por año calendario, según ciudades de 10.000 habitantes y más, 2005–2010', p. 160.

50 Ibid., cuadro 3.06.01.01, 'Bolivia: Indicadores de pobreza moderada, según área geográfica, 1999–2007', at www.ine.gov.bo/indice/indice.aspx?d1=0406&d2=6

51 INEB, cuadro 3.06.01.03, 'Bolivia: indicadores de distribución del ingreso per cápita mensual [sic], 1999–2007', at www.ine.gov.bo/indice/indice.aspx?d1=0406&d2=6. The Gini coefficient, developed by the Italian statistician Corrado Gini, is commonly used as a measure of inequality of income or wealth.

52 CEPAL, *Panorama Social de America Latina en 2009* (Santiago de Chile: 2009), Anexo Cuadro 4 'Magnitud de la pobreza y la indigencia, 1990–2008'.

could not meet the minimum standards of housing, food, access to water, and sanitation. In the rural area this number reached 77 per cent and even in the urban area over half of the homes were below the minimum standard.[53]

Urbanisation in the second half of the 20th century also brought about profound changes in the distribution of the national population. At the beginning of the 20th century the primary axis of the nation was La Paz-Oruro-Potosí, a north-south line, which was the dynamic heartland of the nation. Here was the centre of mining, commerce and agriculture, whereas Santa Cruz was an isolated and depressed region, and Cochabamba a relatively enclosed and backward economy. With the progressive decline of mining, especially after the mid-20th century, the commercial heartland has slowly moved in an easterly direction from La Paz, and now encompasses the departments of La Paz, Cochabamba and Santa Cruz, while the Oruro-Potosí-Sucre axis has gone into severe decline. Essentially, the new NE-SW corridor connecting the three cities of La Paz-El Alto, Cochabamba, and Santa Cruz and their respective provinces accounts for most of the economic activity of the nation. These three departments provided 93 per cent of state taxes in 2009,[54] and produced 71 per cent of the GDP of Bolivia in 2000.[55] The three provinces also had the most advanced and fastest growing cities. The old mining centres of Potosí and Oruro have stagnated and their urban and rural populations are now the poorest in the country. The government recently estimated that over 80 per cent of the populations resident in these two formerly wealthy mining provinces were poor, and over 60 per cent were living in extreme poverty, so that even their urban populations were considerably poorer than the norm. Whereas Potosí, Chuquisaca and Cochabamba accounted for 34 per cent of the nation's population in 1950, similar to the 1900 figure, by the 2001 census these three provinces only accounted for 20 per cent of the population. Santa Cruz, which in 1950 held just 10 per cent of the population, again almost identical to its standing in 1900, by 2001 held a quarter of the country's residents. The total number of inhabitants living in La Paz, Cochabamba and Santa Cruz now increased from just over half the nation's population in 1950, to over 70 per cent in the 2001 census, and an estimated 72 per cent in 2010.[56] Finally, Tarija

---

53   INEB, cuadro 3.06.01.01, 'Bolivia: Indicadores de pobreza moderada'.

54   See Servicio de Impuesto Nacionales, cuadro 4.1, 'Recaudación por Departamento gestiones 1996–2007', at www.impuestos.gov.bo/Institucional/Cifras2009/4.1%20 Recaudaci%C3%B3n%20Hist%C3B3rica%202009.pdf For earlier periods see Miguel Urquiola *et al.*, *Geography and Development in Bolivia: Migration, Urban and Industrial Concentration, Welfare, and Convergence: 1950–1992* (La Paz: Universidad Católica Bolivia, 1999), p. 18, table 11.

55   INEB, *Anuario Estadístico 2000*, cuadro 4.01.03,02, pp. 291–2.

56   INEB, *Anuario Estadístico 2008*, cuadro 2.01.11, p. 159.

has become the new focus of wealth due to its major natural gas reserves — the second largest after Santa Cruz — attracting immigrants and, given its ethnic composition and resources, identifying itself closely with the Santa Cruz elite.[57]

Although the rural population has declined dramatically as a share of total population, Bolivian agriculture, except in well-defined new areas of cultivation, has remained surprisingly backward. As late as 1976, agriculture still absorbed 54 per cent of the male workforce; it now accounts for just 34 per cent (the 2007 figure).[58] Yet farmers were not more efficient, and farming only accounted for 13 per cent of GDP in the same year.[59] Most of that agriculture remained traditional low-productivity foodstuff farming. But this has changed as industrial crops have become a new industry in the Santa Cruz region in recent years. In 1980 industrial crops (above all cotton, sugar, soybeans and sunflower seeds) accounted for 12 per cent of the land devoted to agriculture. By 2008 that ratio had risen to 47 per cent of total land use and was roughly equal to all grains and root crops being farmed in Bolivia.[60] Although soybeans and sunflower seeds — produced in the Santa Cruz lowlands — are commercial crops with output close to world standards, maize productivity per hectare is less than a quarter of output per hectare achieved in the USA, and potatoes yielded but 12 per cent per hectare of North American output levels in 2008. In fact, potato output in Bolivia was just 43 per cent of the potato productivity in neighbouring Peru.[61] Much of this low productivity has to do with the fact

57 Tarija was the second largest producer of royalties (*regalías*) for the state, accounting for
    14% of the total, and with Santa Cruz it made up an impressive 62% of all rights to mineral
    and hydrocarbon production in 2008 (INEB, *Anuario Estadístico 2008*, cuadro 6.04.02,
    p. 680). Growth has also been quite impressive moving from 5% of GDP in 1988 to 13%
    in 2006. The regions of La Paz, Cochabamba, Santa Cruz and Tarija combined went from
    accounting for 77% of GDP in 1988 to 82% in 2006: INEB, cuadro 2.02.01, 'Bolivia:
    Producto Interno Bruto por año según Departamento, 198 2006', at www.ine.gov.bo/indice/
    visualizador.aspx?ah=PC0104010201.HTM

58 Horacio Valencia R., *Tendencias del empleo agropecuario y no agropecuario en Bolivia* (La Paz:
    IDRC-CRDI, Universidad Católica Boliviana, 2009), cuadro 1. It would decline another
    percentage point in 2008, but still ranked with Honduras as the Latin American country
    with the most people involved in agriculture; CEPAL, *Anuario Estadístico de América Latina
    y el Caribe, 2009* (Santiago 2010), p. 42, cuadro 12.5.

59 INEB, cuadro no. 4.02.01.03, 'Bolivia: producto interno bruto a precios corrientes, según
    actividad económica', at www.ine.gov.bo/indice/indice.aspx?d1=0101&d2=6

60 UDAPE, cuadro 1.5.2, 'Superficie cosechada de productos agrícolas: 1980–2009
    (Estructura Porcentual)', at www.udape.gov.bo/

61 For data on land sown to crops see INEB, Anuario Estadístico 2000, cuadro 4.01.04.01,
    p. 362. The comparative Latin American, USA and Bolivian yield per hectare data
    was taken from FAOSTAT, at http://faostat.fao.org/site/567/DesktopDefault.

that Bolivia spends less than any other country in Latin America on agricultural research and extension programmes.[62] Traditional agriculture, which absorbed the bulk of the rural population, has remained undercapitalised and inefficient. For all the recent agricultural transformations in Santa Cruz and some of the valley regions, rural Bolivia is still one of the poorest regions in the Americas.

Social change and 'mestization'

The picture of Bolivia that emerges from this analysis of over a half century of social development is one of major social change, combined with persistent poverty and economic backwardness. Education and health have seen the most dramatic progress. But this continuing poverty and partial betterment of living standards common to all the Americas has occurred within the context of a radically changing social system. If the slow growth of the economy has not promoted much social mobility,[63] urban migration and the rise of rural peasant and urban *mestizo* political power has made a profound difference in the response of all Bolivian governments to demands for improved social conditions. What can only be called the *mestization* of Bolivian society has become an important phenomenon after a half century of social revolution and two periods of hyper-inflation, which have destroyed a great deal of the traditional white economic power. Although monolingual Aymara and Quechua speakers are disappearing, traditional indigenous languages are surviving with a surprising vigour despite the lack of any systematic bilingual education until after the Education Reform of 1994.

In the last few decades the political power of the *mestizo* population has also been finding expression, not only in traditional and radical parties and in the new municipal political arenas, but even in the big cities, with the transformation of a quintessential *mestizo* town into the nation's second largest city. In 1988 the working-class suburb of El Alto on the outskirts of La Paz was finally incorporated as an independent city, whose administration was taken

---

aspx?PageID=567#ancor Even by Bolivian standards, the average output of potato production from La Paz was half a kilo per hectare below the national average in the period 1987–95: Grupo de Desarrollo Rural, *Bolivia: Anuario Estadístico del Sector Rural 1995–1996* (La Paz, 1996), cuadro 10, p. 48.

62   Ricardo Godoy, Mario de Franco, and Ruben G. Echeverria, 'A Brief History of Agricultural Research in Bolivia: Potatoes, Maize, Soybeans, and Wheat Compared', Development Discussion Paper no. 460 (Cambridge MA: Harvard Institute for International Development, July 1993), pp. 6–7.

63   On the theme of social mobility in the post-revolutionary period, see Jonathan Kelley and Herbert S. Klein, *Revolution and the Rebirth of Inequality. A Theory Applied to the National Revolution of Bolivia* (Berkeley: University of California Press, 1981).

over by the new *mestizo* elite. This high-altitude town, which then held some 307,000 persons, was half the size of La Paz, overwhelmingly bilingual and closely associated with the surrounding Aymara rural communities. Fourth largest city when created, by the 2001 census it had become Bolivia's third largest city with 695,000 persons — of whom 86 per cent were counted as being indigenous.[64] By 2005 the population had increased to some 872,000 and had replaced La Paz as the second largest city in the country.[65] Though El Alto had more poverty and worse living conditions than La Paz, its population still had a higher standard of living than the rural altiplano hinterland from which the migrants came, and thus has proved to be an extraordinarily important factor in the increasing social mobility of the *mestizo* class.[66] It is also the centre of intense interactions between indigenous and non-indigenous peoples, where Spanish has become the language of contact even for Aymara speakers.[67]

At the same time, the integration of the regional economies with the central cities and the elimination of the old Spanish rural élites has created a more powerful *mestizo* regional elite. It is from this elite and the upwardly mobile urban *mestizo* population that a whole new generation of *mestizo* merchants, truckers and university-trained professionals has emerged. While there have always been *mestizos* at the university from its earliest days, they were a distinct minority and forced to abandon their language, culture and origins and adapt

64 Despite the overwhelming self-identification of the city population as indigenous, it is worth noting that even then the city was primarily Spanish speaking, with 518,000 persons aged 6 upwards speaking the language as against just 218,000 speakers of Aymara and another 30,000 speakers of Quechua: UDAPE, cuadro 7.9.4, 'Distribución de población por idioma que habla, declaración de auto-pertenencia a algún pueblo indígena, idioma en el que aprendió a hablar y condición étnico lingüística, según municipio', accessed March 2010 at www.udape.gov.bo/

65 Xavier Albó, 'El Alto, La Vorágine de Una Ciudad Única', *Journal of Latin American Anthropology*, 11:2 (2006), pp. 329–50; and Juan M. Arbona and Benjamin Kohl, 'City profile: La Paz–El Alto', *Cities* 21:3 (2004), pp. 255–65.

66 In 2001, for example, infant mortality in La Paz was 54 deaths per thousand live births, and 64 in El Alto — but the latter rate was still a good 10 deaths less than the national average and than most of the rural areas as well. The illiteracy in El Alto in that same year among those aged 15–44 (3.1%) was double the rate of the city of La Paz — but again below the national rate and well below the general rural rate of the zone. The same was true of the incidence of extreme poverty in both cities that year — at 17% in La Paz and 40% in El Alto — but again the former rate was below the national average and much below the local rural zones. UDAPE, cuadros 7.9.1a and 7.9.1b, 'Indicadores alineados a las metas del milenio, 2001-2008', at www.udape.gov.bo/

67 Xavier Albó C. and Franz X. Barrios Suvelza, *Por un Bolivia plurinacional e intercultural con autonomías* (La Paz: Programa de las Naciones Unidas para el Desarrollo, 2006), p. 85.

to the norms of 'white' culture. The new breed of educated *mestizos* — far more numerous than ever before — now seems to have the option of retaining ethnic ties, traditional identities and original indigenous languages along with Spanish, which many of them choose to do.

Thus the particularly significant social changes which have occurred in Bolivia have led to an educated popular class, in both the rural and urban areas. In the urban centres, now comprising the majority of the nation, there have emerged important middle *mestizo* groups closely identifying with traditional culture even as they became fundamental parts of the modern urban economy and slowly abandoned their native languages. This growth of an articulate popular class, highly organised into communal and syndical organisations on the one hand and highly mobile on the other, has created a majority of the population willing and able to challenge traditional leadership and dominant ideologies. This is combined with an exceptionally high level of poverty and inequality, which has only moderately declined despite all the social and economic changes. It is also an economy which has had both fast growth and abrupt declines over the past six decades, thus creating ever more demands on the government for controlling risk and protecting its citizens. It can thus be argued that literacy and poverty have created a highly volatile political environment.

Politics, economy, and indigenous movements, 1982–2002

While the 1952 Revolution unleashed modernising forces into society, the political forces let loose by the revolution brought ever more conflict and economic insecurity. The MNR and its traditional leaders kept a firm hold on power with the support of the peasant groups and its long term alliance with the US. But the inherent economic and political instability of the nationalised economy and alienation of the urban white classes allowed the military to intervene. In November 1964, the army ousted Victor Paz Estenssoro after his third term in office and, given the Cold War ideologies of the era, the army would remain the dominant force in the nation from 1964 until 1982 even during temporary periods of civilian rule. But the military regimes which followed moved in quick succession from Peronist-style popular regimes to far right-wing virulent anti-communist ones. Until the massacre of peasant farmers in the Cochabamba valley in 1974, there remained an informal military-peasant alliance during which time the government continually granted land titles. But this alliance collapsed when peasant farmers made demands for price liberalisation and the government, now fortified by rising exports, was able to control the nation without traditional peasant support.

The forced resignation of the last military junta in September 1982 finally brought an end to the era of military authoritarian regimes. Hernán Siles Zuazo, one of the elder statesmen of the MNR and the leader of its radical wing, was made President and Jaime Paz Zamora, the head of the MIR party of radical intellectuals, became his Vice-President. In the centre was the historic MNR — led by Víctor Paz Estenssoro — which incorporated both the older centre and right of the party, and finally there was the ADN (*Acción Democrática Nacionalista*), the party that was founded by Hugo Banzer at the end of his military rule and proved more forceful than expected. It had gathered together the new economic elites, such as the private mining entrepreneurs and large-scale farmers of Santa Cruz, as well as many of the highly trained technocrats who had emerged in the 25 years since the National Revolution. The military interregnum had delayed the emergence of a younger civilian political leadership and thus gave one last chance for the old leaders of the National Revolutionary period to rule.

Siles dismantled the ferocious paramilitary apparatus that the last military juntas had constructed and the government moved quickly to remove the more authoritarian leaders from the army. Thus the initial national and world reaction to the government was quite enthusiastic. But the economy inherited by the Siles Zuazo regime in August of 1982 was in tatters and the situation would only worsen in the rest of the decade. The end of OPEC price inflation in the late 1970s and the decline of mineral and petroleum production combined with the state mismanagement of the junta period to create a bankrupt public sector and a deeply depressed private economy. Even more significantly, tin production went into a severe and permanent decline for the first time in the 20th century. Annual production was still averaging above 30,000 metric tons in the 1970s, and in the upper 20,000 tonnage range in the first four years of the decade, but in 1984 it dropped below 20,000 and continued to decline. In 1983, for the first time, hydrocarbons — natural gas in particular — replaced tin as Bolivia's primary export, and in that same year Brazil overtook Bolivia as Latin America's largest tin producer and the latter was down to just 6 per cent of world production. By the last years of the decade, production fell below 10,000 tons per annum, and in 1986 private mine owners (grouped into *minería mediana* and *minería chica* — middle- and small-size mines) outproduced COMIBOL (the Bolivian Mining Corporation) for the first time. The era of tin in Bolivian history could be said to have officially ended by the second half of the 1980s, and petroleum and natural gas exports along with non-traditional products (mostly industrial agricultural crops) had replaced it in importance by the 1990s (see graph 4).

Although international demand for cocaine would begin to generate an important parallel market for Bolivian exports, even this highly profitable

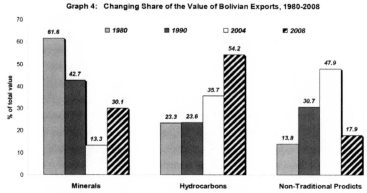

Graph 4: Changing Share of the Value of Bolivian Exports, 1980-2008

Source: Humérez & Dorador, "Una aproximación...del crecimiento económico en Bolivia 1960-2004," pp.8-9; and BCB
"Volumen y Valor de Exportaciones"at http://www.bcb.gov.bo/index.php?q=estadisticas/sector_externo (3/2010)

export could not compensate for the general decline in the mining economy and the disappearance of foreign loan funds. At the same time, the government proved incapable of controlling costs despite the decline of state revenues. The inevitable solution for the Siles government was to print more money, and by May of 1984 Bolivia was officially entering hyperinflation, which lasted until 1985. Whereas growth in the decade of the 1970s had averaged 4.7 per cent per annum and inflation just 15.9 per cent, in the decade of the 1980s growth was declining rapidly and reached negative numbers (see graph 5). In such a context of total fiscal crisis, Siles Zuazo was forced to hold early presidential elections in July 1985.

The election of 1985 was the first to create the balanced three-party arrangement of the MNR, MIR and ADN which would control national government until the 2002 election. But also emerging at this time was the *Movimiento Revolucionario Túpaq Katari*, which represented a straight indigenous rights party and was to gain 2 per cent of the popular vote.

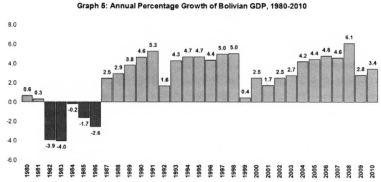

Graph 5: Annual Percentage Growth of Bolivian GDP, 1980-2010

Source: IMF World Economic Outlook Database, Oct 2009 (2008 & after are estimates)

Indigenous leadership had been alienated by the Bolivian Labour Central (COB) for many years and associated in the mind of the left with the military-peasant alliance but, in fact, an autonomous new indigenous leadership had been developing.

The rise of indigenous politics

Even as the peasant-military alliance was ending in 1974, indigenous leaders developed new political ties, not only with the traditional parties as they would emerge in the new democratic era, but also with new political movements. In 1976 Aymara peasant leaders organised the *Túpaq Katari* movement in the La Paz region. By the end of the 1970s it had taken over most of the official government peasant unions, and organised in 1979 its own Unified Syndical Confederation of Peasant Workers of Bolivia (CSUTCB). By 1981 the *kataristas* had seized control of the Aymara peasant unions and obtained representation in the COB. In that year, the COB for the first time appointed an indigenous peasant leader and a member of the movement, Jenaro Flores, as its leader. This shift in the COB was permanent as the peasant leaders, government workers and urban trade unionists now replaced the previously all-powerful mine workers as key groups in the national confederation of workers. In the altiplano, indigenous intellectuals and educated leaders formed the *Túpaq Katari* movement, which would support the increasing articulation of indigenous demands on the national political scene, including a voice in the labour movement, recognition of traditional authorities, and support for the Aymara language and culture. They also opposed the military-campesino pact. In the several national labour congresses it held under the new democratic rule, the CSUTCB and the *kataristas* proposed a new land reform decree, and even suggested an end to cultural homogenisation and the need to create a 'plurinational' and 'pluricultural' society. The dismantling of the state mining sector (COMIBOL) also had a profound impact on the popular movements. It created a new group of former miners who created peasant syndical organisations in the eastern lowlands to which they migrated. The appointment of Evo Morales to head one of the big *cocalero* federations in 1988, and the ascension ten years later of Felipe Quispe as head of the CSUTCB, marked a new more aggressive radicalism among these indigenous leaders. They now presented a series of demands relating to their perceived unequal treatment from the state in terms of agricultural prices, provisions for credit, education and health. They also proposed a change in the nature of Bolivian identity and in the role of the indigenous peoples in modern society.[68]

68   For a good survey of indigenous movements in this period see Xavier Albó's most recent
      essay, '25 años de democracia, participación campesino — indígena y cambios reales en la

Initially it appeared that the traditional parties were able to harness this new political movement and direct it from above with classic non-indigenous elite political leaders. From the early 1980s a complex political system emerged which no one party dominated. In every election from 1985 on, the electorate usually divided into three rough groupings of left, centre and right — with each political alignment made up of a complex of parties. To resolve this impasse, an informal second-turn voting for the presidency occurred in Congress. Thus every presidential election involved complex post-electoral negotiations.

Neo-liberal shock and the 'New Economic Plan'

It was the election of 1985 which brought an abrupt change to the national economic policy, with Victor Paz Estenssoro, now in his fourth term, rejecting all the models which had guided government action since 1952. In a response to hyperinflation, and under US pressure, it adopted the so-called 'Washington consensus' of neo-liberal economic policies. In his New Economic Plan of August 1985, Paz Estenssoro adopted a traditional 'orthodox shock' treatment, through which currency would be devalued, the government would stop controlling prices, and exchange rates and new taxes would be imposed, all coinciding with severe reductions in government expenditure and its role in the economy. This was a response to the impact of hyperinflation for the second time in modern Bolivian history and to the total collapse of the expensive state mining system, constructed from the base of a tin industry that was rapidly declining in importance. The only 'heterodox' aspect to the plan was that payments on Bolivia's foreign debt were temporarily halted. With prices rising and investments at a standstill, the economy went into a severe recession. An attempted general strike was stopped by a state of siege, and the general popularity of the end to hyperinflation gave Paz Estenssoro the support he needed to force through the reform.

Paz Estenssoro then went on to attack the state bureaucracy. With gas replacing tin as the primary export, the very purpose of COMIBOL was questionable. Paz Estenssoro, who had initially founded this institution, began

sociedad', in Xavier Albó (ed.), *25 años construyendo Democracia* (La Paz: Vicepresidencia de la Republica, 2008b), pp. 39–58. For new viewpoints and organisations among the *mestizo* and indigenous Aymara-origin groups and leaders, see also Esteban Ticona Alejo, *Organización y liderazgo aymara, La experiencia indígena en la política boliviana 1979–1996* (La Paz: AGRUCO y Universidad de la Cordillera, 2000); Rafael Archondo, 'Comunidad y divergencia de miradas en el Katarismo', *Revista Umbrales* (La Paz: CIDES-UMSA) 7 (July 2000), pp. 120–47; and George Grey Molina, 'Ethnic Politics in Bolivia: "Harmony of Inequalities", 1900–2000', at http://hdr.undp.org/docs/events/global_forum/2005/papers/George_Gray_Molina.pdf

the dismantling of the once powerful state agency. The reform of COMIBOL also meant the emasculation of its labour unions. Between 1985 and 1987, COMIBOL was reduced from 30,000 workers to only 7,000.

But the political and fiscal success of the so-called New Economic Plan was achieved at the cost of economic growth and the increase of social misery. Unemployment soared to over 20 per cent and the traditional mining centres of Oruro and Potosí went into severe economic decline. But the rise of an illegal and parallel coca economy provided Bolivia with some crucial resources to lessen the impact of this harsh shock treatment. Although coca leaf production was native to Bolivia and had been a major domestic crop produced in the Yungas valleys of the department of La Paz since pre-colonial times, it slowly emerged as a major export crop in the 1970s with the rising world demand for cocaine — its principal derivative — and with the opening up of new coca-producing lands in the tropical eastern lowlands.

The coca economy

The construction of the first modern roads in the 1950s to the Amazonian foothills region of the Chapare, a lowland tropical district in the eastern end of the province of Cochabamba, brought highland peasant migrants in large numbers to these undeveloped lands, and coca was one of the traditional crops produced. With higher alkaloid content than Yungas-produced leaf, the Chapare product was not highly prized for local consumption by the Andean indigenous populations, and initially the Cochabamba migrants who farmed the area were not major coca producers. But the Chapare leaf proved ideal for producing cocaine. The changing drug consumption fashions of the populations of the advanced world economies, and above all that of the US, moved towards cocaine as the drug of choice in the 1970s. This proved to be a boon for Bolivian producers, who accounted for more than a third of world production. With Chapare leaf more highly desired on the international than on the national market, and with its location far from traditional urban centres, from the mid 1970s the Chapare region became the dominant centre for coca leaf supplies being used for illegal cocaine exports. Not only was coca native to the region, and a highly labour-intensive product, but it was for the most part produced on small farms, with an estimated two-thirds of production coming from plots of six hectares or less. These peasant-owned plots were grouped into colonies and organised into large unions which were an effective voice for the small landowners. Thus, for the first time in modern Bolivian history, output of a primary export was dominated by small peasant producers. Given the labour-intensive nature of the crop and the powerful peasant syndical movement, international traders were content to leave the cultivation of the leaf in the hands of small farmers, and confined themselves to processing and marketing the output of peasant producers. Although eventually Bolivian merchants would produce cocaine base (or paste) from the peasant-produced leaf by the mid-1980s, final crystallisation and commercialisation of the product on the world market remained in the hands of Colombian middlemen. The Chapare and the neighbouring region of the Beni and the cities of Santa Cruz and Cochabamba became the centres of this new export trade, while the Yungas continued to produce coca leaf for its traditional internal markets.

Although there are obviously problems with estimating the size and importance of this 'clandestine' economy, which forms part of the so-called informal or unregistered market, it is evident that even by conservative calculations, coca exports were as important as legal exports by the mid-1980s. Physical output followed rising exports. Whereas only some 4,100 hectares were devoted to coca-leaf production in 1976, by the mid-1980s coca was being produced on some 48,000 hectares.[69] In this same period, the number of farmers dedicated to the crop went from 7,600 to 40,000. Without question, coca-leaf production had become the single most important agricultural crop, although, even in the Chapare, coca peasant farmers also grow food crops. But the quid pro quo support of the US government to the post-1982 democratic regimes was the progressive acceptance of anti-coca campaigns. By 1983 the government had set up military units to eradicate coca bushes in the Chapare. At the same time the local organisations of coca growers became ever more confrontational, and in self defence organised increasingly powerful unions and confederations, mounted strikes and road blockages and negotiated constantly with the government. Simultaneously a major effort was made to nationalise the conflict and present it as a defence of Bolivian values. By 1988 there was a FCT or *Federación de Cocaleros del Trópico* and Evo Morales was appointed Executive Secretary.[70]

In the 1980s, there was little question that coca paste and cocaine exports were extremely important for the Bolivian economy and the government did everything possible to encourage reinvestment of these clandestine profits into the national economy. These profits provided Bolivia with the only major source of economic growth in the 1980s, especially as new growth sectors

---

69   Rex A. Hudson and Dennis M. Hanratty (eds.), *Bolivia: A Country Study* (Washington DC: GPO for the Library of Congress, 1989).

70   In the 1960s the first local *sindicatos* were established in the region and by the 1980s there were 160 of them organised into 30 sub-federations (or centrals) and 5 federations. Kevin Healy, 'Political Ascent of Bolivia's Peasant Coca Leaf Producers', *Journal of Interamerican Studies and World Affairs*, 33:1 (Spring, 1991), pp. 88–9; see also Deborah J. Yashar, *Contesting Citizenship in Latin America: The Rise of Indigenous Movements and the Postliberal Challenge* (New York: Cambridge University Press, 2005), p. 185.

such as natural gas and commercial agriculture were just beginning to become important. But the combination of the growth of new exports and major US pressure finally brought about a major decline in production. By the mid-1990s the area dedicated to coca had dropped below 50,000 hectares and by the first decade of the new century it had dropped again by half.[71]

Economic change since the 1990s

By the last decade of the 20th century, a profound reorganisation of the national economy occurred that had a great deal to do with government policies and investments. The two new areas of growth that eventually came to dominate exports were natural gas, developed by *Yacimientos Petrolíferos Fiscales Bolivianos* (YPFB, the state-owned oil company) in conjunction with foreign firms, and commercial crop exports, above all of soybeans. The construction of a natural gas pipeline from Santa Cruz to the Argentine frontier in 1972 was eventually followed by the joint construction of a similar pipeline by YPFB and Brazil's Petrobras from the Santa Cruz fields to the industrial metropolis of São Paulo. Finished in 1999, the new pipeline created a new outlet for Bolivian gas, and exports to Brazil quickly surpassed natural gas exports to Argentina — with total volume climbing from around 100 billion cubic feet in the late 1990s, to over 500 billion cubic feet in 2008. In that year natural gas exports represented 49 per cent of the value of all exports, and although gas exports have recently declined, they still represent Bolivia's single most important export, accounting for 11 per cent of the total (US$ 5.2 billion) in 2009, or 2.7 times more than tin exports.[72]

Even the traditional minerals export area has seen basic change. Zinc has become the single most important traditional mineral (accounting for 13 per cent of the value of total exports), and was over three times as valuable an export in 2009 as tin, despite the fact that Bolivia is a minor world producer of the metal. Even silver exports were twice as valuable as the once mighty metal,

71 UN Office of Drug Control, *World Drug Report 2009*, table 6, 'Global illicit cultivation of coca bush and production of coca leaf and cocaine, 1994–2008', p. 64. For information on the confrontations and syndicalisation movement in the Chapare, see Sarká Malá, 'El movimiento "cocaleros" en Bolivia durante los años 80 y 90: sus causas y su desarrollo', *Revista Esbozos* (UFSC, Santa Catarina, Brazil) 20, pp. 101–17.

72 The data on natural gas production come from US Energy Information Administration, at http://tonto.eia.doe.gov/cfapps/ipdbproject/iedindex3.cfm?tid=3&pid=26&aid=2&cid=BL,&syid=1980&eyid=2008&unit=BCF and that on the value of exports from the Instituto Boliviano de Comercio Exterior (hereafter, IBCE), 'Bolivia: principales productos exportados al mundo según volumen y valor gestiones 2008–2009 (Datos preliminares)', at www.ibce.org.bo/informacion-mercados/estad_bol.asp

although Bolivia continues to have major reserves of tin and a steady output.[73] Bolivia has even exported some refined tin from its underutilised smelters. Although traditional minerals continue to lose their share of exports, the rapid growth of natural gas exports has meant that the overwhelming majority of Bolivia's exports are still made up of nonrenewable resources. Gas exports, which were slow to develop, finally became Bolivia's principal export in 2001, and grew rapidly thereafter.[74] But there has also been a steady growth of renewable and non-traditional exports, from woods and cashew nuts, to coffee, sugar, cotton, soybeans and sunflower oils. Soybeans and vegetable oils now make up 8 per cent of the value of exports. The growth of these new industries, which came into full production in the late 1990s, meant that the economy of Bolivia began expanding at rates not seen since the early 1970s. Nevertheless, although by 2008 the value of Bolivia's total exports of goods and services had more than doubled in just a few years, Bolivia still ranked at the bottom of the countries of Latin America in the total value of such exports, just above most of the Central American republics and Haiti, but behind Honduras and Paraguay.

Thus, despite the growth of new sources of wealth from gas to soybeans, Bolivia remains a poor country. While per capita income has grown from $901 in 1990 (in terms of 2000 US dollars) to $1,656 in 2008, Bolivia is still ranked third lowest income country in Latin America, just ahead of Haiti and Nicaragua (see graph 6). It also scores among the highest Gini index of inequality — about 0.6 — in the hemisphere. But as Lykke Andersen has pointed out, the standard Gini coefficients measure inequality of income and this makes it a complicated measure of reality for Bolivia. Given that only about a third of the economically active population receive regular salaries, the majority of Bolivians are either subsistence farmers or self-employed in the informal sector, 'who generate hardly any profit (income), but which may generate sufficient goods for auto-consumption'. She thus proposed to measure the Gini coefficient on consumption, which comes out to just 0.44 — high, but not as high as in other societies in Latin America.[75]

73 In 2008, the value of natural gas exports peaked at 46% of total exports, and the decline in the value of such exports (mostly to Argentina) was the principal cause for the $US 1.6 billion decline of total exports in 2009. All data for volume and value of Bolivian exports are taken from IBCE, 'Bolivia: principales productos … 2008–2009'.

74 INEB, 'Bolivia: producción nacional de minerales por año', at www.ine.gov.bo/indice/general.aspx?codigo=40106

75 Lykke E. Andersen, 'How unequal is Bolivia really?', in *Monday Morning Development Newsletter from INESAD* (La Paz: Universidad Católica de Bolivia, 11 Feb. 2008), at www.inesad.edu.bo/mmblog/mm_20080211.htm

Graph 6: Per Capital GDP in Constant $US dollars, 1980-2010

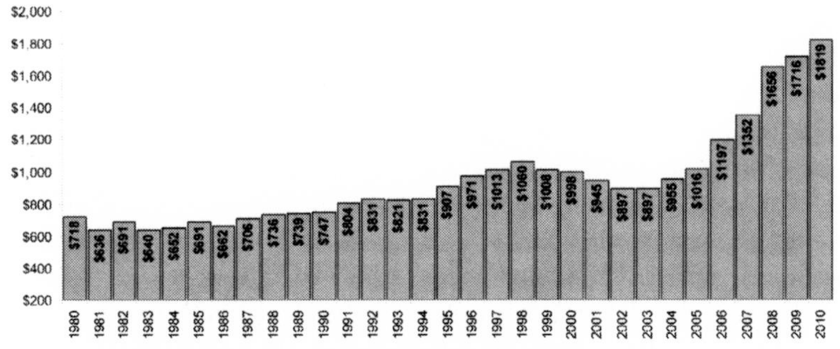

Source: International Monetary Fund, World Economic Outlook Database, October 2009

In countries without such a large informal economy the consumption and income Gini are close together. While this does mean that the Gini index measuring income and wages is not an adequate measure of inequality, at the same time it stresses the generalised poverty of Bolivia and the extraordinary importance of the informal labour market. Equally, there has been a relatively low level of socio-economic mobility until quite recently. As Andersen and others have shown, the impact of education has slowly improved mobility of the rural peasant and urban *mestizo* classes.[76]

Social and political change since 1989

Between the massive economic and political changes unleashed by the last administration of Víctor Paz Estenssoro and the major changes which would occur in the next decade, a major socio-political change was occurring in Bolivia which would eventually lead to the rise to power of the *mestizo* classes. The election of 1989 marked the passage of an entire generation of political leaders who had dominated national life since the 1940s. The presidential candidates of all three parties were men who had come to political prominence after the Revolution of 1952. With the miners' union leader Juan Lechín out of the labour movement, Siles disgraced, and Paz Estenssoro too old to govern again, Banzer alone remained from an earlier generation, and he had only entered the political scene in the late 1960s. For the MNR the most important of the new younger leaders was the US-educated Gonzalo Sánchez de Lozada, one of the new entrepreneurial miners to emerge in the post-1952 period, who served as head of Paz Estenssoro's economic team.

76 Lykke E. Andersen, 'Social Mobility in Bolivia is Finally Improving!', Development Research Working Paper Series no. 16/2009 (La Paz: INESAD/UCB, Dec. 2009); and Alejandro F. Mercado and Jorge G.M. Leitón-Quiroga, 'The Dynamics of Poverty in Bolivia', Documento de Trabajo no. 02/09 (La Paz: IISEC/UCB, 2009).

The election also revealed the massive electoral support the emergence of the first indigenous parties could generate. The CONDEPA (Consciousness of the Fatherland) party was created just prior to the 1989 election by *compadre* (Godfather) Carlos Palenque and his second in command Remedios Loza, the so-called *Cholita Remedios*. In 1991, CONDEPA captured the city government of La Paz, and in 1989 Remedios Loza was the first *mujer de pollera* (traditional *mestiza* dress) to be elected to parliament, and headed the party after the death of Palenque in 1997. New political actors now appeared on the scene. In 1990, leading a dramatic march to La Paz from the Beni, some 800 men, women, and children from 12 indigenous nations of the Oriente region demanded protection of their lands against invasion and exploitation by non-indigenous people. The CSUTCB for the first time joined forces with these new indigenous groups representing the Guaraní and other previously ignored peoples.[77]

Every government in the 1990s followed and strengthened the neo-liberal economic policies carried out by Paz Estenssoro. But significant political changes were also discussed and brought to completion by the new MNR government which came to power in the election of 1993. During this first Gonzalo Sánchez de Lozada presidency, the privatisation of state enterprises was carried out on a major scale. Although the previous regime had enacted a Privatization Law in 1992, it was the Sánchez de Lozada government which sold off numerous small firms to private investors, as well as finally privatising the big government companies which were sold through 'capitalisation' schemes. This meant that the state retained 50 per cent of each company but sold the other 50 per cent to private groups which also would administer it. Of all these actions, the one which would have the most impact was the privatisation of YPFB in 1996.[78] Upon capitalisation, the organisation immediately dropped from almost 6,000 workers to 2,000 and eventually gave up active exploration, production and transportation of oil and gas, in a period when it was transformed into what was called YPFB-Residual. Contracts were signed with numerous private and governmental foreign companies and royalties for new finds of oil and gas were drastically reduced.

It was these contracts and the passive role of YPFB that would generate enormous political conflict in the coming years. The government even enacted

---

77 For more on the *katarista* movement, see Xavier Albó, *Pueblos indios en la política* (La Paz: Centro de Investigación y Promoción del Campesinado, 2002), and Álvaro Bello's comparative study, *Etnicidad y ciudadanía en América Latina: La acción colectiva de los pueblos indígenas* (Santiago de Chile: CEPAL, 2004).

78 Alberto Chong and Florencio López-de-Silanes (eds.), *Privatization in Latin America: Myths and Reality* (Washington DC: World Bank, 2005), ch. 3.

a private accounts pension plan based on the Chilean model.[79] But to make these privatisation reforms palatable, the government created BONOSOL in 1997 (later changed to Renta Dignidad in 2007) which was a straight income-transfer programme giving a minimum pension to all persons over 65, even if they did not pay into the social security system.[80] This programme had a major impact on reducing extreme rural poverty, and also initially reduced opposition to these neo-liberal policies.[81] But even before the election, the MNR had to rely on the *kataristas* in the rural areas to win, and in recompense gave the Vice-Presidency to one of their leaders, Victor Hugo Cardenas. This actual and symbolic victory of the Aymara peasant movement provided recognition of the new importance of the *mestizos* and indigenous peasants in national politics. Not only did the Vice-President's wife make it a custom to dress for political and social occasions in traditional indigenous dress, but the Constitution of 1967 was quite concretely reformed in 1994. In its first article the terms 'multi-ethnic and pluricultural' were added to the traditional definition of Bolivia as a 'free, independent, sovereign' country — the first time this had been formally recognised in republican history. A major group of laws was also approved that not only recognised the legal personality of the *comunidades indígenas*, but also that of the peasant associations and *sindicatos campesinos*. It also guaranteed the *ayllus* and the *comunidades* their rights to local traditional laws and unequivocally guaranteed the existence of the *propiedades comunarias*, that is, the communal property rights of the traditional rural communities.

In support of this new emerging vision of a multi-ethnic and decentralised nation, the Sánchez de Lozada regime was to make a fundamental change in state organisation and political participation. With the decrees of the Popular Participation law (1994) and the Law of Decentralization (1995), the MNR attempted to change the centralist nature of the state by giving far more economic and political autonomy to the municipalities. Whereas there had been just a few dozen municipalities in existence prior to the law, and all of these located in major urban centres, the government announced the creation of 311 municipal governments spread throughout the nation — rural as well as

---

79 The private retirement scheme which Bolivia adapted at this time from the Chilean model had a limited impact. As of 2000 only 19% of the economically active population was enrolled and only 40% of these enrollees were actively paying into their accounts. Rubém Suárez and Claudia Pescetto, 'Sistemas de protección social para el adulto mayor en América Latina y el Caribe', *Revista Panamericana de Salud Publica* 17:5-6 (2005), cuadros 4, p. 424.

80 See Katarina Müller, 'Contested universalism: from Bonosol to Renta Dignidad in Bolivia', *International Journal of Social Welfare* 18 (2009), pp. 163–72.

81 Sebastian Martinez, 'Pensions, Poverty and Household Investments in Bolivia', unpublished manuscript, University of California, Berkeley, Department of Economics, 2004, at http://emlab.berkeley.edu/users/webfac/bardhan/e271_f04/martinez.pdf

urban, each with its own mayor and town council. By this act they increased the number of local elected officials from 262 before the law, to 2,900 afterward. At the same time, these new local regimes were to be overseen by legally appointed vigilance committees made up of registered local grass roots organisations. In the next three years, the government formally recognised 13,827 such territorial organisations, from urban neighbourhood committees to peasant *sindicatos*. These newly-elected governments had finally been given serious economic power for the first time. Municipalities now controlled their own budgets, and 20 per cent of state revenues were devolved to them and granted sums on the basis of population, to expend as they saw fit. Municipalities were also given some control over local education in an Education Reform Law of 1994, having authority over the non-core curriculum, all costs of infrastructure, and school supplies.[82]

So significant was this administrative change it was estimated that almost two-thirds of the 1,624 municipal mayors and councilmen, elected to office after the enactment of the Popular Participation law, were peasants or indigenous peoples. For the first time in republican history, there was a serious growth of local and regional parties. The fact that these new municipality governments had close to 3,000 patronage jobs to distribute became important for even nationally based political parties. The government also decided to increase democratic representation by dividing the deputies into those elected from national party lists (plurinominal) and those running, like the US system, under their own single ticket (uninominal), even if they belonged to a national party. Whatever the short-term problems faced by this programme, there is little doubt that it started one of the most profound processes of political change in contemporary Latin America.

82   There is a large body of literature on these reforms. See, for example: Merilee S. Grindle, *Audacious Reforms: Institutional Invention and Democracy in Latin America* (Baltimore: Johns Hopkins University Press, 2000), ch. 5; several studies by George Gray Molina including: 'The Offspring of 1952: Poverty, Exclusion and the Promise of Popular Participation', in Merilee Grindle and Pilar Domingo (eds.), *Proclaiming Revolution: Bolivia in Comparative Perspective* (London and Cambridge MA: Institute of Latin American Studies/David Rockefeller Center for Latin American Studies, 2003), pp. 345–63; and 'Popular Participation, Social Service Delivery and Poverty Reduction 1994–2000', presented at the conference, 'Citizen Participation in the Context of Fiscal Decentralization: Best Practices in Municipal Administration', Tokyo and Kobe, Japan, 2–6 Sept. 2002. Also: Miriam Seemann, 'The Bolivian Decentralization Process and the Role of Municipal Associations', Discussion Paper no. 271, Hamburgisches Welt-Wirtschafts-Archiv (HWWA), Hamburg Institute of International Economics, 2004; and Carmen Medeiros, 'Civilizing the Popular? The Law of Popular Participation and the Design of a New Civil Society in 1990s Bolivia', *Critique of Anthropology* 21:4 (2001), pp. 401–25, among others.

While many indigenous leaders were initially opposed to the Popular Participation law, many local peasant leaders quickly gained power. The most notable of these new movements was that of the *cocaleros* of the Chapare region under the leadership of Evo Morales, which soon created the *Asamblea por la Soberanía de los Pueblos* (ASP), an immediate antecedent to the MAS party. Using the peasant *sindicatos* as a base, this new party was able to capture municipal governments not only in the coca zones but throughout the department of Cochabamba. As Albó has suggested, the law was clearly a turning point in the career of Morales, who was elected to the National Congress from Chapare in 1997.[83]

In this regard, political decentralisation has undeniably provided indigenous and rural peoples with new opportunities for political participation, leading to the increased presence of *campesino* and indigenous peoples in formal politics since the late 1990s — certainly an unintended outcome of the law of Popular Participation. The multiplicity of new legally recognised communal organisations also provided a fresh outlet for *mestizo* and indigenous mobilisation. Thus neighbourhood federations in El Alto and La Paz, organised according to the Popular Participation law, led widespread street protests against neo-liberal resource policies in 2003 and 2005. Equally the popular protests over the sale of Cochabamba's waterworks to a multinational in 2000, the march of the *cocaleros* to Cochabamba in 2002, and the subsequent expulsion of Morales from congress, anticipated the ever-increasing intensity of popular violence and road blockages after 2003. This intense period of mobilisation united urban and rural workers and indigenous and *mestizo* populations as never before.[84]

It was the election of June 2002 which finally spelled the end of the traditional system and heralded the arrival on the national scene of new political movements led by indigenous political figures. Sánchez de Lozada gained the presidency with less than a quarter of the 2.8 million votes cast, while the new indigenous parties together got more votes than the victorious MNR. Felipe Quispe and his Aymara-based party the MIP (Indigenous Pachakuti Movement) gained 169,000 votes, and Evo Morales and his new party MAS (Movement Towards Socialism) obtained 582,000 votes. Both indigenous parties also gained significant representation in the newly elected congress.[85] The MAS party first emerged as a regional political force in municipal elections

---

83 Xavier Albó and Victor Quispe, *Quiénes son indígenas en los gobiernos municipales* (La Paz: CIPCA and Plural, 2004), cuadro 8.1 and ch. 9.

84 Albó, '25 años de democracia', p. 52.

85 For a useful summary of the mobilisations and the rise of MAS in this period, see Albó, '25 años de democracia', pp. 54ff., and Robert Albro, 'The Indigenous in the Plural in Bolivian Oppositional Politics', *Bulletin of Latin American Research* 24:4 (2005), pp. 43–53.

in the late 1990s. From its electoral base in the tropical coca-growing region of the Chapare in Cochabamba, its influence grew to include much of the altiplano and highland valleys, especially after the 2002 election and popular mobilisations. The election also began a process of ongoing mobilisations and protests, which finally resulted in the 'Gas War' of October 2003 over government plans to construct a natural gas pipeline to Chilean Pacific ports. The confrontations and strikes generated by this plan led to the resignation of President Sánchez de Lozada in 2003, and eventually that of his successor Carlos Mesa in 2004, and to the overwhelming victory of MAS and Evo Morales in the election of December 2005.

Conclusion

As I have tried to suggest in this survey of the social, economic and political changes which have occurred in Bolivia since 1952, increasing urbanisation, education and persistent poverty of even the urban populations, has created an explosive mix of factors which helps to explain the emergence of pro-indigenous radical movements demanding state control over basic public services and natural resources, and the empowerment of the indigenous population. The retention of indigenous identity even as language has been lost, and the systematic drive of Aymara leaders from the 1970s for acceptance of a national identity that includes an indigenous culture independent of the dominant western one — recognised in formal dress as much as in language and communal organisation — is another long-term development that helps define the series of demands around which the *mestizo* and indigenous groups have been mobilised. And last, the decades-long mobilisation of *cocaleros* against government eradication programmes finally provided a sophisticated leadership which could mobilise and propose the defence of traditional coca consumption as a symbol of national autonomous identity. It was this combination of movements and demands which brought down the Sánchez de Lozada government and ultimately led to the establishment of MAS as the leading party in Bolivia.

This massive mobilisation of the 2000–5 period concerned a whole range of issues aside from the traditional ones of better social and economic conditions for the poor. These popular protest movements now included demands for a change in basic state policy on the economy that had little immediate influence on the lives of the lower classes. In the better economic times of the late 1990s and early 2000s, with prices stable and government revenues increasing at an ever faster pace, these popular groups took up the anti-neo-liberal platform, with demands for greater state control over natural resources. They also articulated a need for the state to provide formal explicit recognition of indigenous rights to their own culture, government, distinctive dress and native language, as a basic definition of what constituted Bolivia itself. Many of these ideas were eventually incorporated into MAS's ideology when it finally came to power in the presidential election of December 2005.

2

TOWARDS A 'TRADITIONAL PARTY'? INTERNAL ORGANISATION AND CHANGE IN THE MAS IN BOLIVIA

Sven Harten

Introduction

Bolivia, in the 1990s considered an example of successful democratic consolidation, has since experienced several large-scale social protests, which on two occasions (in 2003 and 2005) resulted in the resignation of the President. What is more, the *Movimiento al Socialismo* — a political party in large part opposed to the established order, founded out of a social movement among coca producers in the tropical region of Cochabamba — surprised even its own leaders when in the 2002 elections it became the second largest party. This in turn was merely the prelude to its historic victory, with 53.7 per cent of the vote, in the elections of 2005. This result was historic for two reasons: first, in a country plagued by political instability and weak parties, where none was normally capable of attracting more than a quarter of the vote, for the MAS to obtain a clear majority represented significant progress. Without precedent since Bolivia's return to democracy in 1982, this result obviated the discredited process of negotiations in Congress, whereby support was mustered for weak Presidents through the clientelistic distribution of public offices. Secondly, the 2005 elections set the historic precedent of the election of a native Bolivian to the Presidency, in a country where the indigenous majority has been marginalised from the political process since the Spanish Conquest. For the first time, indigenous candidates became more than simple tokens designed to attract a few more votes and actually reached power through their own political vehicle.

Yet what was at the time an astonishing achievement for a political party — to receive more than 50 per cent of the popular vote — has since become almost a normal fact of Bolivian politics. Morales and the MAS have repeated their electoral success several times since: in the election of the Constituent Assembly (2006), in the recall referendum (2008), in the referendum on the new Constitution (2009), in the general elections in December 2009 and in the regional and municipal elections in 2010. Morales and the MAS remained widely popular, in particular with the rural indigenous population, and even made inroads in regions dominated by the opposition. The 2010 elections even showed signs that the MAS was able to attract some votes from previously hardened opposition supporters (Crabtree, this volume).

Since the victory in 2005 of Evo Morales and his party, the MAS, and the political and economic policies introduced by his government (such as the nationalisation of hydrocarbons and the new Constitution), much has been written about Bolivia's first native President. Rather less effort has been devoted, however, to dedicated research on his political vehicle, the MAS itself. For that reason, this chapter presents an analysis of the MAS's internal organisation, with emphasis on a comparison of the party before and after 2004 — which, despite all that has happened since 2005, is still seen as the period of most significant development. Drawing on participant observations and in-depth interviews undertaken between 2002–5 and in 2009, the main aim is to examine changes in the internal organisation of the MAS with regard to aspects such as the selection of candidates, policy formulation and internal control. Within this panorama, it is possible to shed light on the challenges facing a process of institutionalisation understood by Randall and Svåsand as one 'in which a party becomes established both in terms of integrated patterns of behaviour and of attitudes, or culture'.[1] The MAS case demonstrates that there are other paths to the establishment of party structures than the traditional model, which emphasises the development of a formal configuration. The current essay suggests that *in*formality is not per se a negative feature of party structures, and that decentralisation is beneficial for internal democracy only up to a point. While the MAS's structure continues to be an asset for contesting elections, it has not contributed to stability and predictability of the Morales administration.

A socio-organisational assessment of the MAS, with identification of its chief actors, geographical coverage, and political and ideological discourses, contributes inter alia to the detection of newly-evolving forms of participation and control of society. In making such an assessment, it is crucial to describe and gauge the nature and characteristics of the interactions between social movements and the MAS. This in turn will shed light on both the limitations and the strengths of the organisational and leadership structure of the MAS, and above all will offer a promising route for delineating the characteristics of the MAS's identity.

The MAS is, in my view, the product of the accumulation of social forces around a political project which even today commands scant consensus and

---

1   Vicky Randall and Lars Svåsand, 'Party Institutionalization in New Democracies', *Party Politics* 8:1 (2002), p. 12.

remains poorly defined with regard to its precise political and ideological aims. What is more, the political project of the MAS has been articulated with significant lacunae, which necessarily implies a degree of uncertainty vis-à-vis the discursive inclusion of diverse interest groups in a 'chain of equivalence'.[2] The logic of this articulation was crucial to secure the electoral victories of the MAS, because it permitted the party to benefit from the complex combination of a reaction of frustration and anger among the population towards the neoliberal model, and an accumulation of power by actors outside the official political institutions, especially by what could be broadly defined as social movements (mainly indigenous and peasant-based). It is not possible to analyse the discourse of the MAS in these pages, but it should be noted that discourse formed part of a popular struggle to broaden the concept of citizenship.[3] The MAS played a crucial role with a discourse of agglomerational equivalence of a range of unmet social demands, which created a new popular identity by constructing a border between the people and its oppressors. Fundamental to this model of articulation is the creation of a common political imaginary which organises social demands according to Laclau's logic of equivalence. Thus, the discourse of the MAS has proved instrumental not only in its electoral victories since 2005; it has also had an impact on the political system itself in Bolivia, through this reformulation of the notion of citizenship (as I have argued elsewhere).[4] Discourse analysis will show that the logic of its mode of articulation and a discursive process of identity construction resulted in a change to the internal organisation of the MAS.

This essay, then, will seek to examine in greater depth the impact of discourse on the internal organisation of the MAS. When the party took office, the reality it faced not only obliged it tendentiously to articulate an alternative logic — that of difference[5] — but this alternative type of articulation encouraged changes in the internal organisation of the party. As a result, the decision of the leadership to radically open the party's electoral lists to newcomers from 2004 is understood here as a critical juncture in the development of the party, which contributed to its electoral success in 2005. This strategy continued with the decision in 2009 to allow people formerly allied with 'traditional' parties to become MAS candidates, and it contributed to increasing the MAS's share of votes in the *Media Luna* departments of the east of the country. In the

2   Ernesto Laclau, 'Populism: What's in a Name', in Francisco Panizza (ed.), *Populism and the Mirror of Democracy* (London: Verso, 2005).

3   Sven Harten, *The Rise of Evo Morales and the MAS*, (London: Zed, forthcoming 2010).

4   See e.g. Sven Harten, 'Social Movements and Democracy in Bolivia: A Discursive Interpretation', paper presented at the Cortona Colloquium, Cortona, Italy, 19–22 Oct. 2006.

5   Laclau, 'Populism'.

middle term, the consequence of this opening up of the party without any simultaneous implementation of effective means of control over new members has been a disorderly proliferation of routes to participation. In consequence, the influence of social movements has diminished since these organisations lost their monopoly over the MAS's decision-making process. At the same time, alternative structural channels for participation were not institutionalised, which implied a concentration of power in the hands of a small group of leaders.

This scenario leads us to ponder the following questions: what were, and are at the current time, the main sources of tension between the social movements and the party structure? What political capacity do the social movements have to challenge, by means of their 'political instrument', the discourse of the country's dominant developmental model? If we accept the interpretation that the social movements have been victorious, and include the MAS's victory as a political and ideological triumph over the neoliberal model, and a profound challenge to the developmental model introduced since 1985, then the following questions at the very least require an answer: does the MAS articulate and constitute the organic representation of social movements? If the answer to this question is 'yes', then what lessons can the country learn from the demands and victories of the social movements?

In sum, this essay seeks to analyse the interactions between the discourse of the MAS and its organisational change. It will highlight a tendency towards the institutionalisation of centralised party structures, accompanied by a relative reduction in the impact of informal politics in the functioning of the party. Nevertheless, on the basis of these processes, the principal argument is that the internal structure of the MAS has been rather different to that of a 'traditional' party, in its informality, decentralisation, and the huge influence of informal organisations.[6] In this light, a certain degree of institutionalisation should ensure that the MAS has a positive impact on the quality of democracy, without reproducing the deficiencies of other Bolivian parties.

A brief history of the MAS

Around 1987, the first leaders of the farmers' social movement in the tropical zone of Cochabamba, the so-called *Trópico de Cochabamba*,[7] suggested that a start be made in integrating the movement into formal politics, but through their own party rather than as the lesser partner of an established party. In

6   'Traditional' is used here in the sense of hegemonic discourse in Bolivia, as a party with a formalised/centralised structure, a vertical hierarchy, and a strong role for the leader.

7   Sometimes this region is also referred to as the Chapare. However, this term is inaccurate since the Chapare is only part of the *Trópico de Cochabamba*.

1989, Evo Morales was among the first leaders to favour founding a political branch of the social movement so as to work more effectively towards its goals, though it was not until 1993 that a consensus could be built around this issue. This was partly because several leaders were anxious to maintain the autonomy of the movement and avoid involving it in the corrupt play of party politics. But once the movement agreed on the new strategy, its strong position within the national peasants' union (CSUTCB) obliged it to go on and approve the formation of the Assembly for the Sovereignty of the Peoples (ASP) during its 7th Congress (held 25–27 March 1995). However, manipulation by the dominant political parties (ADN, MNR, MIR) of the politicised National Electoral Tribunal (CNE) meant that the Tribunal exploited minor technicalities to reject the registration of the ASP. The peasants circumvented this electoral obstacle in the municipal elections of 1995 by using the ticket of the United Left (IU).[8] The pre-negotiated participation of peasant candidates then ensured an overwhelming victory in the movement's strongholds. In 11 municipalities, peasant leaders were elected as mayors, 49 candidates were elected as municipal councillors, and six won posts in the departmental council of Cochabamba. In the national elections of 1997, the coca producers won four 'uninominal' seats in Congress on the IU-ASP ticket. While IU won a reasonable 3.7 per cent of the vote nationally, in the department of Cochabamba it won a thoroughly respectable 17.46 per cent, which made IU-ASP the second party in the department. Before the 1999 elections, ASP split into two when Alejo Véliz — the ASP candidate for the presidency in 1997 — refused to resign the leadership in favour of Evo Morales, who had been accorded this role by the movement's popular base. At a large meeting of the Six Federations of the Tropics of Cochabamba[9], it was thus decided to leave Véliz with the ASP and to contest the elections under the name of Political Instrument for the Sovereignty of the Peoples (IPSP).[10] Yet again, the CNE seemed determined to place obstacles in the path of an independent peasants' party, since it not only rejected the registration of the IPSP, but also annulled the IU's electoral licence. But once again, the coca producers found a creative solution to overcome the difficulty of access to the ballot box, when they adopted the name of Movement Towards Socialism (MAS).

8   IU was formed in 1988 to unite the Left.

9   The social movement of the coca producers has three main organisational levels: local community-level *Sindicatos*, canton-wide *Centrales*, and six (approximately) provincial-level *Federaciones*.

10   Véliz allied himself with the Bolivian Communist Party (PCB) and others for the municipal elections. Once the party base decided to support Morales, Véliz calculated that his future would be more secure as candidate of the populist New Republican Force (NFR).

Ironically, the MAS had been established in 1985 when the nationalist and occasionally fascist Bolivian Socialist Falange (FSB), among the oldest parties on the extreme right, split into two. The FSB was founded in 1937, and was behind several plots to overthrow the MNR after the Revolution of 1952. But David Añez Pedraza, the founder of the MAS, failed in his socialist project, and the MAS became little more than a 'taxi-party'.[11] Being unwell, Añez Pedraza offered Morales and the Six Federations control of the MAS. In extraordinary congress, the members of the Six Federations approved the take-over. At last, the CNE permitted this maneouvre, on the condition that no changes could be made to the party's name, symbols, organic statutes, or programme. The peasants respected this ruling — at least in theory, as will be seen hereafter.

The MAS's first electoral experience, in the municipal elections of 1999, was relatively successful, with 79 counsellors and ten mayors elected. Approximately 70 per cent of the MAS vote was in the tropical zone of Cochabamba, while nationally the party won 3.27 per cent of the vote. Now with experience of local government, the MAS prepared more methodically for the elections of 2002. Networks of social movements supplied hardworking volunteers, compensating to some extent for the lack of funds available to mount a large-scale campaign.[12] Although the MAS leadership hoped for success with the help of the volunteers, the skilful use of networks of social movements and alliances, and the mixture of indigenous, worker, and intellectual candidates, 'nobody dreamt of coming so close to winning the elections' (Oscar C. Antezana, Minister of the Presidency, interview with the author, Chimoré, 1 August 2002). With 20.94 per cent of the ballot (equivalent to 581,884 votes), the MAS came just 1.5 per cent behind the winning MNR. The MAS became the biggest party in the departments of La Paz, Cochabamba, Oruro, and Potosí, winning eight seats in the Senate and 27 seats in Congress.[13] The pre-electoral period was overshadowed by an instance of foreign interference which exacerbated fears that the results would be annulled. It came as a real shock to democrats in the country when the US Ambassador, Manuel Rocha,

11   Eduardo Gamarra and James M. Malloy, 'The patrimonial dynamics of party politics
     in Bolivia', in S. S. Mainwaring (ed.), *Building Democratic Institutions: Party Systems in
     Latin America* (Stanford: Stanford University Press, 1995). 'Taxi-parties' are so small that
     their national conventions could be held in a taxi. Between 1990 and 1994 the MAS had
     approximately 20 permanent members according to Sabino Aroyo (the former mayor of
     Shinaota), who was present during negotiations by the coca farmers' social movement to
     take over the MAS; interview with the author, 23 Aug. 2004.

12   The MAS lacked the funds to give out flags, t-shirts, and other gifts to its militants, as was
     common in other parties. Its base thus organised production and sale of these items for the
     good of the party. As a rule, candidates contributed two months' salary to party funds.

13   See www.bolivia.com/cne/

'reminded' Bolivians that a vote for Evo Morales, characterised as having links to drugs trafficking, could result in US aid being cut off.[14] Ironically, this incident appears to have brought the MAS an additional 2 per cent of the vote,[15] enough to deprive Reyes Villa's NFR of second place in the elections. For this reason, Morales later 'officially named Ambassador Rocha his head of campaign'.[16]

Following these results, expectations were high that the MAS would do well in the municipal elections of 2004, especially in view of the crisis affecting the other parties. Perhaps too high; Xavier Albó, for example, concluded that the MAS fared poorly in 2004: 'I think that here, the MAS did quite badly; in the municipal elections it hasn't got a single mayor in the big cities. Not even in El Alto' (interview with the author, 30 November 2005). In Albó's opinion, the main reason was that the MAS's candidates were too ideological and insufficiently pragmatic to convince a municipal electorate preoccupied with the problems of daily life in the cities. Similarly, Álvaro García Linera (2004) — before he became a candidate for the MAS — suggested that the elections revealed the failure of the party to form lasting alliances with the urban middle class. Despite this criticism, my own view is that the electoral performance of the MAS in 2004 was far from poor: the party's vote clearly grew in comparison with 1999, and it became the largest party at the national level, with 28.6 per cent of counsellors, an absolute majority in 15 per cent of municipalities, control of one in three municipalities, and at least one counsellor in 70 per cent of municipalities. Nevertheless, clearly, the MAS failed to meet the expectations held for it, and did not achieve massive support all over Bolivia at the ballot box. This was acknowledged by party leaders in interviews in 2005, though they still considered the elections a triumph, making the MAS the only victor in the elections: 'So it's urban and rural, the MAS is now an option nationally. Not just an option for the social sectors', that is to say for groups such as workers (in particular miners), or peasants (Morales Olivera, interview with the author, La Paz, 21 November 2005).

The criticism, justified or not, became irrelevant following the MAS's victory in the 2005 elections with 53.7 per cent of the vote. I have already mentioned the historical relevance of the MAS's triumph and the election of Evo Morales, in his youth a llama-herd, as the first indigenous President. Amalia Pando is representative of many analysts in perceiving the great importance of having an 'Indian' as Head of State:

14 Rocha's comments were made during a public speech in Chimoré, 26 June 2002: *Los Tiempos*, Cochabamba, 27 June 2002.

15 Walter Chávez, 'La persecución de Rocha. ¿Favoreció o perjudicó al MAS?', *El Juguete Rabioso*, 21 July 2002.

16 In a speech during festivities held in Chimoré after victory in the elections.

Evo Morales represents that historic dimension, extraordinary, that in
500 years in Latin America for the first time an Indian is going to take
the reins of power ... Now, beyond that, if I had to make a comparison,
it's with Mandela ... The symbolism seems to me to point to that great
achievement, when the marginalised majority takes power. And that's very
similar to the achievement of Mandela (interview with the author, La Paz,
17 November 2005).

The election of Evo Morales, then, is understood here as the culmination of
the political strategy of the coca-growers' social movement, and marks the end
of a developing process of organisation from extra-institutional opposition to
governmental responsibility.

Political parties and change

Several authors have pointed to the importance of the institutionalisation of
parties,[17] which is seen as necessary to avoid erratic changes in response to
external shocks (such as the loss of elections) or a change of leader.[18] In general,
the institutionalisation of parties may be conceptualised following the criteria
of Huntington[19] as, for example, in Dix.[20] The idea here is to examine changes
within the MAS with regard to implications for the institutionalisation of the
party. One of the MAS's strengths has been its high degree of informality or
'spontaneous germination' from the party base,[21] but one current within the
party seeks to institutionalise and formalise its structures. In Huntington and
Dix, *adaptability*, *complexity*, *coherence*, and *autonomy* are important indicators.
Adaptability is measured by the age of the party, the existence of generational
succession in the leadership, and change in the party's role (for example, from
opposition to government). Complexity signifies the degree of existence of

17 See, for example, Larry Diamond, *Developing Democracy. Towards Consolidation*
     (Baltimore: John Hopkins University Press, 1999); Robert Dix, 'Democratisation and
     the Institutionalisation of Latin American Political Parties', *Comparative Political Studies*,
     24:4 (1992), 488–511; and Scott Mainwaring and Timothy Scully, *Building Democratic
     Institutions. Party Systems in Latin America* (Stanford, Stanford University Press, 1995).

18 In this work, I use Sartori's simple definition of a party as 'any political group identified by
     an official label that presents at elections, and is capable of placing through elections (free
     or non-free), candidates for public office': Giovanni Sartori, *Parties and party systems: a
     framework for analysis* (Cambridge and New York: Cambridge University Press, 1976), p. 63.

19 Samuel Huntington, *Political Order in Changing Societies* (New Haven: Yale University Press,
     1968).

20 Dix, 'Democratisation and the Institutionalisation of Latin American Political Parties', 1992.

21 Angelo Panebianco, *Political Parties: Organization and Power* (Cambridge: Cambridge
     University Press, 1988).

multiple functions exercised by the party and its type of internal structure. For example, the prevalence of paternalism is understood to indicate a low degree of complexity, because it arises from a structure mainly oriented to the service of the leader and lacking in a plurality or diversity of functions. The third indicator, coherence, has to do with the degree of consensus within the party over the limits of its functions and over procedures to resolve internal conflicts. Lastly, autonomy is an indicator of 'the extent to which political parties exist independent of other social groupings'.[22] A party which appeals to various classes and social interests is considered relatively autonomous of particular interests. However, as Mainwaring and Scully suggest, it is important for political parties to have strong roots in society, manifest in links with (several) civil organisations. One general problem with Dix's view is his linear and progressive understanding of institutionalisation, which leaves little space for a developmental model which includes both forward and backward steps. Moreover, no differential weighting is accorded his indicators, making any more precise analysis elusive. Similarly, Huntington has been criticised on the grounds that his model is ultimately tautological, since it does not set out with sufficient clarity the relation between its dimensions and institutionalisation.

An interesting step towards clarification of the concept of institutionalisation is the notion developed by Randall and Svåsand.[23] This proposes a model based on four dimensions: firstly, *systemness* denotes the density and regularity of the interactions which constitute the party as a structure. Secondly, *infusion of values* is the degree to which militants and leaders feel an identity and commitment to the party beyond simple opportunism. While these first two dimensions are internal, the next two are external: thirdly, *autonomy of decisions* is a more moderate concept than that of Huntington and signifies the possibility of taking decisions on policy without external interference. Lastly, *reification* means that the existence of a party is taken for granted in the public imaginary. As my discussion of the MAS hereafter will show, its party structure is not institutionalised, although some steps have been taken along this path. With respect to 'systemness', it can be seen that the MAS's development has displayed a high degree of 'spontaneous germination' from the base[24] which is not very favourable to institutionalisation. More important still, there exists a tension between two logics of political action and two discursive logics, which hinder the acceptance of agreed modes of behaviour. There is also the

22 Dix, 'Democratisation', p. 500.

23 Randall and Svåsand, 'Party Institutionalization', pp. 13–14.

24 Panebianco, *Political Parties: Organization and Power*, 1988.

question of resources, for which the MAS long remained quite dependent on contributions from its base, with this tendency only diminishing recently.[25]

So far as leadership is concerned — a determinant of 'systemness', according to these authors — one can observe that the MAS does not have a charismatic/personalist leadership, and is built on a pre-existing identity and organisational base. Though Morales has a certain amount of charisma, this is by no means the main, let alone the only element, of his leadership. Regarding the 'infusion of values', it can be argued that the MAS has achieved good results because the vast majority of its members are involved out of ideological motivation and an identification with the objectives of the party. In this respect, the MAS clearly differentiates itself from the other parties, whose organisational logic is opportunism; that is to say, they were founded as vehicles for the use of participation in government for the personal benefit of their members.[26] That said, it should also be pointed out that since the MAS has been in government, its organisation has continued to grow primarily in a decentralised and bottom-up manner with local branches being established all over Bolivia. In this process, it has been impossible to avoid a considerable number of opportunists joining its ranks. However, it still holds that the chief organisational logic is not opportunism — at least not yet. As will be seen hereafter, 'autonomy of decisions' is the most controversial aspect for the MAS, because a part of the new urban intellectual leadership sought to eliminate interference from the social movements in strategic decision-making. This has caused some tension within the party because the concentration of power was not accompanied by mechanisms for the productive channelling of the participatory spirit of the base. 'Autonomy of decisions' generates some ambiguity, then; by contrast, the final dimension (reification) militates very clearly in favour of institutionalisation. It is now inconceivable in the public imaginary that the party system might exist without the MAS; for the past eight years — a considerable period in an unstable political context — the MAS has been the only constant in the political panorama.

To summarise, then, a brief examination of the institutionalisation of the MAS yields a partially positive response. It has demonstrated a certain degree of adaptability, with its new role in government, and much complexity

---

25 One should note that this dependence was maintained after 2002 through a conscious decision of the leadership, which preferred to remain dependent on its party base rather than use the resources of a system it did not agree with. However, since 2006 the Morales administration has begun to use state resources for its own campaign, an action which has been criticised, for instance, by the EU Electoral Observation Mission: *Elecciones Generales y Referendos Autonómicos. Informe Final* (2009), at http://ec.europa.eu/external_relations/human_rights/election_observation/bolivia_2009/final_report_es.pdf, p. 2.

26 The possible exception is Felipe Quispe's *Movimiento Indígena Pachakuti*.

through structural links with social movements. While 'infusion of values' and 'reification' point clearly to an institutionalisation of the MAS, 'autonomy of decisions' and 'systemness' suggest that the MAS still has far to travel along this road. It has yet to achieve a generational succession in the leadership; its autonomy has increased recently with the reduction of the influence of the social movements, and in 'systemness' only the absence of leadership built exclusively around the charisma of a single leader is an advantageous factor.

Political Opportunity Structure and mobilisation of resources

As this essay will seek to demonstrate, the theories mentioned leave some questions unanswered in the attempt to conceptualise the relationship between institutionalisation and change within parties. This is particularly the case, given the need for a non-linear, non-teleological model for better explaining internal change. One solution might be to combine the notion of Political Opportunity Structure (POS) with the theory of mobilisation of resources that Van Cott uses to explain the formation of 'ethnic' parties.[27] Firstly, we find here once more the idea that parties respond (rationally) to changes in their institutional and structural context. The second variable, according to Van Cott, is the degree to which the party system is 'open', which implies that there is space for new parties, for example, due to the disappearance of parties on the traditional left.[28] The disintegration of the left in Bolivia freed up intellectuals and advisors who contributed to internal change through their ideological coherence and organisational skills. According to the theory of POS, internal change within the MAS would be caused by alterations in the institutional system (such as the new electoral code), by the perception of a capacity to occupy the space left free by other parties, and by the influence of intellectuals and advisers in the party. Van Cott concludes that the presence of leftist activists was one of the main factors in the MAS's electoral success, on an ample platform also attractive to the middle class.[29] Thirdly, Van Cott highlights the role of resources, such as the support of the bases of the social movements, as necessary for political effectiveness. Skill in mobilising resources is not only a determinant of the success of a party; also influential are the possibility and form of internal organisational changes. In the case of the MAS, the network of social movements was crucial to sustain the electoral campaigns before 2004 and, given the lack of financial resources, it would not have been

---

27   Donna Lee Van Cott, *From Movements to Parties in Latin America: The Evolution of Ethnic Politics* (New York: Cambridge University Press, 2005).

28   Ibid., pp. 26–35.

29   Ibid., pp. 88, 215–9.

possible to change the internal organisation in such a way as to diminish the influence of the social movements.[30] In view of the importance of these movements, Van Cott's analysis of the formation of the MAS is persuasive, and could also be applied in explaining the absence of significant organisational change prior to 2004. Its emphasis on the decline of the left is also interesting, because it is evident that the MAS made approaches to a notable number of intellectuals and some politicians on the left, who now play an important role in the government. Nevertheless, POS theory does not offer any complete understanding of the internal dynamic of the party. The MAS was founded in highly hostile circumstances, which made it impossible to establish a party on the basis of rational calculation of anticipated benefits. What is more, it is unfortunate to interpret decisions by the leaders of the MAS as a rational reaction to changes in the POS, because this would imply paying insufficient attention to the dynamics of internal debate, with reference particularly to the impact of different ways of formulating demands regarding the form of organisation. My aim here, then, is to add an element of discourse analysis which might help to understand the role of 'agency' in its relation to 'structure'.

Discourse analysis

The reason for applying discourse analysis in the present context is that it helps to understand organisational change in the MAS, and its yet incomplete journey towards the institutionalisation of its party structures, as a non-linear and non-teleological process with multiple steps both forwards and backwards. The basic motor of that process is an internal struggle for power between two factions, which remain ill-defined in absolute terms with regard to their membership, but *are* defined in terms of the logic of articulation. For this reason, only an analysis based on discourse theory can permit us to understand the power relations behind organisational change in the MAS.

The relation of this to the theme of the current essay is thus the idea that within the MAS, a discursive struggle for hegemony took place between two modes of articulation: between Laclau's logics of equivalence and difference.[31] Since these imply two different ways of organising the programme represented by the MAS, they at the same time imply tangible consequences for the internal organisation of the party. Thus, discourse is linked to the exercise of power, since the definition of meaning and the consequent structuring of social relations implies a (temporary) exclusion of alternatives. The construction and

---

30 Until approximately 2003, none of the most important MAS leaders so much as considered moving the party away from the bases of the social movements.

31 Ernesto Laclau and Chantal Mouffe, *Hegemony and Socialist Strategy* (London, Verso, 1985); Laclau, 'Populism'; Laclau, *On Populist Reason* (London, Verso, 2005b).

questioning of discourses reveals power relations when given political forces seek to impose interpretations and meanings, while those formerly excluded in the construction of a discourse may seek to criticise the meanings proposed. Seen in this light, the question of internal change within the MAS goes beyond a simple administrative affair: it is fundamentally a struggle for power, and as such bears important implications for democracy in Bolivia.

The internal organisation of the MAS

To gain a thorough idea of how the MAS functions, it is important to take three related but separate issues into account: the social movement in the Tropics of Cochabamba (hereafter simply 'the Tropics') which founded the MAS, the party structure, and the process of organisational change which gave rise to the current structure. Until approximately mid-2004, the MAS was governed along similar lines to the organisations of the coca producers in the Tropics, and displayed the same organisational culture. As already explained, when the Federations of coca producers took control of the MAS, they were not able to alter its organisational structure in any significant way. Consequently, we must exercise caution in our assessment of the statutes of the MAS. There is in practice a double structure to the party: first, the 'official' structure as formulated in the party statutes, with a complex and hierarchical structure along fairly typical party political lines, with a national office and departmental and local branches. This structure also incorporates a clear and rigid description and distribution of responsibilities. Although provision is made for party offices throughout the country, it is clear that the structure is far from decentralised and the local agents are not autonomous — in fact, they are simply executors of decisions made at the centre. Almost all decisions are made by the national leadership and there is little provision for an effective mechanism for participation from the party base.[32]

The second part of this double structure, however, consists of an 'informal' line in the governance of the party, with informal understood here as not forming part of the statutes registered with the CNE. What is interesting about this structure is that in reality, it is not a part of the MAS itself, but rather should be thought of as pertaining to the social movements which include the MAS as one aspect of their own organisations. Before 2004, this held in particular with respect to the coca producers' movement, while during 2005 other social movements also established branches dealing with the 'political instrument' (as the MAS is also referred to). Even while alliances with social movements proliferated, the most important decisions were taken during the *Ampliado*

---

32 Of course, the original MAS, prior to its takeover by the coca producers, was so small that it did not have a significant 'party base' to consult.

(or largest meeting) of the Six Federations of the Tropical Zone, which since the 1990s had included debate over its 'instrument' on its agendas. Thus, at all meetings of the movement in the Tropics there has been an agenda item devoted to the 'political instrument'. In this way, the base organisations are informed of decisions or developments relating to the MAS and are involved in the decision-making process. Participation operates in the same way as in the social movement, which is to say there is a bottom-up dynamic for discussing and reaching agreement on topics of importance to the 'political instrument'. The most noteworthy example is probably the fact that the MAS candidates for elections prior to 2004 were chosen by the coca producers' base, which played a particularly important role in defining ideological and programmatic priorities. It also took part in the decisions of the party, for example relating to the electoral campaign (including the selection of a slogan and how to establish relations with other social organisations). It is not possible to analyse here in detail the organisational culture of the coca producers' movement, but data from fieldwork conducted between 2002 and 2005 confirm that the notion 'the base decides, the leaders execute' operates in practice in the movement, even if at times the idea of any real 'dictatorship of the base' over the leaders seems rather exaggerated. Nevertheless, it remains true that its influence is far from trivial; and even when some leaders well understand how to convince the base of their opinion, it is not possible for any leader to take several consecutive decisions against the will of the base.

In summary, prior to 2004 a participatory culture characterised the internal functioning of the MAS, with a structurally-guaranteed contribution from the base in the most important decisions. For the base, the MAS, as its 'political instrument', is a branch of the social movement. In organisational terms, the MAS used to be perceived prior to 2004 as located parallel to the Federations and subordinate to the Coordinating Committee of the Six Federations (CCSF), the highest organ of the coca producers. After 2004, the MAS became *de facto* and in the perception of its militants increasingly independent of the structure of the coca producers' movement, and functioned more as the political expression of several social movements. The consequence of this double structure, as explained by Manuel Morales Olivera, an advisor (but not related) to Evo Morales, is that 'the MAS is a chaotic organisation, where the name of a commission or of someone's post can be irrelevant' (interview with the author, 21 November 2005). This particular connection between the party and the social movements is probably the central characteristic of the MAS structure, although it should be noted that the connection varies in intensity with different movements and is not always as pronounced as in the case of the coca producers of the Tropics. As part of its strategy of setting down roots throughout the country, the MAS has formed alliances with various social movements, but the connection is sometimes limited to giving the organisation room on its electoral list and asking it to make the arrangements for a local campaign in the MAS's name.

Organisational change

The image of the operation of the MAS sketched thus far is appropriate to the first ten years of its existence as the 'political instrument' of the coca producers. From 2004, however, the party launched itself on a process of institutionalising its own structures. This course of action remains incomplete, and some structures still appear to be provisional and to have been improvised. But, notwithstanding its 'scant institutionalisation' (Fernando Mayorga, interview with the author, Cochabamba, 10 July 2007), the MAS now has a vibrant and relatively autonomous structure, characterised by multiple commissions established at national, departmental and local levels. The intention is to channel citizens' demands upwards through the party hierarchy and to develop concrete policy proposals.

The critical conjuncture in the MAS's organisational change was the decision to radically open the electoral lists in the run-up to the municipal elections of 2004 and to transfer control over the selection of candidates to local organisations (Ivan Iporre, advisor to Morales and central figure behind the 2005 campaign, interview with the author, La Paz, 2 December 2005). At the same time, the MAS leadership did not introduce any system of controls, even in the case of the new candidates' backgrounds. No controls were imposed on entrants to the party, either in the period before or that immediately following victory in 2005. This last was a particularly significant time, since people joining the party then were likely to benefit from its incumbency — a common phenomenon in Bolivia. High-ranking leaders of the party, including Morales and García Linera, acknowledged this lack of a control mechanism in interviews with the author (La Paz and Cochabamba, 22 and 25 November 2005), but it seems that no-one regarded it as important. In any case, behind the opening of the lists lay the strategic decision of the MAS's National Political Commission to unlock the doors of the party so as to attract the maximum number of allies. These alliances were built upon a political project defined in ever more general terms, for example articulating the idea of working in the interests of all those marginalised under the *ancien régime*. In other words, the discourse of the MAS moved tendentiously from representing the interests of a well-defined group — albeit one which swelled with the years — towards the articulation of a wide range of grievances and demands. From being the 'political instrument' of the coca producers (though they continued to perceive it in that way) the MAS became a party attracting all sectors disillusioned with the prevalent political and economic system, and one which paid special attention to subaltern urban interests (for example, in the transport sector, miners, teachers, the young, or low-level public servants). For the political scientist Susana Seleme, the MAS opened up an alternative for the middle sectors seeking a party on the centre-left:

> I imagine that some parts of the middle classes identify themselves with the MAS as a reaction against the other parties on the right and centre-right (Susana Seleme, interview with the author, Santa Cruz, 15 July 2007).

In general, the opening consisted of two aspects. Firstly, a process of discursive opening or broadening articulated a growing variety of demands in a 'chain of equivalence',[33] under the term 'defence of natural resources'. Secondly, the decision was taken not to attempt to articulate the demands of other groups with the existing candidates — as is usual in Bolivian political parties — but to include the very representatives of those interests in the party, and allow them to give voice to their own demands. As a result, the MAS leaders decided that the party would seek to draw up its electoral lists with local candidates in every constituency. To achieve this, Evo Morales asked local social organisations to agree on their candidate and to inform the MAS's National Political Committee. In rural areas where either the *Sindicatos Campesinos* (peasant unions, an invention of the MNR) or a revived *ayllu* structure existed,[34] making decisions on candidates for the MAS lists was relatively straightforward since, in these cases, a hegemonic territorial organisation for choosing a candidate already existed, and once one was selected (sometimes after long and stormy debates, in other cases simply by the decision of the local elder or leader), no-one could effectively place their position in doubt. In addition, rivalries could sometimes be placated by means of the nomination not only of uninominal candidates, but also plurinominal and supplementary ones (though the position of supplementary candidate has become distinctly less attractive with the new Constitution in place that eliminated their salaries).

In the cities the situation was rather more complex, because here various organisations competed for the right to nominate MAS candidates. The different social structure in the urban areas caused numerous problems for these candidates, the great majority of which were related to the lack of any control mechanism over the entry of new individuals, which gave rise, for example, to such scandals as the candidate who had previously been a member of congress

33 Laclau, 'Populism'; Laclau, *On Populist Reason*.

34 *Ayllu* is an ancient indigenous concept of a discontinuous social space, which cannot be mapped with clearly defined boundaries. Rather, it consists of territorial journeys across different *pisos ecológicos* (roughly geographical and climatological zones), a social space that moves together with the population, 'materially spreading the cultural immanence' (Prada Alcoreza, 2002: 90) with its rituals, festivities, collective imaginaries and so on.

for the ADN, or the one who simultaneously stood to represent another party. Another type of problem arose when, say, 300 people arrived for the election of the candidate of a social organisation that might have a total of 600 members. The 300 proposed their candidate, who paid them to do just that, and as a far more united bloc than the rest of the organisation, they secured his or her election. As the analyst Xavier Albó explains (interview with the author, La Paz, 21 July 2007), this type of fraud explained the significantly low level of votes for some MAS candidates in El Alto in 2004 and 2005. It seems the leadership thought that the risk of problems with some candidates would be compensated for by the benefit of being able to attract new interest groups, especially among the urban middle class and, particularly in 2009, people voting for the main opposition parties in the *Media Luna* departments. According to a senior MAS leader, some influential people within the party warned that there would be problems with opening the party lists without effective controls. But the most important leaders ignored these warnings, because they were convinced that victory in the elections required the support of the middle class, even if this carried with it the risk of losing some militants in its rural heartlands. Towards the end of Morales' first term in office, it is apparent that the MAS indeed had to cope with mounting criticism from some core supporter groups. While this was primarily caused by unrealistic expectations as to what the MAS could achieve, another factor was its strategy of appealing to the urban middle class and interests linked to the autonomy movement particularly in Santa Cruz and Tarija.

Thus, the decision to open up the MAS was motivated primarily by strategic and electoral considerations aimed at maximising the possibility of winning the 2005 elections. In the 2009 and 2010 elections, this strategy was intensified in the sense that the MAS semi-openly sought to attract former candidates from parties opposed to it, whereas this would have been unthinkable in 2004. Many militants and some cadres (who preferred to remain anonymous) mentioned to the author that they disagreed with this strategy, since they feared that the party might 'lose face' with the influx of so many newcomers, for example intellectuals like García Linera, who ostensibly had little interest in the historic demands of the MAS. A comparison between the electoral lists before and after 2004 indeed proves that the public face of the party — that is to say, its candidates — changed:

> It's said that the success of the MAS and the MIP [Pachakuti Indigenous Movement] was to include Indians in parliament. It's striking that in the lists for this election, that's gone down. It's not necessarily a problem, because it's one thing to have indigenous candidates in the parliament. But it doesn't mean they have a project to favour the indigenous population. Not necessarily. (Fernando Mayorga, interview with the author, 10 July 2007).

The MAS, then, now has fewer indigenous parliamentarians in relative terms, which does not necessarily imply that it has no ideological project in favour of indigenous demands. But it gives a different impression to the party base if they have candidates drawn from the organisation itself, or by contrast are represented by intellectuals who claim to understand and speak for the indigenous peoples. So, although it seems to be the case that opening the party lists helped to win elections, it might also be noted that this introduced friction and tensions, both with respect to which demands were articulated by the MAS and how this was done, as well as when choosing who would be allowed on its electoral list. The latter is a more recent phenomenon since for most of its history the MAS faced the problem of not being able to attract enough people from outside its core supporters. Yet, the logic of being the party in power has caused the opposite problem: now a large number of people want to join the MAS for completely different reasons. As noted above, the MAS had no generally applied mechanisms for controlling who the first newcomers were after its victory in 2005. This resulted in some cases where individuals, experienced in switching party affiliation in line with the political tide, set up new barriers for joining the party in order to avoid the dilution of their newly-won power. As a consequence, some people sympathetic to the MAS for a long time have been barred from entering.

From the perspective of the coca growers' movement, this change on the whole implied the reduction of its influence over the development of the MAS. Instead of being able to decide the affairs of the party directly in the *Ampliados* of the Federations of the Tropical Zone, after 2004 they were relegated to having a representative on the National Political Commission (CPN). And while beforehand the base exercised direct influence over decision-making, either in the *Ampliados* or in the Coordinating Committee of the Six Federations (CCSF), from 2005 they had to be content with being represented by the *Executive* of one of the Federations, Julio Salazar, who was nominated by Evo Morales rather than being elected by the base:

> Before, comrades, it was basically you who decided. Now the National Political Commission decides a lot. The other day one or two comrades, from the Six Federations, said quite rightly that they should participate in this National Political Commission. And I want you to know, comrades, that comrade Julio Salazar is there as a member of the Six Federations, and also of the CSUTCB. (Evo Morales, during the *Ampliado* of the CCSF in Lauca Eñe, November 2005).

This meant that the coca growers lost much of their structural representation in the crucial period between mid-2004 and late 2005. This is not to say they lost all influence, nor that their priorities were completed neglected; indeed, even as President, Morales continued frequently attending meetings of the coca producers' movement. Yet the opening of the MAS lists introduced other priorities and other principal leaders. In truth, no steps were taken at the time to safeguard against the neglect of the demands of the party's founders; once more the problem of squaring a well structured and effective internal organisation with rapid organisational growth came to the fore.

The consequence was the concentration of power in what is now the most powerful body: the National Directory, composed of some ten individuals for most of the first Morales government. These include Evo Morales, Álvaro García Linera, Félix Santos Ramírez, Iván Iporre, Ramón Quintana, Manuel Morales Olivera and Julio Salazar. The National Directory takes the majority of strategic decisions and coordinates party activities. Also influential is the National Political Commission, which basically coordinates and approves the policy work of other commissions at both national and sub-national levels. It remains clear that in theory the party base takes part in these bodies by means of a representative but, in practice, the lack of any structural mechanisms for consulting with the base (*ex ante* and *ex post*) over decisions taken should be noted. Though the MAS created a vice-Ministry for coordination with social movements as an interesting attempt to bring them closer into 'official' politics (as opposed to street politics), this new institution has not been functioning according to expectations. Furthermore, it is of course a mechanism for coordination with the government and is no substitute for any MAS-internal structure. This said, I should add that there *are* mechanisms for informal consultation, and that Evo Morales seems extremely skilful at using these channels to capture the demands of the base. Indeed, Morales has a very good sense for the perceptions of ordinary Bolivians and he makes a constant effort to remain in touch with social movements. Nevertheless, President Morales has fewer opportunities for direct contact with the base, something that would be facilitated by the construction of channels for formally structured participation both inside the MAS and between civil society and the government. The new Constitution actually demands multiple mechanisms for direct participation, but it is not yet clear how they will be designed and implemented in practice.

The leadership of the MAS, both in the National Directory and the party at large, is less personalist than was the case with the ADN of Hugo Banzer, the MNR of Gonzalo Sánchez de Lozada, Jaime Paz Zamora's MIR, Samuel Doria Medina's UN or Jorge Quiroga's PODEMOS. But even so, it is Evo Morales' word that counts in the end, the more so since he does not take decisions alone or without deliberation. To risk excessive simplification, he seeks counsel among his closest circle of advisors first so that he can subsequently discuss his position in the relevant commissions and with the representatives of the interest groups affected. Elsewhere, Morales learns on the job with gusto, appearing conscious of his limitations in terms of formal education. His enormous work rhythm as President, with meetings usually starting at 6am, means that he compensates to some extent for his lack of experience in government.[35] In any case, it is clear that the provisional nature of autonomous party structures gives him and the other members of the National Directory considerable room for manoeuvre and, in the selection of candidates at least, Morales has been accused of making nominations from above and by fiat. For recent campaigns, including the election of the Constituent Assembly and the 2005 and 2009 general elections, there was a trend towards MAS leaders choosing the candidates and having them confirmed by local organisations. A number of leaders of *ayllus*, social movements and *juntas vecinales* (neighbourhood associations) stated in interviews with the author (telephone interviews, December 2009) that their organisations effectively did not determine the candidate for their electoral district. Nevertheless, it has to be said the MAS has made more effort than any other Bolivian party to consistently include representatives of civil society organisations in its electoral lists. In addition, the voices of those who did not make it on to the lists have to be considered with some care in the sense that their recollection of the choice of the candidate might be biased by their unfulfilled wish of becoming the candidate. Taking all this into account, the most important challenge in the coming years will be to bring about the installation of a new generation of leaders. For the moment, it seems possible for the MAS to continue existing without Morales; yet it also seems difficult to imagine another leader guiding the party to comparable success.

Between 2005 and 2009, one could observe a number of measures being introduced which aimed to institutionalise the party structure as the social movements gained greater independence. This was necessary to attempt to introduce some order in its overlapping parts and functions. The aim was to retain a decentralised structure, with considerable influence from the base organisations, but with the requirement of working more efficiently to produce policy proposals. At the same time, in order to channel the energy of so many militants, there was a call for a stronger organisational centre capable of directing all the commissions and related organisations. As a consequence, bodies such as the CPN or the Central Executive Committee won greater power but, despite the efforts of Iván Iporre (a member of the CPN), no effective mechanism for structured and coordinated participation had as yet been established. My informal conversations with high-ranking MAS leaders in 2006 and 2008 indicated that the improvised nature of party structures had not changed significantly, and that there were no significant efforts to improve this situation.

35 One telling anecdote is that in Dec. 2009, Morales met the EU Electoral Observation Mission team at 6.30 am, which included members of the European Parliament, European Commission and the EU Delegation to Bolivia.

In the view of the analyst Fernando Mayorga, the failure of the party structures' institutionalisation meant that the MAS remained an atypical organisation, halfway between a political party and a social movement (interview with the author, 10 July 2007). To an extent, this has been intentional with a view to avoid becoming seen as just another political party in power and exclusively active within the official political sphere (as opposed to the important sphere of street politics). This hybrid status, in-between social movement and political party, resulted in unprecedented steps being taken by President Morales, such as his hunger strike in 2009. Contrary to the frequently-portrayed image of these actions, rooted in the social movements, I contend that they were the result of the hybrid structure of the MAS.

Taken as a whole, the opening of the MAS ultimately had ambiguous results: it helped the party win the elections and attract people who did not identify with the demands of the rural and indigenous population. On the other hand, the opening was made in such an abrupt and uncontrolled way that inappropriate individuals could win positions of power or space on the electoral lists. It also resulted in individuals with merely a superficial understanding of the life-world of the MAS's core supporters rising to high political office between 2005 and 2009. This caused problems for President Morales when those individuals took a stance that was at variance with the core political line of the MAS. Though there are many other factors, I contend that this influx of people ultimately contributed to the frequent re-shuffling of senior officials in the Morales administration.[36] It also generated the problem of a lack of structural guarantees protecting the interests of its founding social movement. Moreover, we should note the conflict inherent in the attempts to autonomise and institutionalise the party structure, and the continuance of its strong roots in the social movements, who still press for the maintenance of a spirit of participation and deliberative decision-making. The challenge is thus to find a balance between a 'bottom up' dynamic and an efficient party structure. The MAS still has to demonstrate its capacity to achieve institutionalisation by means of consolidation of the autonomous party structure and the need for mechanisms to prepare for the generational change in the leadership. While it has failed to free itself entirely of the Bolivian traditions of personalism and close control of a small party elite, internal democracy and effective connections with society offer better opportunities than for other Bolivian parties. At local

---

36 However, this should be qualified in the sense that the MAS still only has a limited number of highly-qualified people to staff key offices. Hence, opening the party was inevitable to attract people to fill the many offices, while moving competent people from one ministry to the other was a strategy to have them where they were most needed in accordance with political urgencies. Yet the downside of this was of course a loss in continuity in parts of the state bureaucracy.

level, initiatives have been taken to establish an autonomous party structure, yet this structure needs checks and balances from the national leadership, and the national strategy concerning the party structure needs to be in place and implemented.

Analysis

In this section, I aim to use a description of the nature and characteristics of the interactions between the social movements and the 'political instrument' of the MAS to shed light upon the capacity and limitations of the organisational and representative structure of the party, and above all upon a promising path towards the construction of distinctive aspects of the MAS's identity. To begin with, the question of the relations of the MAS with the social movements should be addressed, and specifically whether the MAS articulates and constitutes the organic representation of social movements. An analysis of the waves of social conflict after the year 2000 suggests that the emergence of the social movements, without any single organisational leadership representing national or regional coherence, has demonstrated more than once the path to political victory and social power. I refer here to the indigenous/peasant movements for land and territory (*tierra y territorio*), the social mobilisation around the struggle for water, the struggles of the social organisations over oil and gas and for coca and its decriminalisation, the fight of cultural movements for the defence of cultural heritage, the demand for a new Constitution drafted with the participation of civil society, and other movements. The victory of the MAS is understood here as a consequence of the sum of the battles fought by all these social movements. In this sense, the party's victory in the elections of 2005 was a reflection of the power of the social movements and of the inability of the traditional political parties to capture this political energy and represent those disenchanted with the status quo.

In these social conflicts, the MAS managed to broaden its discourse so as to incorporate the demands of the protest movements and to situate itself, if not at the head of the protests, then at least as an acknowledged point of reference within them. The protests developed an idiosyncratic dynamic, since they had no centralised leadership and functioned according to a logic of spontaneous agglomeration. The role of the MAS was to articulate the different demands under a 'logic of equivalence';[37] that is to say, to represent them without introducing a hierarchy and to present them as similar in their opposition to the status quo. This logic of articulation was key to the electoral success of the party, because it permitted it to exploit 'social power' without any futile attempt at leadership of the protest movements. Thus, the key to

---

37 Laclau, 'Populism'.

the relationship between the MAS and the social movements lies not in a strict organic representation as is the case with the coca producers. Rather, relations between the MAS and the other social movements are quite variable in intensity, with alliances between movements and the party being the closest form. That is to say, the MAS has learned that the path to political power depends upon the mobilisation of the social power of the movements, but not in a vertical fashion (with the incorporation of social actors in a party structure with an internal hierarchy of demands). Rather, the proposal is for a relationship of equality with the movements, in which all demands form a discursive chain opposed to the status quo. The role of the MAS consists, then, in articulating this chain in the political and institutional sphere.

Thus far I have attempted to show how the relationship between the MAS and the social movements changed the internal operation of the party, especially after the opening of the party lists in 2004. It should be stressed once more that this opening brought new leaders to the party, which tended towards the construction of a more coherent, centralised and hierarchical structure which would produce firmer leadership over the militants. During the first Morales administration, the difficulty of squaring the reality of government with the multiple demands of social movements resulted in proponents of a more hierarchical leadership being able to argue their case more forcefully. Frequently, these new individuals, many of them professionals and urban intellectuals, came with experience of other parties of the left or an aptitude for business management, for which there was a need within the MAS. For this reason, they were in an advantageous position vis-à-vis leaders drawn from the social movements, and rose rapidly to influential positions, where they argued for a more vertical hierarchy within the demands articulated by the MAS. Partially explicable by their Marxist training or study of the Cuban or Russian Communist parties, they preferred a Gramscian approach in which the revolutionary party would organise the masses.[38]

It is striking that a logic of articulation is thus found which is different to the MAS's usual one: a logic of 'differential' articulation.[39] The logic of difference stands in contrast to the logic of equivalence since it does not articulate any common and unifying signifier under which a variety of demands can be articulated. The logic of difference assigns each demand to a clearly defined category and tries to satisfy it by turn and selectively, that is to say, by introducing a hierarchy that defines which demands will be satisfied first. The discourse of the new group of leaders reveals the notion that the native peoples should be the new vanguard that guides Bolivia towards revolutionary change and that all

38 Antonio Gramsci, 'Some aspects of the southern question', in A. Gramsci (Q. Hoare, trans.), *Selections from political writings (1921–1926)* (London: Lawrence and Wishart, 1978).

39 Laclau and Mouffe, *Hegemony*; Laclau, 'Populism'.

other demands should be subordinate to this. Clearly, this type of logic is better suited to a party in government, since it is impossible to satisfy all demands at once and thus the introduction of some sort of hierarchy is unavoidable. But one consequence of this mode of articulation is that it avoids any amalgam of particular demands into broader protests that might constitute a menace to the established order. Between 2005 and 2009 the MAS had to tackle the problem that its project of fundamental reforms constituted a challenge to the status quo and to many powerful interests linked to it. It thus also needed a discourse capable of motivating the base behind a common political project, and maintaining a broad front supporting fundamental changes. Besides, the differential logic did not concord with the discourse of the social movements, which had formed a chain of equivalence uniting various demands without clear leadership. This is comparable to the notion of Rosa Luxemburg, who argued that for achieving revolution the masses should be allowed to float freely without centralised leadership and that this would facilitate the spread of the 'revolutionary spirit'.[40]

In consequence, a tension exists within the MAS between two strategies for achieving radical political change. As I have shown, both logics include elements both favourable and harmful to the MAS as the party in power. As Laclau indicates, the tension between these two logics cannot be resolved completely, for example through either having the monopoly, because elements of the other are always present.[41] But in the MAS there is strong tension between the two logics, of approximately equal strength, and this does limit the capacity of the organisational structure and representation within the party. Under the hegemony of the logic of equivalence, the MAS developed an organisation which ensured the militancy of the grass-roots organisations and meant the party could compete successfully in the elections. With the conflict that followed the introduction of a differential logic, the links with the social movements have been weakened, while no effective party organisation has been fully institutionalised. As a result, the MAS suffers from the 'organisational chaos' described by Morales Olivera (above), which limits consistent internal representation of the diverse interests articulated by the party. Although the MAS is more open and accessible than any other party in Bolivia, it has no coherent and transparent mechanism for responding to the interests, demands, or proposals that are formulated. That is to say that, during my time spent observing the MAS from within, I witnessed tremendous energy and will to take the party forward in ideological, programmatic and organisational terms. Regrettably, it appears that the party leadership was incapable of exploiting this situation to the maximum, and the interpretation advanced in these pages is

40   Rosa Luxemburg, *The Russian Revolution* (New York: Workers Age Publishers, 1940).
41   Laclau, *On Populist Reason*.

that the fundamental cause of this failure is the unresolved tension between the logics of difference and equivalence.

It is not possible to resolve this question here, but I would emphasise that a path towards resolution would lie in a revision of the construction of the MAS's identity. This is because the articulation of the logic of equivalence implied the construction of a common identity (of opposition to an oppressive status quo) for all interest groups included in the discursive chain. With the differential articulation, this identity came under attack, while the new discourse did not achieve any hegemonic position from which to build an alternative identity. In this way, the MAS retains an identity that shows a strong face when directed against the established order and its political and economic institutions, but which in practice is no longer so clearly defined when compared with the years of hegemonic leadership of the coca producers. In addition, its understanding of itself is to a large extent based on what it opposes, namely the political and economic 'model' represented by the previously dominant Neo-Liberal parties. It might be said that the MAS's identity is partly 'relational'; it is defined by what it is *not*. Similarly, the identity of the MAS as an 'indigenist party' still retains an element of truth, but it is also diluted for two reasons. Firstly, this is due to the very mechanism already encountered, of the deconstruction of its identity through another discursive logic. Secondly, it is because 'indigenous peoples' has become a 'empty signifier'[42] and is articulated in such broad terms that even liberal *q'aras* ('whites' in Aymara) could identify themselves as indigenous, because 'indigenous' has been articulated as the essence of plurinational Bolivia.

The image of the MAS presented hitherto may seem rather negative, but I would wish to emphasise that the party has sought to maintain the spirit of an open and participatory movement. This is true despite all the changes and especially the opening of the party lists, which brought in many new people and reduced the attention devoted to the previous internal dynamic, similar to that of a social movement. Through this endeavour, the MAS managed to build a bridge between the spheres of official and extra-institutional politics. In other words, the MAS always kept one foot outside official institutions, even if it was obliged to give considerable ground in the face of pressure to build a structure more like that of a traditional political party.[43] Building a bridge between the two spheres of political action means having individuals

---

42 Laclau, 'Populism'.

43 As President, Evo Morales joined demonstrations, in effect transforming what were anti-governmental protests into pro-MAS marches. This is also exemplified by Ministers such as Abel Mamani (former Minister for Water), who, if obliged to choose between the interests of the social movement or those of the institution they head, do not hesitate to support the movement.

in official institutions who act as though they are still part of 'street politics'. This behaviour is troubling to traditional politicians because it poses, from within the institutions, the question of their legitimacy. Put more simply, since the MAS continues to have an open-ended project of redesigning the political institutions and the economic systems, it can sustain the paradox of two (extra- and inter-institutional) political actions.

And so the challenge facing the MAS is this: it has a mode of articulation that seeks to change the status quo in favour of all who suffer by it and it has a logic of political action that does not even trust the redesigned official institutions to bring about the changes demanded. But paradoxically, to respond to the various demands, the MAS has welcomed some actors who have a 'differential' mode of articulation and a logic of political action that prioritises institutional changes driven from within. This implies that internal change within the MAS, or the solution to the tension between the logics of equivalence and difference, is not only of interest with respect to the survival of the party. If the MAS wants to succeed in its reforms of public institutions it needs to draft and implement a significant number of bylaws in order to specify the new Constitution, which contains many vaguely or ambiguously formulated articles. In order to make those changes acceptable to its supporters and avoid giving the impression that the new regulatory framework is drafted by isolated experts, it is vitally important that it resolves its internal tensions and establishes more efficient internal institutional channels for the participation of its base. In my view, only the MAS can guide Bolivia during this crucial process of redesigning the institutions so that they once more win the support and trust of the people, since the idiosyncrasy of its internal structure has great potential, having links to civil society and an organisational culture that emphasises deliberation and participation. During Morales' first term, certain fundamental changes were realised but sometimes at the price of increasing polarisation in the country and the risk of alienating some core supporters. If the MAS is to successfully and sustainably implement its project of redesigning the institutions, it must be clear about its identity and organisational culture.

Conclusions

This work has presented a diagnostic of the MAS encompassing the identity and composition of its actors, including the oldest group of leaders related to social movements and another more recent group of urban intellectuals who have risen rapidly to positions of considerable influence. With regard to the establishment of relations and the exercise of power, I have indicated that these two groups are still divided by a dispute over internal power, which manifests itself in the struggle between two modes of articulation (equivalence versus difference). Regarding coverage and geographical influence, I have suggested that the MAS remains mainly a rural organisation, but that since 2004 its leadership should be characterised as partially rural at most. The reality of government has reinforced the trend of using professionals who are broadly sympathetic to the MAS cause but who rarely have an indigenous or rural background. Similarly, there has been a gradual dilution of the socio-cultural values of the coca producers in the MAS's political and ideological discourse, in favour of the incorporation of other interest groups. This was done quite successfully even up to 2009, yet — somewhat problematically — for electoral-strategic reasons the decision was made to appeal, in the campaigns of 2009 and 2010, to groups formerly closely linked to the opposition (especially in Santa Cruz and Tarija), although it is not clear how their interests can be successfully included in the discourse of the MAS.

Nevertheless, for the first time in Bolivian party-political history, the MAS can legitimately claim to have roots in civil society and to represent a great part of a population that barely existed before in the perception of the parties established as independent political actors. The persistence of informality in the structure of the MAS was one of the most important factors behind the successful inclusion of organisations from civil society. Despite all the internal changes, the party base can still hold candidates accountable for their actions and parliamentary decisions, which reduces possibilities for purely opportunist political alliances or those based on personalism. Furthermore, the MAS can count on a stable base of support, which has reduced electoral volatility in the past five years, and which conferred the popular support indispensable to implement the MAS's structural reforms. However, I have also demonstrated how organisational changes since 2004 have created tensions between the social movement and the party structure, owing to people from other sectors having reached influential positions, and arguing for a more hierarchical approach to party-movement relations. For some militants, this organisational change gave the impression of betraying the principles and goals originally established by the social movement of the coca producers, in that the party became independent of the movement and embarked between 2005–10 on a process of establishing more independent party structures. Similarly, the demands of the core social movements at the grass-roots of the MAS were articulated by other people and in different terms, that is to say, increasingly under the logic of difference and introducing a scale of priorities in demands partly as a consequence of being in government. These problems highlight the danger of losing the voluntary support of the social organisations if the MAS makes much progress in formalising its structures and is increasingly pressured to make policy choices thus following a logic of difference. This is a critically difficult balancing act for President Morales and it is quite an achievement that he managed to maintain an equivalential logic in his discourse whilst incumbent. It could in fact be argued that his controversial annual nationalisations on 1 May are to a significant extent intended to maintain or renew the equivalential chain of demands united against a common antagonist (in this case 'transnational' companies and their 'anti-nationalist' Bolivian allies exploiting Bolivian natural resources).

Evo Morales has identified that an important challenge for the MAS is managing the transition from 'protests to proposals' and finding ways to implement the latter; I argue here that these proposals have been articulated increasingly after the MAS came to power under Laclau's 'logic of difference'.[44] In terms of the conditions of articulation of the social movements and their political capacity to question (by means of their 'political instrument') the discourse of the dominant economic model in the country, this implies that it is no longer the movement that has hegemony in defining the discourse, and that its logic of equivalence has been confronted with an alternative discursive logic.

Interestingly, however, the tension between the two modes actually increased (at least for some time) the capacity to challenge the dominant economic model. This is for the simple reason that differential articulation has been necessary to achieve a programme of government, because it divides demands into elements capable of being implemented. That is to say, there is a more realistic dimension here which could point to an alternative path to neo-liberal discourse. I see the victory of the MAS in 2005 as a political and ideological triumph over the model for development implemented since 1985, by the articulation by equivalence of all the protests generated by discontent with this model. Thus, we have our answer to the question of what the country can learn from these protests and victories. Discourse analysis has demonstrated that the equivalential agglomeration of several demands in a discourse directed against the established order was crucial to the first election of an indigenous person as President. Only this mode of articulation made possible the union of the fragmented actors of civil society and the establishment of an alternative political project to the existing neo-liberal hegemony. At the same time, the MAS leadership realised that in the aftermath of electoral victory the logic of equivalence would be ineffective in implementing the changes that were planned. As already seen, the reorganisation of the MAS and the reality of being in government thus implied the introduction of a different logic in its mode of articulation of demands, and this change of discourse gives us the clues with which to begin to understand the evolution of new forms of participation and control of society in the process of strengthening democracy as a political system of social life.

44   Laclau, 'Populism'.

The case of the MAS poses the dilemma of an apparent necessity for a growing institutionalisation of more centralised party structures and the danger of a simultaneous loss of social support, accompanied by a reduction in the impact of informal politics. Greater formalisation in the party was needed, for example, because informality implied such a degree of inclusivity that problems arose with the selection of inappropriate candidates whose background came under insufficient scrutiny. In general terms, hybrid organisational forms mid-way between party and social movement can win elections in Bolivia, but to build an effective government they have to shift their organisation more towards the party form. Despite these processes, the main conclusion of this work is that the internal structure of the MAS has remained quite different from that of a traditional party, because of its decentralised nature and the massive influence of the informal organisations. For this reason, a certain amount of institutionalisation should assist the MAS in having a positive impact on the quality of democracy, without replicating the deficiencies of other Bolivian parties. But at the same time, this change will not make the MAS a 'traditional' party.

3

BOLIVIA'S NEW CONSTITUTION AND ITS IMPLICATIONS[1]

Willem Assies

From neo-liberal multiculturalism to post-neo-liberal plurinationalism in Latin America

Bolivia's new Constitution, approved in a popular referendum on 25 January 2009, reflects a new turn in Latin American constitutionalism, in which some form of multiculturalism, or rather plurinationalism — which suggests some form of consociationalism or institutionalised power sharing that would allow for the self-determination or autonomy of the peoples and nations that inhabit a state — is a noteworthy feature. Thus, whereas multiculturalism points to a certain recognition of the multiethnic and pluricultural composition of society, reflected for example in bilingual education, the recognition of the legal personality of indigenous and peasant organisations at a community level, and a limited recognition of territorial rights, plurinationalism suggests a profound reconfiguration of the state itself.[2]

During a presentation at the VI Congress of the *Red Latinoamericana de Antropología Jurídica* (RELAJU) in Bogotá in October 2008, Raquel Yrigoyen suggested that the spread of multicultural constitutionalism in the region over the past quarter-century can be divided into three cycles. The right to 'identity and cultural diversity' characterised the 1980s, examples being the Constitutions of Guatemala (1985), Nicaragua (1987) and Brazil (1988). It is important to note that the first two cases were the result of attempts to resolve a situation of violent conflict, whereas in the case of Brazil a new chapter on indigenous rights was included in the Constitution after a period

---

1 I thank the anonymous reviewer of this chapter for her/his thoughtful comments, which I have tried to take into account. Responsibility for the final result is, of course, all mine.

2 The thinking about indigenous peoples in terms of nationalities or nations partly draws on European Marxist thinking on the 'national question'. In 1998 the Ecuadorian Constitution for the first time referred to 'indigenous peoples who define themselves as nationalities with ancestral roots'.

of authoritarian military rule. Furthermore it should be noted that, at least in the case of Brazil, the inclusion of indigenous rights was part of a broad constitutional reform that also included (for example) housing entitlements and a range of social rights.[3]

A second cycle, during the 1990s, was characterised by formulations that pointed to the 'multi-ethnic and pluri-cultural' composition of the nation, and included the formal recognition of legal pluralism and of a special indigenous jurisdiction, as well as (to some extent) of indigenous territorialities.[4] Examples of this second 'wave', each with its own particular history, would be Colombia (1991), Peru (1993), Bolivia (1994), Ecuador (1998) and Venezuela (1999). Some particularities can be noted. The case of Ecuador stands out, as the new Constitution for the first time included specifically indigenous notions in Quechua language: *Ama quilla, ama llulla, ama shua* (don't be lazy, don't lie, don't steal) (art. 97:20). Another feature of the 1998 Ecuadorian Constitution is that it refers to 'indigenous peoples, who define themselves as nationalities with ancestral roots' (art. 83). The theme of 'plurinationalism' thus was incipiently present.[5] It should also be noted, however, that Venezuela presents a 'transitional' case in this cycle in that it clearly, or at least rhetorically, broke away from the neo-liberal framework and heralded the 'Left Turn' in Latin America. The other cases rather exemplify what Charles Hale, basically referring to Guatemala,

3   It is beyond the scope of this paper to outline the particular national-level processes of constitutional reform and their dynamics. Yrigoyen's view is thought-provoking but also very much focused on indigenous peoples' rights. Further comparative research is needed on national-level processes and region-wide processes, that not only takes account of the impact of indigenous peoples' mobilisations but also of their interaction with the so-called 'Left Turn' in Latin America and the implicated modification of citizenship regimes, but such a research programme is still only in the early stages (see Deborah Yashar, *Contesting Citizenship in Latin America: The Rise of Indigenous Movements and the Postliberal Challenge*). My chapter seeks to provide a modest contribution to this emerging agenda.

4   Note that in 1989 the International Labour Organization Convention 169 on the Rights of Indigenous and Tribal Peoples in Independent Countries was adopted and subsequently was ratified by over a dozen Latin American countries. The convention became an important reference in the wording of constitutional and other legislative reforms. One of its innovations was the use of the term 'peoples' instead of 'populations', already suggesting some measure of self-determination as understood under international law. The Convention, which considered the developments that had taken place since the ILO adopted the Indigenous and Tribal Populations Convention (No. 107) in 1957, explicitly took leave of the 'assimilationist orientation of the earlier standards'.

5   In the case of Ecuador the framing of the issue in such terms probably has its roots in early 20th century debates on the 'national question' influenced by the polemics on the issue in the context of the Second and Third International.

has called 'neo-liberal multiculturalism', which involves a limited recognition of cultural rights but no significant redistribution of power and resources.[6] From the 'top-down', this was very much about constructing a new mode of governance that would fit the overall Washington Consensus framework.[7] In the case of Ecuador, the initial celebration by the indigenous movement of its 'gains' in the 1998 Constitution gradually gave way to more sober assessment, or even a sort of hangover; rhetorical gains had been achieved but the absence of indigenous representatives in the commissions preparing an outline for a new economic model was also noted.[8] At that juncture Stavenhagen recorded:

> It has now become clearer that what began as demands for specific rights and compensatory measures has turned into a new view of the nation and the state (...). After the enthusiastic groundswell of the 1990s, the first decades of the twenty-first century may find new and more pragmatic forms of accommodation between Indians and various political and economic forces.[9]

6   Charles Hale, 'Does Multiculturalism Menace? Governance, Cultural Rights and the Politics of Identity in Guatemala', *Journal of Latin American Studies* 34:3 (Aug. 2002), pp. 485–524.

7   The term 'Washington Consensus' was coined by Williamson to refer to what he perceived as the basic tenets of policy prescriptions adopted by the Washington-based multilateral financial institutions: 1) reducing fiscal deficits; 2) switching public expenditure from subsidies towards education and health and infrastructure investment; 3) tax reform; 4) interest rates that should be market determined but at the same time should be positive in order to discourage capital flight and increase savings; 5) achieving competitive exchange rates; 6) import liberalisation under some conditions; 7) lifting restrictions on foreign direct investment; 8) privatisation; 9) deregulation; and 10) security of property rights; see John Williamson, 'What Washington Means by Policy Reform', in same author (ed.), *Latin American Adjustment: How Much has Happened?* (Washington: Institute for International Economics, 1990). In Bolivia most of these policy guidelines — except for all-out privatisation — were followed in the New Economic Policy introduced in 1985, which brought an end to reeling inflation but hardly alleviated the hardships of most of the population. Under the Gonzalo Sánchez de Lozada presidency (1993–7) these measures aimed at establishing macro-economic stability would be followed by a round of 'second generation' reforms that included extensive privatisations and a reform of the state through decentralisation to the municipal level, as well as a certain recognition of indigenous rights, including some territorial rights and the introduction of bilingual education.

8   For a critical assessment of Ecuador's position see Carmen Martínez (ed.), *Repensando los movimientos indígenas* (Quito: FLACSO, sede Ecuador/Ministerio de Cultura del Ecuador, 2009) and the comparative study of Bolivia and Ecuador by José Antonio Lucero, *Struggles of Voice: The Politics of Indigenous Representation in the Andes* (Pittsburgh: University of Pittsburgh Press, 2008).

9   Rodolfo Stavenhagen, 'Indigenous Peoples and the State in Latin America: An Ongoing Debate', in Rachel Sieder (ed.), *Multiculturalism in Latin America: Indigenous Rights,*

By the end of the past century indigenous movements found themselves at a cross-roads. Some gains had been made in terms of specific demands, but such gains were framed in the context of what Hale has called neo-liberal multiculturalism in the 'Era of the *Indio Permitido*'.[10] Hale, however, also points out that the indigenous may be somewhat unruly subjects and may contribute to subverting the neo-liberal scheme. Van Cott highlights the evolution of 'ethnic politics' in Latin America and their impact in Bolivia and Ecuador as well as their mitigated impact in Peru, Argentina, Colombia and Venezuela.[11] She seeks to assess the transformation from ethnic movements into parties and their impact on national-level political systems, and thus to some extent she anticipated what Yrigoyen identified as a 'third cycle'.

Diversity and Democracy (Houndmills and New York: Palgrave Macmillan, 2002), p. 41.

10   Hale, 'Does Multiculturalism Menace?'; also Charles Hale, 'Rethinking Indigenous Politics in the Era of the *Indio Permitido*', *NACLA Report on the Americas* 38:2 (2004), pp. 16–21. See also Yashar, *Contesting Citizenship*, on the development of citizenship regimes in Latin America. The collection by Salvador Martí i Puig (ed.), *Pueblos indígenas y política en América Latina: El reconocimiento de sus derechos y el impacto de sus demandas a inicios del siglo XXI* (Barcelona: Fundació CIDOB, 2007), presents an excellent panorama of the state of affairs at the beginning of the 21st century. The collections by Jesús Espasandín López and Pablo Iglesias Turrión (eds.), *Bolivia en movimiento: Acción colectiva y poder político* (Madrid: El Viejo Topo, 2007), and by Martínez (ed.), *Repensando los movimientos indígenas*, respectively, provide valuable insights on Bolivia and Ecuador. Lucero, *Struggles of Voice*, presents an interesting comparison between these countries.

11   This is partly due to the size of indigenous populations, which are quite small in Colombia and Venezuela, but rather large in Bolivia and in the controversial case of Ecuador, where estimates of the indigenous population range between 6% and 32%. In Peru the size of the indigenous population is estimated between 17% — Heather Marie Layton and Harry Anthony Patrinos, 'Estimating the Number of Indigenous Peoples in Latin America', in Gilette Hall and Harry Anthony Patrinos (eds.), *Indigenous Peoples, Poverty and Development in Latin America* (Houndmills and New York: Palgrave MacMillan, 2006) — and 47%, see Cletus Gregor Barié, *Pueblos indígenas y derechos constitucionales en América Latina: un panorama* 2nd ed. (Mexico City and Quito: Instituto Interamericano Indigenista/ Comisión Nacional para el Desarrollo de los Pueblos Indígenas/Editorial Abya-Yala, 2003), p. 44, but the dynamics of indigenous mobilisation seem to be quite different from those in neighbouring countries due to particular historical circumstances; see Donna Lee Van Cott, *From Movements to Parties in Latin America*, pp. 140–76. Nonetheless, the impact of indigenous movements does not depend solely on the size of the indigenous population but also on their moral status, as became clear in the debates on the constitutional reform in Colombia in 1992, where indigenous organisations had an important impact, despite the small size of the indigenous population: Van Cott, *The Friendly Liquidation of the Past: The Politics of Diversity in Latin America* (Pittsburgh: University of Pittsburgh Press, 2000).

Yrigoyen notes that this third cycle would be exemplified by the processes of constitutional reform in Bolivia and Ecuador. The focus of her presentation, however, is above all on the recognition of legal pluralism. This is valuable as such, but also somewhat limited because it bypasses the debate on development 'paradigms' and the contribution of Latin American indigenous and popular movements in challenging the dominant neo-liberal paradigm. In order to assess the Bolivian constitutional reform from a comparative perspective it is necessary to move beyond the issue of legal pluralism and include the question of 'development' and the construction of a post-(neo)liberal framework as well as the issue of autonomies and the construction of a post-colonial and pluri-national state, future prospects and the role of indigenous movements and parties[12] in constructing such prospects and a new citizenship regime.[13]

Bolivian constitutionalism and citizenship

Ever since independence in 1825, Bolivia has been a quite prolific producer of Constitutions: 'sixteen of them plus six constitutional reforms between 1826 and 2004', according to Kohl and Farthing.[14] Its last Constitution was adopted in 1967 during the government of general René Barrientos (1966–9), and was reformed in 1994 during the government of Gonzalo Sánchez de Lozada and again in 2004 during the brief government of Carlos Mesa (2003–5).

The 1938 Constitution, adopted under the government of Germán Busch — an exponent of post-Chaco War (1932–5) 'military socialism' — marked a turning point in Bolivian constitutionalism, in departing from the liberal orientation of previous Constitutions by introducing the concept of the social function of property and more generally of social constitutionalism and a nationalist redefinition of the role of the state in the economy and its originary possession of natural resources. In this the Constitution was inspired by the Mexican Constitution of 1917 and the political thinking about social constitutionalism that followed in its wake, but also by European fascism. The 1938 Constituent Convention also stood out, for the first and only time in Bolivian history, for the direct representation of certain functional, corporative

---

12 Van Cott, *From Movements to Parties in Latin America*.

13 Yashar, *Contesting Citizenship in Latin America*.

14 Benjamin Kohl and Linda Farthing, *Impasse in Bolivia: Neoliberal Hegemony and Popular Resistance* (London: Zed, 2006), p. 41. The precise number of Constitutions remains a matter of debate. See also Rossana Barragán, 'Ciudadania y elecciones, convenciones y debates', in Rossana Barragán and José Luis Roca, *Regiones y poder constituyente en Bolivia: Una historia de pactos y disputas* (La Paz: Programa de la Naciones Unidas para el Desarrollo, 2005), pp. 335–6, and Carlos Romero Bonifaz, *El proceso constituyente boliviano: El hito de la cuarta marcha de tierras bajas* (Santa Cruz de la Sierra: CEJIS, 2005), pp. 338–51.

sectors: the workers and Chaco War veterans.[15] The issues debated at this juncture foreshadowed the themes that were central to Bolivian political debate for decades to come.[16] The 1938 Constitution introduced the minimum salary, established the length of the working day, paid holidays, social security and other labour rights. It also included the idea of universal free education, as well as progressive family rights, and strengthened the position of peasant and indigenous communities, thus prefiguring many aspects that would take further shape with the 1952 revolution. The 1938 Constitution was reformed in 1945 and 1947, mainly so as to consolidate its content and introduce some institutional reforms.[17]

New reforms came about in 1961, in the wake of the 1952 Bolivian Revolution and to consolidate its gains. These included: the universal vote and the consolidation of electoral institutions; the declaration that nationalised mines are part of the national patrimony and will be exploited by an autarchic entity; the fundamental principles of the 1953 agrarian reform according to which the land belongs to those who work it, agrarian enterprises and middle-sized properties should comply with a social-economic function and *latifundios* are prohibited; the educational reform; social rights; and urban reform.[18]

In 1967, under the government of René Barrientos — then in power — a new Constitution was adopted, though this document's deliberations drew little public attention as the capture and killing of Che Guevara was dominating the headlines.[19] A major feature of this reform was the revision of the Constitution's structure. The first part, containing general dispositions, was followed by three other sections: 1) the person as member of the state (personal guarantees and nationality and citizenship rules); 2) the Bolivian state (division of powers and organisations of the legislative, executive and judiciary); and 3) special regimes (e.g. economic and financial organisation, social, agrarian-peasant, cultural, family law, and so on). In its final part, the 1967 Constitution introduced a procedure requiring a law of necessity for constitutional reform to be adopted by a two-thirds majority in both the Chamber of Deputies and the Senate, stipulating the articles to be modified. This law would then set the framework for reform under a new government, after general elections. The 1967 Constitution retained many of the stipulations of the 1961 Constitution that had enshrined the major gains of the 1952 revolution and put particularly strong emphasis on the agrarian regime — the Barrientos government relied

15 Barragán, 'Ciudadania y elecciones, convenciones y debates'.

16 Laura Gotkowitz, *A Revolution for our Rights: Indigenous Struggles for Land and Justice in Bolivia, 1880–1952* (Durham, NC: Duke University Press, 2007), pp. 114–30.

17 Romero Bonifaz, *El proceso constituyente boliviano*, pp. 346–7.

18 Ibid, pp. 348–9.

19 Barragán, 'Ciudadania y elecciones, convenciones y debates', p. 374.

heavily upon the peasantry, while the heavily-oppressed miners were its main enemy. Under Barrientos, ties with the USA were strengthened and some measures of economic liberalisation and promotion of foreign investment were implemented. After his death in 1969 the Constitution remained officially in force but the right-wing authoritarian regimes that governed the country between 1971 and 1982 only paid lip-service to it.

The 1967 Constitution remained unchanged until 1994. By then Bolivia had experienced the roller-coaster transition to elected government, which was finally established in 1982. The first years saw an attempt to revive the economic model introduced in 1952, but were characterised by governmental instability and inflation, which eventually reached 25,000 per cent. Under a new government a harsh shock-therapy was applied in 1985. This inaugurated a progressive liberalisation of the economy and the abolition of the 'State of 1952' through structural adjustment measures that were largely inspired by the Washington Consensus agenda. From 1985 onward, politics came to be dominated by what has become known as 'pacted democracy' or 'parliamentary presidentialism'. According to the electoral system, in the case that no candidate gained an absolute majority, Congress would elect the President from among the three run-off candidates in general elections. It is unique to Latin America in combining features of presidentialism and parliamentarism and has strong coalition-inducing effects. The arrangement resulted in back-room dealings among party chiefs negotiating a division of the spoils according to a patronage system, while at the same time agreeing that the neo-liberal policies introduced in 1985 would not be called into question.[20] The controversial 1989 elections brought the third-placed candidate Jaime Paz Zamora of the *Movimiento de la Izquierda Revolucionaria* (MIR) to the presidency in a curious coalition with ex-dictator Hugo Banzer's *Acción Democrática Nacionalista* (ADN), crossing 'rivers of blood'.[21]

---

20   Betilde Muñoz-Pogossian, *Electoral Rules and the Transformation of Bolivian Politics: The Rise of Evo Morales* (New York: Palgrave Macmillan, 2008).

21   Ibid, p. 63. Following a unilateral decision the *Movimiento Nacionalista Revolucionario* (MNR) had broken up its earlier Pact for Democracy with Banzer's ADN, which then decided to team up with its former arch-enemy the MIR in an *Acuerdo Patriótico* which lasted from 1989 to 1993. After the 1993 elections Gonzalo Sánchez de Lozada brokered a Pact for Governance with the *Unión Cívica Solidaridad* of beer brewer Max Fernández, as well as a Pact for Change with the *Movimiento Bolivia Libre* (MBL), a split-off from the MIR. After the 1997 elections Hugo Banzer governed with the support of a 'mega-coalition' that exacerbated the spoils system, and after the 2002 elections the established parties mostly banded together in support of Sánchez de Lozada as the best alternative to Evo Morales, who came in second in these elections.

The 1989 elections were among the issues that put constitutional reform — and revision of the electoral system — on the agenda. But there were other questions to be dealt with. In 1990 indigenous peoples from the oriental lowlands staged a spectacular March for Territory and Dignity to protest at the incursions of logging companies into what they considered to be their territories.[22] The latent issue of Bolivia as a 'pluri-cultural' and 'multi-ethnic' society thus acquired new prominence, and the demand for a constituent assembly emerged way up on the agenda.[23] And then there was the issue of pursuing the structural adjustment agenda and going for a 'second generation' of reforms that focused on institutional re-engineering.

By early 1991 preparations were begun for a reform of the Constitution. The *Fundación Milenio* — a think-tank founded by Sánchez de Lozada — played a key role in these preparations, and by August 1992 had come up with a final proposal which provided the basis for further backroom negotiations among three party chiefs.[24] In March 1993 a Law of Necessity for Constitutional Reform was rubber-stamped by Congress during an extraordinary session.[25] That paved the way for a reform of the Constitution after the 1993 elections that brought Gonzalo Sánchez de Lozada to the presidency. The reform was carried out during the course of 1994 in highly 'top-down' fashion, which

22 In response to the march, President Jaime Paz Zamora recognised a series of indigenous territories in the eastern lowlands, and in 1991 Bolivia ratified ILO Convention 169 on the rights of indigenous and tribal peoples in independent countries.

23 The issue first arose in the 1960s when the *Katarista* movement — named after a key leader of the Great Rebellion in the late 18th century which sought to restore the Inca empire — emerged in the highlands and gained influence in the *Confederación Nacional de Trabajadores Campesinos de Bolivia* (CNTCB). In 1979 the CNTCB was renamed the *Confederación Sindical Única de Trabajadores Campesinos de Bolivia* (CSUTCB), signifying the definitive joining of opposition groups against the military regimes. *Katarismo*, which consisted of a variety of factions, sought to combine the struggle against colonial oppression with the struggle against class exploitation. For an account see Víctor Hugo Cárdenas, 'La lucha de un pueblo', in Xavier Albó (ed.) *Raíces de América: El mundo Aymara* (Madrid: Alianza América/UNESCO, 1988).

24 The proposal was published later on by Fundación Milenio, *Proyecto de reforma a la Constitución Política del Estado 1991–1992* (La Paz: Fundación Milenio, 1997).

25 Van Cott, *The Friendly Liquidation of the Past*, pp. 141–3. The Bolivian Constitution establishes a rigid procedure for constitutional reform. A law of necessity for constitutional reform has to be approved by congress and then, after general elections, the reform must be approved by the new legislature. This procedure, however, was followed on only four occasions (1947, 1961, 1994 and 2004). Other reforms were carried out by national conventions or constituent assemblies in the wake of revolutions or military coups, see Ana Cecilia Betancur, *Diez temas de reforma constitucional* (Santa Cruz: CEJIS, 2004), p. 49.

is markedly different from the ethos of a Constitutional Assembly or a re-founding of Bolivia as demanded by indigenous movements. Important features included:

- the state was denominated multicultural and pluri-ethnic;
- the electoral system was reformed through the introduction of a mixed system. Sixty-eight single member (uninominal) districts were created, while another 60 (plurinominal) deputies were to be elected through a national-level closed list system;
- the presidential term was extended from four to five years;
- a Constitutional Court and a Judicial Council were created as well as the office of a *Defensor del Pueblo* (ombudsman in charge of monitoring the constitutional rights and guarantees of the person in relation to the administrative activities of the public sector as well as defence, promotion and awareness-raising regarding human rights);
- the agrarian and peasant regime recognised the rights of indigenous peoples to *Tierras Comunitarias de Origen* (TCO), as well as the legal personality of the communities, associations and unions and their authorities, which may exercise administrative and judicial functions;
- the Constitution contained a chapter on municipalities actually sanctioning the Law of Popular Participation that had been adopted in April 1994. This was a measure of administrative decentralisation towards the municipal level, and provided for municipal autonomy.[26] Bolivia's nine departments, however, remained part of the executive with prefects designed by the President.[27]

Bolivia thus joined the Latin American trend towards the recognition of indigenous peoples' rights and the 'pluri-multi' composition of their populations, in the context of a new package of 'second generation' adjustment reforms focused on institutional engineering, to complement the earlier economic reform package introduced in 1985.[28] It is beyond the scope of this

26 The Law of Popular Participation actually turned the provincial sections, which only existed on paper, into municipalities. Whereas up to that time only some 20 municipalities had in effect existed, their number increased to over 300.

27 The Constitution thus did not respond to the demand for greater departmental autonomy that had been on the political agenda for some time. A partial response only to this demand came in 1995 with a Law on Administrative Decentralization.

28 The initial Washington Consensus, as described by Williamson, 'What Washington Means by Policy Reform', subsequently evolved into an 'augmented Washington Consensus' in which the emphasis shifted to institutional reforms that should complement the original consensus, see Dani Rodrik, 'Goodbye Washington Consensus, Hello Washington

chapter to discuss how this recognition percolated into secondary legislation, such as the new agrarian and forestry legislation adopted in 1996, or the administrative set-up of the state and the implementation of such policies under the first Sánchez de Lozada government (1993–7) and the Banzer government (1997–2002). What should be kept in mind here is the transition from a liberal framework to social constitutionalism in 1938, reconfirmed in the wake of the 1952 Bolivian Revolution in the 1961 Constitution. In 1967 this Constitution was reorganised and this remained the formal framework for a subsequent reform in 1994 in the context of structural adjustment reforms and 'neo-liberal multiculturalism'. These reforms reflected the move from a liberal to a social and then neo-liberal and multiculturalist citizenship regime. Demands for further reform were voiced with growing insistence by the late 1990s, but their prominence increased by the turn of the century.

The demise of pacted democracy and the search for new ways

The year 2000 can be considered as marking a turning point in recent Bolivian history. The early months of that year saw the development of the 'Water War' in the city of Cochabamba, a series of protests against the privatisation of water exploitation and supply in the region. The protests resulted in the expulsion of Aguas del Tunari, a subsidiary of the Bechtel Company and a substantial modification of recently-adopted new legislation regarding sanitation and water supply. This outcome was regarded as a first victory of popular movements after 15 years of Washington Consensus-inspired structural adjustment policies. The Cochabamba events were paralleled by widespread peasant-indigenous protests in the highland region and with coca-growers' protests in Cochabamba, which continued through the following years.

Meanwhile, party representation in the National Electoral Court gave rise to controversy at another level in the course of 2001. After mediation by the Catholic Church, the government (then still headed by Hugo Banzer)[29] and other political parties agreed on some measures to solve the political crisis.[30] One of them was the intention to convoke a Constitutional Assembly. The government proceeded to create a nine-member commission of 'notable' citizens — the Citizen's Council — to prepare a reform of the Constitution, while peasant-indigenous groups with support from some non-governmental

---

Confusion? A Review of the World Bank's *Economic Growth in the 1990s: Learning from a Decade of Reform*', *Journal of Economic Literature* 44 (Dec. 2006), pp. 969–83.

29   In August 2001 Banzer stepped down as he was diagnosed with cancer and was succeeded by his Vice-President Jorge Quiroga.

30   Muñoz-Pogossian, *Electoral Rules and the Transformation of Bolivian Politics*, p. 136.

organisations (NGOs) started to develop their own proposal.[31] By November 2001 the Citizen's Council had presented its proposal for a constitutional reform,[32] which was heavily criticised by social movements basically for endorsing the neo-liberal model topped up with some rather restricted forms of popular participation such as the legislative initiative, the popular referendum, and the plebiscite. It also opened up the possibility for citizen associations to present candidates, but only in municipal elections. At the same time, it sought to liberalise the agrarian regime and to eliminate the obligation of the state to promote a better distribution of land, and it proposed to further liberalise the natural resources regime. The Citizen's Council proposal soon faded into oblivion in the context of the run-up to the general elections due to take place on 30 June 2002.[33]

In May of that year indigenous-peasant organisations of the oriental lowlands started their 'fourth' march 'For Popular Sovereignty, Territory and Natural Resources',[34] which resulted in an *Acto de Acuerdo Nacional* subscribed to by a series of indigenous-peasant organisations, traditional authorities, executive and legislative powers, and human rights defenders on 21 June 2002. The principal objective of this agreement was to make possible the convocation of a National Constituent Assembly for a total reform of the Constitution. It implied a partial departure from the procedure for constitutional reform enshrined in the 1967 Constitution. And it foreshadowed later debates over the nature of the Constituent Assembly; would it be 'originary' (starting from scratch) or 'derived' (following the procedure for partial reform of the existing Constitution according to the 1967 formula)?[35]

The elections in June 2002 were suggestive of the unraveling of the party system and the model of 'pacted democracy' that had been in place since 1985. In these elections Evo Morales surprisingly garnered nearly 21 per cent of the votes and came in second after Gonzalo Sánchez de Lozada of the *Movimiento Nacionalista Revolucionario* (MNR), who got 22.5 per cent of the votes. In such

31 Betancur, *Diez temas de reforma constitucional*, p. 37.

32 Consejo Ciudadano para la Reforma Constitucional, *Anteproyecto de Ley de Necesidad de Reforma Constitucional* (La Paz: H. Cámara de Diputados, Programa de las Naciones Unidas para el Desarollo/PRONAGOB-BID, 2001).

33 A Necessity of Constitutional Reform law was eventually adopted in August 2002, two days before President Jorge Quiroga handed over power to his successor Gonzalo Sánchez de Lozada. This law basically related to the political regime and would open the way for a reform of the Constitution. The law should have been ratified during the first sessions of the newly elected Congress, but this proved impossible and political conditions further deteriorated in the course of 2002 ending in the crisis of October 2003.

34   Romero Bonifaz, *El proceso constituyente boliviano*.

35   Ibid., pp. 229–32.

cases, where none of the candidates wins an absolute majority, the Bolivian Congress elects the President from among the two most voted candidates,[36] which as already noted is the occasion for inter-party coalition making.[37] In 2002 Sánchez de Lozada was elected. The 'pacted democracy' model still seemed to work, but at the price of an ever-increasing disconnect between the party leaderships and their parties and with the electorate in general, which expressed itself in growing street protests against unpopular measures and the failure to deliver tangible benefits to the population. In early 2003 the introduction of a new income tax prompted a round of protests, including a shoot-out between protesting police and the military followed by crowd attacks against various government offices and the looting of shops in La Paz and El Alto. In October of that same year, a variety of protest movements coalesced in the massive protests against the intended sale of natural gas to the US, by way of Chile. The protests met with heavy-handed repression which claimed some 60 lives. The 'Gas War' or 'Black October' forced Sánchez de Lozada to flee the country and Vice-President Carlos Mesa assumed the presidency.

Mesa seemed to embrace the 'October Agenda', which included the demand for nationalisation of the gas industry,[38] the holding of a Constituent Assembly,[39] and a trial of responsibilities against Sánchez de Lozada. Moreover, Mesa sought to govern without parties in order to allow for a re-composition of the party system. Initially that agenda bought him some relief from pressures from the MAS, which informally supported his government.

In the meantime, however, another agenda had begun to emerge in opposition to the popular movements of 2000 and the following years. A main protagonist of this agenda is the Civic Committee of Santa Cruz, together with similar organisations and groups in the eastern lowland departments of Beni, Pando and Tarija (and to a certain extent Chuquisaca). In February 2003 the

---

36 Until the constitutional reform of 1994 the three candidates with the most votes.

37 This mechanism resulted in what has been characterised as 'parliamentarised presidentialism' or a 'hybrid presidential system'. What is known as 'pacted democracy' emerged in 1985, relying on more or less formal agreements among party leaders. Its main features were a commitment to electoral democracy and support for Washington Consensus policies.

38 In the context of the 'second generation' reforms the State hydrocarbon company *Yacimientos Petrolíferos Fiscales Bolivianos* (YPFB) had been virtually dismantled through the 'capitalisation policy', the Bolivian version of privatisation, which was linked to the introduction of a new pension scheme. A new Law on Hydrocarbons of 1996 reduces taxes and royalties in order to attract foreign investment and was actually very generous in comparison to other countries.

39 The demand for the holding of a Constituent Assembly had been in the air for some time but had been forcefully put on the agenda by indigenous peoples' mobilisations during the run-up to the 2002 general elections.

Civic Committees of what became known as the *Media Luna* (Half Moon, or Crescent, for its geographical shape) had declared their support for the gas export plans and suggested that they might declare 'regional autonomy'. During the September–October crisis the Santa Cruz Civic Committee's president, Rubén Costas, declared that he doubted whether Santa Cruz would remain within the current structures of the Bolivian state. And by June 2004, on the eve of the referendum on the gas issue organised by the Mesa government, the Santa Cruz Civic Committee organised a public meeting calling for departmental autonomy, which became known as the 'June Agenda'.[40]

Later that year the Mesa government decided to reduce subsidies to gasoline (including diesel) in order to combat contraband to neighbouring countries and to reduce the fiscal deficit. Although that generated discontent throughout the country, the Santa Cruz Civic Committee managed to capture local discontent by presenting itself as defender of the 'popular economy'.[41] And it succeeded in transforming initial protests into a movement in favour of autonomy, culminating in a *cabildo*, an open popular assembly, on 28 January 2005, at which between 200,000 and 350,000 persons were present. The 'June (2004) Agenda' was now transformed into the 'January Agenda'. In response, Carlos Mesa fixed a date for the election of departmental prefects, which until then had been appointed by the executive.[42]

At the same time, the Mesa government faced protest movements centred in El Alto — La Paz's sister city, largely composed of recent rural-urban migrants of Aymara origin — against the Illimani water company, a subsidiary of the Suez Company that had acquired a concession for water supply and sanitation in La Paz and El Alto in 1997. The protesters affirmed that the company did not comply with contractual stipulations regarding the extension of water supply to outlying areas of this sprawling city.

The tensions between these two 'agendas' proved to be unmanageable for Carlos Mesa, who in the event also gradually lost support from the MAS. After

40 The referendum on the gas issue was held on 18 July 2004 and its outcomes were considered an expression of support for the Mesa government, although the questions posed raised controversy since they were considered ambiguous and no direct question regarding nationalisation had been included.

41 In fact, the local agro-industries benefited hugely from this subsidy.

42 For a recent account of the Santa Cruz movement see Martín Sivak, *Santa Cruz: Una tesis; El conflicto regional en Bolivia (2003–2006)* (La Paz: Plural, 2007). See also Bret Gustafson, 'Spectacles of Autonomy and Crisis: Or, What Bulls and Beauty Queens have to do With Regionalism in Eastern Bolivia', *Journal of Latin American Anthropology* 11:2 (2006), pp. 351–79; *T'inkazos*, 'Dossier debate: La media luna: autonomía regional y comités cívicos', *T'inkazos* 16 (2004), pp. 9–64; and Juan Carlos Urenda Díaz, *El sueño imperturbable: El proceso autonómico boliviano* (Santa Cruz de la Sierra: El País, 2009).

earlier attempts his letter of resignation was finally accepted by the Bolivian Congress on 6 June 2005. Following popular pressure, the institutional successors lined up — the president of the Senate and the president of the Chamber of Deputies — resigned, opening the way for the appointment of Eduardo Rodríguez Veltzé, president of the Supreme Court, to assume the presidency with a mandate to organise general elections within 180 days.

The December 2005 elections and the Constituent Assembly: a chronological summary

These elections were finally held on 18 December 2005 and resulted in the landslide victory of Evo Morales and the MAS, with nearly 54 per cent of the vote, followed by Jorge Quiroga of PODEMOS with nearly 29 per cent of the vote. However, while the MAS won 72 seats out of 130 in the Chamber of Deputies, it won 12 out of 27 Senate seats. Thirteen seats were won by PODEMOS and one each by UN and the MNR.

That same day prefects were elected in Bolivia's nine departments. It was the first time they had been directly elected, and then installed by the new President a day after he assumed office on 22 January 2006. Until then prefects had been nominated by the executive. In these elections the MAS only won three prefectures.

Department	Elected candidate	Party
Chuquisaca	David Sánchez	MAS
La Paz	José Luis Paredes	PODEMOS
Cochabamba	Manfred Reyes Villa	Alianza de Unidad Nacional
Oruro	Alberto Luis Aguilar	MAS
Potosí	Mario Virreira	MAS
Tarija	Mario Adel Cossío	Camino al Cambio-MNR
Santa Cruz	Rubén Darío Costas	Autonomía para Bolivia
Beni	Ernesto Suárez	PODEMOS
Pando	Leopoldo Fernández	PODEMOS

Elections for a Constituent Assembly were to take place six months later and were to coincide with a referendum on autonomies.[43] The elections and the referendum took place on 2 July 2006. In the elections the MAS obtained nearly 51 per cent of the vote, translating into 137 seats, so that together with allied groups it could count on some 151 out of the 255 Assembly members, but no two-thirds majority. In the simultaneous referendum on autonomies the

43   The Santa Cruz Civic Committee had gathered signatures in support of a popular initiative for a referendum on autonomies, which had been handed to the National Electoral Court in Feb. 2005.

NO vote prevailed at the national level (57.6 per cent), but in four departments the YES vote won: Santa Cruz (71 per cent), Beni (74 per cent), Pando (58 per cent) and Tarija (61 per cent). The outcome of the referendum was supposed to be binding for the Constituent Assembly, but the general guidelines for autonomy statutes were to be defined by the Assembly.

The Constituent Assembly was inaugurated on 6 August in Sucre, Bolivia's capital.[44] That same day indigenous-peasant organisations, which had formed a Unity Pact, presented their proposal for a new Constitution for a plurinational state that would allow for the self-determination of Bolivia's indigenous peoples.[45] The proposal also contained the concept of *vivir bien* (living well), inspired in indigenous concepts and also present in MAS proposals and discourse.[46]

The Assembly initiated its sessions on 16 August 2006 and was due to conclude its work by August 2007, after which the text of a new Constitution would be submitted to a popular referendum. From the beginning, however, frictions between the MAS and the main opposition party PODEMOS made themselves felt, mainly focusing on issues of procedure and the nature of the Assembly. Whereas the MAS argued that articles should be adopted by majority and that the final text should be adopted by two-thirds of the Assembly, the opposition argued that each of the articles should be adopted by two-thirds of the vote in each of the commissions involved in redacting the Constitution. And whereas the MAS argued that the Assembly should be 'originary', reflecting its proposal to 're-found' the state through the exercise of the sovereign will of the people not limited by any of the constituted powers

---

44 After the Federal War (1898–9) La Paz became the seat of government, reflecting the emerging power of the tin magnates and the declining importance of silver mining.

45 Asamblea nacional de organizaciones indígenas, originarias, campesinas y de colonizadores de Bolivia, *Propuesta para la nueva Constitución Política del Estado* (Sucre: Asamblea Nacional, 2006). Bolivia counts some 36 indigenous peoples, and in the 2001 census, 62% of the population over 15 identified with some indigenous people. The highland Quechuas and Aymara are demographically most important whereas in the eastern lowlands a smattering of indigenous peoples of numerically different sizes can be found. The outcomes of the 2001 census are controversial since no option to identify as *mestizo* was offered. For further discussion see, for example, Ramiro Molina B. and Xavier Albó (eds.), *Gama étnica y lingüística de la población boliviana*.

46 MAS, Instrumento, *Refundar Bolivia para vivir bien: propuesta para la Asamblea Constituyente* (La Paz: Movimiento al Socialismo, Instrumento Político por la Soberania de los Pueblos, 2006).

of the state,[47] the opposition argued that it should be 'derived' and follow the outline and procedures laid down in the existing Constitution.

Polarisation increased when by the end of the year a PODEMOS delegate from Chuquisaca proposed that Sucre should become the 'full capital' of the country, a surprising proposal that gained support from the Civic Committees of the *Media Luna* who found it a useful device to divide the MAS in Chuquisaca and garner support for their oppositional stance. The issue came to a head between March and July 2007 and resulted in the Assembly's work coming to a virtual standstill. This included violent attacks against indigenous people and indigenous Assembly delegates. By early July the Assembly agreed to postpone submission of a final draft Constitution by four months, until December 2007. The question of the 'full capital' demand for Sucre would continue to polarise relations between the majority and the minority during the following months, resulting in further violence and attacks against indigenous people. Meanwhile, the continuation of the work of the Assembly was negotiated among the different groups under the presidency of Vice-President Álvaro García Linera.

As a result of the violence against delegates, by the end of November 2007 the directory of the Constituent Assembly decided that a final session would be held at a military compound outside the centre of Sucre, which continued to be a scene of violence, eventually claiming various lives. In the absence of the opposition, but reaching the legally established quorum, most of the 21 majority working group reports were ratified and the new text for a Constitution was approved 'at large', with 136 votes out of 138 delegates present.

In view of the violent confrontations in Sucre the Assembly Directory then decided to summon the Assembly delegates for a final session in Oruro, in the highland department of Potosí. Though the decision was approved by the National Congress it was not in line with the original convocation for a Constituent Assembly and was therefore denounced as illegal by the opposition, which was not present in Oruro. On 9 December 2007, in the presence of 164 Assembly members a new constitutional text was approved by two-thirds of the vote, with the exception of an article on the maximal extent of agrarian properties. That would then be decided through a popular referendum coinciding with a popular referendum on the Constitution.

That was not the end of the story, however. By February 2008 dialogue between the government and the *Media Luna* prefects failed and the latter

---

47 For some, however, the notion of 'originary' suggested that the Assembly would be based in the 'originary' peoples of Bolivia. The designations of 'indigenous' and 'originary' are a matter of some controversy in the country. While eastern lowland peoples do not object to the term 'indigenous' some highland movements argue that 'indigenous' applies to anyone born in the country and therefore favour the term 'originary', which suggests that they were there 'first' and thus have special rights.

decided unilaterally to call for popular referenda on the autonomy statutes that had been drawn up for their departments. On the other hand, in the absence of the opposition the National Congress called for a referendum on the new Constitution to take place on 4 May. Both initiatives were rejected by the National Electoral Court. The government accepted postponement of the referendum on the Constitution, while the prefects of the *Media Luna* departments continued to prepare for the referenda on the autonomy statutes, which were held in May (Santa Cruz) and June (Beni, Pando, and Tarija). In these referenda the statutes were approved by substantial margins (around 80 per cent), though abstensionism was rather high — averaging about 38 per cent — which is suggestive of support for the government position according to which the referenda were illegal.[48]

Meanwhile, another issue had come up. The government had proposed to submit itself to a recall referendum on the condition that the departmental prefects did the same. The opposition initially rejected the idea but changed its mind after the Santa Cruz autonomy statute had been approved in the local referendum and, in a surprising move, the opposition in the Senate gave its support to the recall referendum initiative, though they soon realised that they had overestimated their strength. The President and Vice-President, as well as the prefects of eight out of the nine departments,[49] would be recalled if they received more no-votes than the number of votes by which they had been elected. The referendum was held on 10 August 2008 and Morales gained an approval rate of 67 per cent, while the prefects of the Cochabamba and La Paz departments were recalled. In the *Media Luna* departments the prefects were ratified and gained important support. At the same time, however, the support for Morales within them also significantly increased as compared to 2005, suggesting that the power base of the elites in these departments is not that solid.

In the wake of the referendum, the government invited the *Media Luna* prefects to discuss the autonomy issue as well as the distribution of the direct tax on hydrocarbons, part of which it wanted to use for a new pension scheme, the Renta Dignidad, meaning that the departments' share would decrease. When these talks collapsed protests began in the four departments, accompanied by attacks on national public offices which were looted and set on fire. The NGOs were also attacked.[50] Such violence in Santa Cruz and

48 The Autonomy Statutes are reproduced in Urenda Díaz, *El sueño imperturbable*.

49 In the case of Chuquisaca, MAS prefect David Sánchez resigned in the midst of the turmoil in Sucre and was succeeded, after elections, by Sabina Cuellar, a Quechua woman who had joined the opposition in support of the 'full capital' demand for Sucre.

50 On 10 Sept. the US Ambassador Philip Goldberg was expelled, having been accused of conspiring with opposition groups in the *Media Luna* to orchestrate a 'civic coup'.

Tarija caused a split among elite sectors as some feared that it might damage the business climate. The spiral of violence culminated in the attack on a group of indigenous peasants heading to a meeting in the city of Cobija in Pando on 11 September. Their objective was to prevent the taking of the offices of the national agrarian reform institute by anti-government protestors, fearing that documentation regarding their land rights would be destroyed. They were stopped in the vicinity of the El Porvenir hamlet, where violent clashes left at least 11 dead (nine indigenous peasants and students and two supporters of the local Prefecture) and some 50 wounded. A state of emergency was declared for the department in the wake of this massacre, and opposition prefect Leopoldo Fernández was arrested a few days later and charged in connection with these events. The UNASUR strongly condemned the massacre and declared its full support for the Morales government.

These events severely undermined any legitimacy the civic and prefectural leaders might have won as they confirmed their reputation for the use of violence.[51] Under these circumstances, and pressured by the international community, the opposition was obliged to come to the negotiation table by the end of September. First, in negotiations in Cochabamba between government delegates and the regional opposition, new formulas were developed regarding the enshrining of departmental autonomies in the new Constitution and regarding the division of rents from oil and gas production. Though these negotiations did not result in a formal document, agreement was reached regarding the legislative capacities of departmental, municipal and indigenous autonomies. And whereas in the Oruro draft Constitution, 12 departmental competencies were included, in the final new Constitution a list of 36 exclusive competencies appears, but land policies and internal migration, for example, remain competencies of the central state.

Negotiations then moved to the national Congress, and representatives of different political parties[52] engaged in revising the text of the draft Constitution. The main points were:

- the characterisation of the Bolivian state as plurinational, which was retained;

- the possibility of re-election of a sitting President for one more term was included, after Morales promised that he would not to stand for re-election in 2014, as had been possible under the Oruro proposal;

51 In particular, the *Unión Juvenil Cruceñista*, the youth branch of the Santa Cruz Civic Committee, is reputed to act as a 'clash group' with activities inside and outside the department.

52 This is suggestive of a split between the more moderate opposition in Congress and its more extremist leaders in the *Media Luna* departments.

- the establishment of a maximum size for landholding — 5,000 or 10,000 hectares — would be resolved through a popular referendum parallel to the referendum on the Constitution, while it was agreed that this size limit would not apply retro-actively if owners could prove that their land complied with its 'social-economic function'. The guarantees for private property were strengthened, and urban properties were expressly exempted from reversion to the state;

- the agreement further included the maintaining of a bi-cameral Congress, now to be called the Plurinational Legislative Assembly. A 130-seat Chamber of Deputies will be elected through a mixed system with 70 single-member seats allocated according to relative majority in their electoral districts, and the other 60 according to a proportional system. The Senate will have 36 seats; four per department according to a proportional system;

- it was agreed that reforms of the Constitution would require two-thirds of the vote, instead of a simple majority;

- similarly, the Plurinational Electoral Organ will have seven members instead of five. One of them will be designated by the President and the others will be elected by the Plurinational Legislative Assembly by two-thirds of the vote, instead of by absolute majority. Two of them should be of indigenous originary peasant origin;

- the scope of the mechanism of 'social control' was circumscribed. The Oruro text anticipated that civil society organisations would participate directly in state decision-making and would have ample attributions in monitoring a variety of public services and state agencies and in approving their accounts. The idea of social control in a way harked back to the systems of co-governance (or dual power) between state agencies and trade (especially miners') unions that had emerged in the wake of the 1952 revolution. In the new Constitution the participation of civil society organisations in the design of public policies is foreseen which may monitor the quality of public policies and may express their views regarding the accounts of state agencies, rather than (dis-)approve them;

- whereas the Oruro text established that verdicts of communitarian justice would not be subject to revision, though they should respect the right to life and other constitutional rights, the new text suggests tighter mechanisms of coordination with the state justice system through a law on jurisdictional delimitation and will be subject to scrutiny by a Supreme Constitutional Court.

These agreements led Congress on 21 October 2008 to set the date for a referendum on the Constitution and on the maximum size of landholding on 25 January 2009. When that referendum was held, the 'yes' option for the Constitution won more than 61 per cent of the valid votes. And regarding the maximum size of landholding, 80 per cent of the voters agreed with a maximum of 5,000 hectares rather than 10,000 hectares.

Bolivia's new Constitution: some reflections

A notable feature of Bolivia's new Constitution is the reference it makes to the 'ethical-moral principles of the plural society: *ama qhilla*, *ama llulla*, *ama suwa* (don't be lazy, don't lie, and don't be a thief),[53] *suma qamaña* (to live well), *ñandereko* (harmonious life), *teko kavi* (good life), *ivi maraei* (land without evil), and *qhapaj ñan* (the noble path or life)'.[54] The concept of 'living well' has also been included in the 2008 Ecuadorian Constitution. It suggests redistribution, reciprocity and living well without being rich. Similarly, both Constitutions make reference to the *Pachamama* (Mother Earth) and the Ecuadorian Constitution explicitly includes the rights of *Pacha Mama*.[55] Despite the tense relations between the Rafael Correa government and the principal indigenous movement, in the end the latter supported the constitutional reform proposal.[56] The Bolivian Constitution incorporates the ideas and proposals of the indigenous movements to a much greater extent and is, for example, much stronger on issues of autonomy and land rights. Both Constitutions, however, reflect the influence of indigenous movements and their thinking.

The new Bolivian Constitution is suggestive of this trend. This is not the place for an exhaustive analysis, which is also complicated by the document's use of somewhat convoluted and elliptic language, sometimes the result of compromises reached in negotiations. It is an extensive document consisting

53 These principles were first included in Ecuador's 1998 Constitution. [This is of course the same phrase as seen in the opening section above; the slightly different forms reflect differences between the Quechua (or 'Quichua') of Bolivia and Ecuador, both in pronunciation and in the national standard orthographies in force at the times when these Constitutions were promulgated. My thanks to Paul Heggarty for advice on this point – ed.]

54 My translation. These are expressions from different indigenous languages of the country.

55 The issue caused controversy because in the Ecuadorian text *Pacha Mama* 'of which we are part and which is vital to our existence' is mentioned before God, who is invoked 'recognising our diverse forms of religiosity and spirituality'.

56 Ecuador's indigenous movement has often been considered one of the strongest in Latin America but was weakened substantially as a result of its ephemeral support for the Lucio Gutiérrez government in 2003.

of 411 articles — compared to the 235 articles in the previous 1994–5 Constitution — and it is divided into five parts instead of four. The first part is about the fundamental bases of the state, rights, obligations and guarantees, and includes stipulations about civil, political, social and economic rights and the entitlements of indigenous nations and peoples.

The second part is dedicated to the structure and functional organisation of the state and, for example, includes stipulations about the composition and attributions of the Plurinational Legislative Assembly which will consist of a 130-member Chamber of Deputies — elected through a mixed system — providing for special 'indigenous originary peasant' representation. The Senate will consist of 36 members: four for each of the nine departments. Furthermore, this part outlines the structure of the executive and the judiciary, in the latter case through the organisation of a Supreme Court of Justice and a Plurinational Constitutional Court. The members of both courts will be elected by popular vote from a shortlist presented by the Plurinational Legislative Assembly, which should take care to assure the presence of 'indigenous originary peasant' representation. This should, for example, ensure the coordination between the ordinary justice system and the 'indigenous originary peasant' jurisdiction. This part, which also covers social control and participation, suggests that control mechanisms for government policies and agencies by structures within organised civil society should be established and include a seven-member plurinational electoral organ, with at least two persons of indigenous origin.

The third part of the new Constitution addresses the structure and territorial organisation of the state and touches upon the controversial issue of autonomies, distinguishing departmental, regional, municipal, and 'indigenous originary peasant' autonomies.[57] It thus adds departmental autonomy, with legislative competencies, to the structure of the state which already included municipal autonomy to a certain degree. As a result of negotiations it was stipulated that regional autonomies may not cross departmental boundaries[58] and that their competencies will be of an administrative-normative and oversight nature. The 'indigenous originary peasant' autonomies may be of a municipal, territorial or regional nature. This points to the possibility of creating indigenous municipalities, converting *Tierras Comunitarias de Origen* into autonomous territories, and creating indigenous regions, though their status is ambiguous in view of the stipulations about regional autonomies. A draft Framework

---

57   For an insightful review of the intricacies of indigenous autonomies, see Xavier Albó and
     Carlos Romero, *Autonomías indígenas en la realidad boliviana y su nueva constitución* (La Paz:
     Vicepresidencia del Estado Plurinacional de Bolivia, 2009).

58   This may be problematic in so far as indigenous territories, partly consolidated as TCO,
     may straddle departmental boundaries. In the case of municipal boundaries some forms of
     re-accommodation are foreseen.

Law on Autonomies and Decentralization was circulated in July 2009, and is currently the subject of debate.[59]

Part four is about the structure and economic organisation of the state and defines the Bolivian economic model as plural and aiming to improve the quality of life and achieve the 'good life' for all Bolivians, female and male. The plural economy consists of various forms of economic organisation: communitarian, state, private and social-cooperative, which will all be protected. At the same time, the role of the state in planning and regulating economic activities is to be enhanced and such activities should contribute to the general well-being. In that context, priority will be given to the communitarian economic organisation and micro-, small- and medium-sized enterprises. The rural economy should be given special attention, the state will play a key role in the exploitation of natural resources and the regulation thereof, and Bolivian investment should be privileged over foreign investment. This part also contains stipulations regarding hydrocarbons, mining and other natural resources, including water, which is defined as a fundamental right for life and will not be subject to privatisation. The issue of water rights and management was forcefully put on the agenda during the 'Water War', centred in Cochabamba in early 2000, which not only resulted in the expulsion of the *Aguas del Tunari* consortium, but also in a substantial revision of the water and sanitation legislation that had been adopted in late 1999. In 2004 a new law on irrigation was adopted, but further regulation was only forthcoming under the MAS government, reversing the previous privatisation orientation and strengthening the role of local communities in water management. An additional innovation was the MAS government's creation of a Ministry of Water.[60] There is also a short article on coca, which is defined as a cultural patrimony and a renewable natural resource that in its natural state is not a drug.

The final fifth section is dedicated to normative hierarchy and reform of the Constitution, establishing the primacy of the Constitution and the procedure for its reform.

The foregoing is intended to give an impression of the general drift of the new Bolivian Constitution. It is beyond the scope of this article to provide an exhaustive analysis of all of its provisions. Though nothing definitive can be

---

59   For a recent discussion of territories and indigenous government, see Juan Pablo Chumacero R. (ed.), *Reconfigurando territorios; reforma agraria, control territorial y gobiernos indígenas en Bolivia* (La Paz: Fundación Tierra, 2010).

60   For a recent discussion of neo-liberal water policies and opposition to them, see Rutgerd Boelens, David Getches, and Armando Guevara-Gil (eds.), *Out of the Mainstream; Water Rights, Politics and Identity* (London and Washington DC: Earthscan, 2010).

said, the Constitution will provide a framework for further political struggle. Some points can, however, be highlighted:

- the rights of indigenous peoples are significantly strengthened, including their political rights, though the claim to representation and a reserved quota according to the 2001 census was turned down;

- a system of departmental autonomies will be introduced, alongside regional, municipal and indigenous autonomies. The relations between these different autonomy regimes will remain controversial, and a draft Framework Law on Autonomies and Decentralization is open to debate;

- a broader recognition of indigenous forms of justice is incorporated, but in its last version the Constitution includes stricter vigilance by the state system which, however, will incorporate indigenous representatives to assure an intercultural dialogue;

- after the era of privatisations and roll-back of the state, the state will take a greater degree of control over the use and exploitation of natural resources and the distribution of revenues;

- the Constitution guarantees the right to private property (in rural areas on the condition that it complies with a social-economic function) alongside communal and state property, suggesting the construction of a mixed economy. This might be construed as a transitory phase towards a socialist-communitarian economy;[61]

- a Plurinational Assembly will be bi-cameral instead of uni-cameral (as suggested in original draft proposals).

A new electoral law was adopted on 14 April 2009, after complex negotiations and a hunger strike by President Morales. The quota for indigenous representatives has been reduced to seven seats. This law set the stage for the general elections held on 6 December 2009 in which the MAS garnered 64.2 per cent of the vote, while the main opposition, *Plan Progreso para Bolivia* (PPB) led by Manfred Reyes Villa, won 26.5 per cent. This implies a reconfiguration of power relations within the legislative, the MAS having gained 26 out of 36 Senate seats and 88 seats in the 130-seat Chamber of Deputies. It will also allow for the adoption of legislation that will further facilitate the implementation of the MAS programme and the new Constitution through secondary legislation that is still in the making. Significantly, these elections also showed that the MAS gained ground in the eastern lowland departments. Simultaneously, a

---

61   Vice-President Álvaro García Linera proposed the idea of Andean-Amazonic capitalism as a transitory phase towards a socialist and communitarian economy.

new referendum on autonomies was held in which all departments as well as a number of municipalities this time voted in favor of autonomy as outlined in the new Constitution. Political struggle will, of course, be ongoing, and the course of future events remains unpredictable. Municipal elections and department-level elections in April 2010 will be indicators of what lies ahead. Meanwhile, further legislation will be elaborated that should give shape to the constitutional framework and should further outline a new citizenship regime in the context of a plurinational state.

4
ELECTORAL VALIDATION FOR MORALES AND THE MAS (1999–2010)

John Crabtree

Introduction

Re-elected as President with over 64 per cent of the vote in December 2009, Evo Morales demonstrated that four years of government had done nothing to dim his political star or that of the ruling *Movimiento al Socialismo* (MAS). His first election triumph in December 2005, which had seen him elected with 54 per cent of the vote, had at the time appeared to be a landslide victory. For the first time in just over two decades of constitutional government, a single party had managed to win sufficient votes to avoid the run-off in the Congress. The MAS won a majority of seats in the Chamber of Deputies, although it narrowly missed achieving this in the Senate. By contrast, in the 2009 presidential elections, the MAS achieved strong majorities in both houses, winning just over two-thirds of both of them combined, the number needed to change the Constitution — should it wish to do so. Based on an organic structure of social movements and, having achieved repeated electoral validation, it had unquestionably established itself as the dominant force in Bolivian politics.

As the MAS government moves into its second term of office, it is pertinent to examine its electoral performance in greater detail so as to better understand its strengths and weaknesses. In particular, it is important to explain the reasons for its popularity in order to assess whether or not it is contingent on any particular factor and the extent to which it is likely to prove durable over the longer term. How successful has the MAS been at extending the radius of its support beyond its natural constituency? How unconditional or uncritical is that traditional support? Is the vote for the MAS primarily an expression of personal support for Morales and his Vice-President, Alvaro García Linera, or is it validation for a political project? Will opposition groups be able to re-establish themselves and present a successful challenge to the MAS over the next few years? Ultimately, does the MAS's electoral success signify that it will outlive its present leaders and convert itself into a permanent feature of the Bolivian political system, at least for the foreseeable future?

Such questions are easier to pose, of course, than to answer. The analysis of electoral data can take us only so far and it would be foolish to read more into it than is warranted, particularly in a country with such a history of political instability and unpredictability. However, on the basis of four years in government, during which the MAS appears to have consolidated its position in politics, it is possible to hazard some preliminary answers to these points. At least that is what this chapter will attempt to do. The first section looks at the results of elections since 1999, a period of unusual electoral activity. There have been three presidential contests (2002, 2005 and 2009); an election to a Constituent Assembly (2006); two elections for departmental prefects/ governors (2005 and 2010); three rounds of local elections for mayors and municipalities (1999, 2004 and 2010); and finally a sequence of referendums on a variety of different issues (2004, 2006, 2008 and 2009), a novelty in Bolivian politics. There is therefore a plethora of electoral data on which to chart the advance of the MAS as a political force. The second section, which will seek to provide some analysis of the reasons for this strong electoral performance, deals with more complex terrain and offers greater scope for interpretation of the data. The factors are multiple and often self-reinforcing.

Charting the growth of the MAS

Presidential and congressional contests

The results from the three presidential elections (see Table 1) held so far in the new millennium show very clearly the electoral advance of the MAS, a party only established as such in time for the 1997 elections.[1] In 2002, to the surprise of most observers, the party polled 20.94 per cent of the total valid vote, narrowly achieving second place in the final results that year. The *Movimiento Nacionalista Revolucionario* (MNR) candidate, Gonzalo Sánchez de Lozada, came first with 22.5 per cent, while the *Nueva Fuerza Republicana* (NFR) of Manfred Reyes Villa, a former mayor of Cochabamba, was squeezed into third place with 20.92 per cent. In fourth place was the *Movimiento de la Izquierda Revolucionaria* (MIR) with 16.3 per cent. No less surprising was the

---

1   The origins of the MAS were to be found in a congress of peasant union leaders in 1995 when the *Asamblea para la Soberanía de los Pueblos* (ASP) was created, just before the municipal elections of that year. Prior to the 1997 presidential and congressional elections, the ASP split in two: one faction led by Alejo Véliz and the other (known as the *Instrumento Político para la Soberanía de los Pueblos* [IPSP]) led by Evo Morales. The IPSP adopted the name of the moribund MAS party in order to achieve electoral registration — the MAS-IPSP to give it its full title; see Donna Lee Van Cott, *From Movements to Parties in Latin America: The Evolution of Ethnic Politics* (New York: Cambridge University Press, 2005), pp. 86–7.

MAS's performance in the 2005 elections. No-one predicted the MAS winning 53.7 per cent that year of valid votes cast — most expected the party to achieve no more than 30 per cent of the vote.

In practice, the 2005 elections demonstrated a collapse in the vote for Bolivia's traditional parties, notably the MNR — the party that more than any other had dominated politics since the 1940s. Support for the traditional parties had shifted to two loose and recently created right/centre-right coalitions, *Podemos* and *Unidad Nacional* (UN). *Podemos* won 28.6 per cent of the vote in 2005 and UN just 7.8 per cent. The results of the December 2009 presidential elections, the first held under the new Constitution, also took observers by surprise, since they again exceeded what most pollsters had anticipated.[2] Morales took 64.2 per cent of the valid vote overall, winning nearly 3 million votes. This was the first election in which some Bolivians living abroad were able to vote and the final figure for Bolivia itself was a shade lower at 63.9 per cent.[3] Since voting is compulsory in Bolivia, participation in all three of these national elections was over 80 per cent, but it reached nearly 95 per cent in the 2009 elections on the basis of a complete overhaul of the electoral register.[4]

Support for Morales and the MAS had always had a strong regional component. Although it was first established in the tropics of Cochabamba in the early 1990s, since 2002 it has continually appealed more to people in the highlands than in the lowland departments of the north and east, the so-called '*Media Luna*' of Santa Cruz, Tarija, Beni and Pando. As Table 1 shows, in all three contests, the voting strength of the MAS was more in evidence in the former than the latter. With the exception of Chuquisaca, the MAS scored more than its national percentage in 2002 in La Paz, Cochabamba, Oruro and Potosí. In 2005, the same pattern is observable, although the percentages in each case are much higher, and on that occasion the MAS vote in Chuquisaca was also higher than the national vote. In 2009, the vote in Chuquisaca was slightly below the national figure. In each case too, and in almost all departments, the MAS vote was higher in rural areas than urban ones, reflecting the MAS's strong

2   The 2009 constitution did not affect the system of presidential elections in any fundamental way. The main innovation was the expansion of the Senate with four members per department (previously three). Within the Chamber of Deputies, seven members were included representing indigenous and ethnic groups, though the overall number of deputies did not change.

3   Elections were held in the four countries with the largest populations of Bolivians living abroad: Argentina, Brazil, Spain and the US.

4   On account of complaints from the opposition, a complete revision of the electoral register was conducted during 2009 with the introduction of biometric ID cards for each voter. Slightly over 5 million electors were registered. This partly explains the large increase in the numbers voting for the MAS compared with previous elections (see Table 1).

Table 1: Presidential Elections (2002, 2005 and 2009): Votes for Morales and the MAS

	2002		2005		2009	
	Percent	Votes	Percent	Votes	Percent	votes
TOTAL*	**20.9**	**581,844**	**53.7**	**1,544,374**	**64.2**	**2,943,209**
					63.9	**2,851,996**
Chuquisaca	17.1	27,823	54.2	84,343	56.1	127,995
La Paz	22.5	197,810	66.6	640,880	80.3	1,099,259
Cochabamba	37.6	182,211	64.8	335,439	68.8	569,257
Oruro	29.2	42,396	62.6	99,648	79.5	178,363
Potosí	27	52,452	57.8	112,068	78.3	243,865
Tarija	6.2	8,372	31.6	43,019	51.1	114,577
Santa Cruz	10.2	67,049	33.1	207,785	40.9	441,705
Beni	3.2	3,159	16.5	16,937	37.7	60,671
Pando	2.9	479	20.9	4,255	44.5	16,334

Source: Corte Nacional Electoral

links with *campesino* and indigenous movements. Not until the 2005 elections did the MAS seek to court candidates and mobilise support in urban areas as a conscious policy, inviting candidates to participate who had no background in social movements, thereby widening its social appeal.

Although comparison of electoral outcomes in these three presidential and legislative elections shows how the vote for the MAS grew exceptionally rapidly nationally (both in terms of absolute numbers of votes cast as well as in percentage terms), it is particularly striking how it managed to build support and attract voters in the departments of the *Media Luna*. In 2002, the MAS won 6.2 per cent of the votes in Tarija and 10.2 per cent in Santa Cruz, while in Beni and Pando its support was weaker. By 2005, its share of the vote had grown in Tarija and Santa Cruz, to 31.6 per cent and 33.1 per cent respectively. In both departments, it had become the second largest electoral force. Even in Beni its share of the vote had tripled to 16.5 per cent and in Pando (a tiny electoral population) it multiplied tenfold to 20.9 per cent of the vote. By 2009, despite the campaign by elite groups to mobilise around the issue of departmental autonomies, electoral support for the MAS continued to expand. In Tarija, the party won more than half (51.1 per cent) of the vote, whilst in Santa Cruz it attracted 40.9 per cent. In Beni and Pando, support continued to grow rapidly, attracting 37.7 per cent and 44.5 per cent respectively. These results challenged the notion that support for the government was concentrated almost entirely in the highlands, with the opposition commanding almost universal support in the *Media Luna*. As Table 2 makes clear, there were fairly strong regional differences within departments like Santa Cruz, with certain parts of the department — notably those with large migrant populations of Andean origin — voting overwhelmingly for the MAS in 2005. Within the city of Santa Cruz, support was particularly high in those low-income neighbourhoods like Plan Tres Mil in which migrants from rural areas to the city are a majority. A similar pattern could be observed in Tarija, with MAS support much stronger in low-income neighbourhoods of the capital city and in rural parts of the department where *campesino* and indigenous social movements have strong traction.

The results of these national elections increased the MAS's presence in Congress. Whereas in 2002, it won seven seats in the Senate (out of 27) and 27 in the Chamber of Deputies (out of 130), in 2005, its share had increased to 12 and 72 seats respectively. The 2005 results gave the party a majority in the Chamber of Deputies but a minority of one in the Senate, where the opposition parties combined had 13 seats. Because of the changes to the Constitution in 2009, the number of seats in the Senate was increased from 27 (three per department) to 36 (four per department). The MAS won 26 Senate seats, picking up two Senate seats in each of the departments of Tarija, Santa Cruz, Beni and Pando. In the Chamber of Deputies, the electoral system remained

Table 2: Voting in Santa Cruz and Tarija: percentage of valid votes cast for the MAS, Presidential elections of 2005 and 2009

	2005	**2009**
Santa Cruz		
Andrés Ibáñez	31.5	36.2
Warnes	26.5	41.2
Velasco	17.7	27.1
Ichilo	63.7	72.6
Chiquitos	15.9	32.5
Sara	29.8	38.8
Cordillera	29.4	54.6
Vallegrande	28.1	40.5
Florida	36.7	49.2
Obispo Santistevan	41.1	53.4
Ñuflo de Chávez	57.7	68.8
Angel Sandóval	20.2	42.3
Caballero	57.9	70.8
Germán Busch	20.7	38.1
Guarayos	28.3	51.9
Tarija		
Cercado	26.9	41
Arce	35.3	64.4
Gran Chaco	36.2	58.1
Avilés	38.4	62.6
Méndez	36.4	60.3
O'Connor	36.6	63.5

Source: Corte Nacional Electoral

unaltered, with somewhat less than half the representatives elected on a list system (*plurinominales*) for departments and the rest for individual constituencies (*uninominales*) and special indigenous constituencies. The number of MAS seats increased to 89 in the new Chamber.[5]

5   Of these, three belong to the *Movimiento sin Miedo* (MSM) who have subsequently split from the MAS. At the time of writing, the extent to which they will lend support in future to MAS legislative initiatives was unclear.

Just six months after the 2005 outcome, the 2006 election to the Constituent Assembly represented a further victory for the MAS, although it failed to achieve the two-thirds majority necessary to pass its text unopposed, giving way to repeated opposition attempts to frustrate the process of rewriting the Constitution. The MAS had 134 members of the Assembly out of a total of 255, winning 50.7 per cent of the vote,[6] thus confirming its status as a truly national political party. This was not just in the western highlands but also in the eastern lowlands, where it gained as many seats as its main conservative rivals. With the exception of the MNR (which picked up a handful of seats), the traditional parties were effectively wiped off the electoral map.[7]

Prefects/governorship elections

Elections to the executive at departmental level are a relative novelty, taking place for the first time in 2005, when prefectural elections were held at the same time as the presidential and legislative ones. Previously, prefects had been named by the President and were mainly responsible for law and order issues and infrastructure at the local level. The change in the law allowing for the election of prefects took place under the interim administration of Carlos Mesa (2003–5) and responded to pressure from regionalist groups, particularly the *Media Luna*, to increase the political powers of individual departments. This move opened up a whole new sphere of political contention, which had not existed previously, and enabled those elected to use their local legitimacy to become independent advocates of departmental interests. This change, as was to become clear, would lead to the development of strong centrifugal tendencies against the centralised state and severe challenges to the authority of Morales and the MAS.

In 2005, notwithstanding its landslide victory in the presidential and legislative elections, the MAS won the prefectural elections in only three departments: Chuquisaca, Potosi and Oruro (see Table 3). Even in these three, the margin of victory was fairly small and in no case did an MAS candidate get elected with an absolute majority of votes. In two departments — La Paz and Cochabamba — opposition prefects were elected, notwithstanding the convincing victories of Morales and the MAS in the presidential elections. These failings, coupled with the relatively small margins of victory elsewhere, showed — for the first (and not the last) time — the importance of selecting candidates in sub-national elections who carry conviction among local electorates. In

6   The system used to elect the 255-member Assembly included the election of 210 members for 70 constituencies with the winning party achieving two seats and the runner-up one. Five per department were elected out of the remaining 45 members.

7   Although many of their leaders joined *Podemos*, led by the former President, Jorge Quiroga, previously from the ADN.

La Paz, victory went to the *Podemos* candidate, José Luis Paredes, a former mayor of El Alto. In Cochabamba, Manfred Reyes Villa, the former mayor of the city of Cochabamba, was elected prefect. Elsewhere, other prominent opposition figures — apparently more aware than the MAS leadership of the future significance of prefectural politics — won fairly easy victories: Rubén Costas in Santa Cruz, Mario Cossío in Tarija, Ernesto Suárez in the Beni, and Leopoldo Fernández in Pando. Of these, Cossío was a former MNR president of the Chamber of Deputies and both Fernández and Suárez were key members of former President Banzer's right-wing party, *Acción Democrática Nacionalista* (ADN).

As we will see below, tensions between the government in La Paz and the departmental prefects of the *Media Luna* peaked in 2008. Acting in close harmony with local elite civic committees, these prefects were key actors behind the holding of unilateral referendums to approve 'statutes of autonomy' in the four departments of the *Media Luna*, a direct challenge to the schemes of autonomy contemplated in the new draft Constitution.[8] However, following the outbreak of widespread violence in September 2008, and amid plots to subvert government authority, a constitutional deal was sealed in Congress which resolved this problem and paved the way towards a referendum on the Constitution in January 2009. Amongst other things, the new Constitution envisaged a complex system of devolution with autonomies granted not just to departments but to regions, municipalities and indigenous groups. The Constitution also perpetuated the new system of elected prefects, thereafter to be known as 'governors', whilst also establishing departmental assemblies.

The April 2010 gubernatorial elections were therefore the first to be held under the new rules. Given the difficulties that had arisen since 2005 because of the failure to elect prefects amenable to the MAS government, considerable efforts were exerted to make amends. In the end, the MAS was successful in electing its candidates in six departments, as opposed to just three in 2005, reducing the opposition to controlling the three departments of Santa Cruz, Tarija and Beni. As we see in Table 3, not only were the percentages higher but so too were the numbers of those voting for MAS candidates.[9]

Perhaps the most significant result was the narrow MAS victory in Pando in the extreme north, a department whose previous prefect had been arrested for his role in fomenting violence in 2008. It also saw a substantial increase in its vote in the Beni. Although support for the MAS in 2010 increased substantially

---

8   The statutes of autonomy were unveiled in Santa Cruz on December 15, 2007, the same day as the draft Constitution was formally unveiled in La Paz. Other M*edia Luna* departments unveiled similar statutes in the following weeks, all modelled on that of Santa Cruz.

9   Like the December presidential elections, these were held using the new electoral role which increased substantially the number of voters able to exercise this right.

Table 3: Election of Prefects/Governors (2005 and 2010): Votes for MAS candidates

	2005		2010	
	Percent	Votes	Percent	Votes
Chuquisaca	**42.3**	66,999	**53.6**	109,270
La Paz	33.8	321,814	**50**	534,255
Cochabamba	43.1	222,895	**61.9**	415,245
Oruro	**41**	63,630	**59.6**	106,948
Potosi	**40.7**	79,710	**66.8**	163,989
Tarija	20.4	28,690	44.1	88,014
Santa Cruz	24.2	151,306	38.2	372,730
Beni	6.7	7,054	40.1	60,477
Pando	6	1,244	**49.7**	17,003

Source: Corte Nacional Electoral

Percentages in bold denote departments where MAS prefects/governors were elected.

Note: Final official votes were still not in as at 29 April 2010.

over 2005, the margins of victory in each department were considerably less than in the presidential elections four months earlier. Some within the MAS expressed disappointment with the results, since they were not the 'clean sweep' that some party strategists had hoped for, and incumbent prefects were returned as governors in the *Media Luna* (with the exception of Pando). Of these, perhaps the results from Tarija were the biggest disappointment. Morales' plurality of votes there in December 2005 had fed hopes that the MAS stood a good chance of winning the Tarija governorship, thereby decisively tilting the balance of regional power away from opponents of the government. Still, the size of the vote polled by the MAS in Santa Cruz, Tarija and the Beni reaffirmed the idea that it could count on a solid social base of support in these departments.

Municipal elections

The strong growth in support for the MAS is also evident from the results of local elections for mayors and municipalities (see Table 4), although levels of support in the country's main urban centres were considerably lower than in other types of election. The local elections of 1999, which took place during the Banzer government, show support for the MAS at extremely incipient levels. Nationally, the MAS won 3.3 per cent of the vote, but of the nine departmental capitals plus El Alto, its highest score was in Sucre where it achieved just 2.27 per cent of the vote. At that time, its support was still largely rural and concentrated in the Chapare in Cochabamba, where it won 70 per cent of the vote. Altogether, it picked up ten mayors and a majority of councillors in five municipalities.

By the time of the municipal elections in December 2004, the party's standing had changed fairly radically following its electoral breakthrough in the 2002 presidential and legislative elections. In 2004, the MAS had — effectively — become the main party of opposition, its standing enhanced by the hiatus in October the previous year when Sánchez de Lozada had been driven from the presidency and replaced by his Vice-President Carlos Mesa. The MAS had emerged as the strongest force in the Congress and used its influence to exert pressure on Mesa and his ministers. But this presence did not translate into a strong campaign for the local elections, particularly in the main cities where the MAS failed to win a single mayoralty. Its best urban result was in the city of Cochabamba, where it won 31 per cent of the vote, not enough to win even there. The MAS's performance suffered from the inexperience of its candidates and the difficulty they encountered in building alliances within the urban milieu. In rural Bolivia, the party fared much better, picking up over 28 per cent of available council seats overall and winning absolute majorities in 15 per cent of municipalities.

Table 4: Municipal Elections (1999, 2004 and 2010):
MAS vote in departmental capitals plus El Alto (percentage)

	1999	2004	2010
Sucre	2.3	8.3	31.3
La Paz	0.9	19.9	34.9
El Alto	1	17.1	**38.7**
Cochabamba	1	31.1	**39.5**
Oruro	2	9.5	33.4
Potosi		4.1	33.6
Tarija	1.9	6.6	24.9
Santa Cruz	0.5	9.5	31.8
Trinidad	0.3	2.3	24.5
Cobija	1	5.6	**53.7**

Source: Corte Nacional Electoral

Figures in bold denote cities where MAS candidates were elected mayor

In 2010, the MAS had a realistic chance of asserting itself more effectively within the structure of local government, taking full advantage of its successful 2009 presidential campaign and its determined drive to win the governorship elections held at the same time. But while its proportion of the vote was well up on 2004, it largely failed to make the hoped-for breakthrough in the country's main cities. Of the ten departmental capitals plus El Alto, it won the mayoralty of only three: El Alto, Cochabamba and Cobija (the minuscule capital of far-away Pando). Opposition candidates won in all the others. In both the cities of La Paz and Oruro, MAS candidates were defeated by the *Movimiento Sin Miedo* (MSM) of former La Paz mayor, Juan del Granado. Up until 2010, the MSM had worked in alliance with the MAS, but decided at this point to break the alliance and field its own candidates against those of the MAS. The MSM had gained a strong foothold in La Paz, but the result in Oruro was a jolt to MAS expectations. In Potosi, the MAS candidate failed to defeat the incumbent mayor, René Joaquino, who had a strong and loyal local following. In Sucre, Tarija, Santa Cruz and Trinidad, other opposition candidates managed to defeat MAS aspirants. In rural Bolivia, the MAS fared better, but rural municipalities lack the funds and political weight of their urban counterparts. Overall, the MAS won in 227 of the 339 municipal races. As in other elections, those of 2010 showed that success depended greatly on the selection of candidates and the standing that these enjoy within their communities. The standing of Morales and the organised presence of the MAS at the local level were no guarantees of success.

Referendums and consultas

Bolivia does not have a history of referendums and it was only as a consequence of amendments to the Constitution in the 1990s (and since) that measures such as referendums, *consultas*, recall referendums and the like have come into use. In part, they were designed to overcome the perceived failings of Bolivian representative democracy in galvanising participation and averting the sort of political alienation that came to characterise politics by the mid- to late-1990s. The demand for more direct involvement by ordinary citizens in political decision-making was made patent by the mobilisation surrounding the downfall of Sánchez de Lozada in 2003. One of the key demands of the so-called October Agenda was for the renationalisation of oil and gas and this was put to the people in a referendum.

So Bolivia's first referendum was held on 18 July 2004, with five questions on the ballot: (1) The repeal of the existing hydrocarbons law, passed during the first administration of Sánchez de Lozada in 1996, granting generous tax conditions to foreign companies to encourage them to invest in Bolivia; (2) the assertion of national ownership over hydrocarbons up until the wellhead (i.e. to the point of commercialisation); (3) the need to strengthen the role of former state oil company *Yacimientos Petrolíferos Fiscales Bolivianos* (YPFB); (4) the use of the country's gas export potential to negotiate with Chile on sovereign access to the Pacific Ocean; and (5) approval of the export of natural gas, subject to conditions on the use of gas for domestic supply and industrialisation. The MAS's position with regard to the referendum was that people should vote 'yes' to the first three questions, but 'no' to the last two. It was the only party to advocate a variegated response. In the event, voters approved all the questions, but not by the same margins: question one was approved by 87 per cent; question two by 92 per cent; question three by 87 per cent; question four by 55 per cent; and question five by 62 per cent. The lower margin of approval for the last two questions was directly attributable to the influence of the MAS. The outcome was a reverse for more radical currents of opinion — especially among the union movement and urban poor — which campaigned for a 'no' vote or abstention. The MAS thus distanced itself from the more radical left.

The second referendum was in July 2006, following the MAS victory at the end of 2005 and taking place at the same time as the elections to the Constituent Assembly. It concerned regional autonomies, and came as a response to pressure from the *Media Luna* departments, particularly Santa Cruz. The Assembly would have the binding obligation to grant greater autonomy to those departments where the 'yes' vote was in a majority, within a 'framework of national unity'. In the event, the four lowland departments voted 'yes', while the five highland ones voted 'no'. The MAS had campaigned for a 'no' vote overall. The result thus set the scene for the showdown in 2008, when the *Media Luna* departments openly challenged the views of the Constituent Assembly and the draft constitution itself, organising referendums to approve de facto 'statutes of autonomy'.

The third, which was a recall referendum, took place in August 2008, effectively a plebiscite on the policies followed by the Morales government, as well as those of each of the nine departmental prefects. It was perhaps the most direct form of political validation of all the electoral processes we have examined. Voters were asked whether they were 'in agreement with the continuity of the process of change led by President Evo Morales and Vice-President Alvaro García Linera'. They were also asked whether they agreed with 'the policies, actions and governance (*gestión*) of the prefect' of their department. The results were a round endorsement for Morales, who received a 67 per cent 'yes' vote (although with 'no' majorities registered in Santa Cruz, Beni and Tarija). Two opposition prefects — Paredes in La Paz and Reyes Villa in Cochabamba — were voted out with large majorities against them. The referendum proved to be something of a turning point in Morales' embattled relations with the opposition, reaffirming the legitimacy of his administration and reducing the number of prefects arrayed against him. Following a bout of violence in Santa Cruz and Tarija in September, the government was able to negotiate agreements with opposition politicians that removed the final legal obstacles to the Constitution being put to the people in a further referendum.

A fourth referendum, ratifying the Constitution, took place on 25 January 2009. The Constitution was approved by 61.4 per cent of voters, well over the 50 per cent required but with a majority in the four *Media Luna* departments voting against it, with the lowest level of support registered in Santa Cruz and the Beni (34.7 per cent and 32.6 per cent respectively). Voters were also asked a supplementary question on this occasion, regarding the upper limit that should prevail on landholding. More than 80 per cent voted that the limit should be 5,000 hectares rather than 10,000 hectares. This had been an issue on which the Constituent Assembly had been unable to agree, but which the MAS government was determined to pursue. Even in Santa Cruz, where landowners' lobby organisations were strongest and most influential, a large majority of voters opted for the 5,000 hectare limit. Many landed estates, especially in Santa Cruz and the Beni, are far larger than the legal limit. The issue of land reform in the *Media Luna* has proved to be one of the more contentious issues in the disputes with the civic committees in the lowlands, through which landowners exert strong influence over the direction of regional politics.

Explaining the growth of the MAS

As pointed out in the introduction, the growth of the MAS since the late 1990s has been a unique experience in Latin American politics, taking place precisely at a time when parties and party systems in Bolivia and elsewhere in the region have suffered crises of credibility and conviction. It is a party which has an organised social base as well as an electoral support that goes well beyond the confines of that base. The election results that we have analysed provide eloquent testament as to this phenomenon, charting as they do the varying performance of party candidates for different types of elective post. In what follows, we will deal with the main reasons for this expansion of electoral support.

Evo Morales and the role of leadership

There can be no denying that the question of leadership, particularly that of Evo Morales, has been a key explanation of the MAS's success at the polls. The electoral data show quite clearly that Evo's popularity far outmatches that of other party figures and that this popularity is not necessarily transferable to others within the MAS. The scale of the 2005 presidential election owed much to Evo's leadership, as did that of 2009.

The story of how Evo emerged as a political figure as leader of the *cocaleros* in the Chapare before setting up what became known as the MAS has been told elsewhere.[10] Here it is worthwhile stressing three factors. The first is that Evo's humble origins give him huge legitimacy in the eyes of most Bolivians who are at once poor and indigenous. He is quintessentially a 'man of the people', 'one of us'. His origins in dire poverty in a village in southern Oruro, his experiences as a boy working on the sugar harvest in Argentina, his passage through military service, his decision to migrate to the tropics of Cochabamba in pursuit of a better life, the struggle to survive in this difficult environment, all parallel the experiences of thousands of ordinary Bolivians. Although not the first person of humble origins to break into the political elite, he has been the first to shatter the 'glass ceiling' by reaching the very top. Secondly, coming from an Aymara family but having grown up in a largely Quechua-speaking environment in the Chapare, he has experience of both ethnicities and is not perceived as being the 'property' of one or the other. Thirdly, and possibly most importantly, Morales straddles two traditions of popular organisation: the *sindicalista* tradition and the *indigenista*. The political culture and organisation of the *cocaleros* of the Chapare was heavily coloured by the country's strong trade union traditions. The influx of former mineworkers who migrated to the Chapare in search of work after the mass closure of the mines in the mid-1980s had a powerful influence on the ideological and organisational development of the *cocaleros*. However, the spirit of resistance was given new meaning by the policies of coca eradication. These were pursued with renewed vigour from 1997 by the Banzer administration, with the coca leaf and its cultural significance becoming emblematic of that spirit. As the MAS grew after 1997, particularly gaining support on the Altiplano, its *sindicalista* roots became suffused with a new identity, particularly within the realm of *campesino* politics and through the *Confederación Sindical Unica de Trabajadores Campesinos de Bolivia* (CSUTCB) out of which Morales emerged as an important leader. The indigenous identity of the MAS became increasingly pronounced as the party managed to win over support within the Aymara world and marginalise its more outspoken leaders such as Felipe Quispe.

It is also difficult to overstate Morales' personal contribution, since the MAS first came to office in 2005, and the ways in which he has used this to good effect at critical junctures. Evo's tireless dedication to duty is well documented,

---

10 See, for example, Darwin Pinto and Roberto Nava, *Un tal Evo: biografía no-autorizada* (Santa Cruz: El País, 2007). Pablo Stefanoni and Hervé do Alto, *Evo Morales, de la coca al palacio* (La Paz: Malatesta, 2006), also describe Morales' political evolution from his days as a *cocalero*.

not least by those who are obliged to keep up with his exhausting routine.[11] The President spends most of his time travelling, maintaining direct and personal contact with the social movements that make up the MAS. He sees this personal contact as key in maintaining a sense of purpose and direction within the ruling party, warding off the danger of splits and fractures and preventing alternative leaderships emerging from the social movements — particularly the more radical among them. It would seem that Morales is acutely aware of the danger of popular contact becoming atrophied with the concerns of state, a problem that helped undermine the legitimacy of his predecessors. There can be little doubt that political power is highly concentrated in the office of the presidency and the relatively small circle of intimate advisors surrounding Morales.[12] However, it is not an absolute power, since Evo is answerable to the social movements which make up the MAS and which have themselves been greatly empowered by the MAS's electoral success. Still, one of the risks facing the MAS is its over-dependence on one person for its continued success, not least in view of the problems of eventual succession. The party's lack of institutionalisation, and the lack of credible alternatives to Evo, may make engineering such a succession problematic.[13]

Filling the political vacuum

It would be wrong, though, to portray the growth of the MAS as simply the success of personalist politics; rather, it is the result of the success of an ideological project that filled a vacuum left by the progressive exhaustion of previous political models.[14] By the 2002 elections, the cracks in the old order were evident. Although Sánchez de Lozada for the MNR narrowly won the elections, it was clear at the time that he lacked the sort of proposals for government that he had produced in 1993 with his Plan de Todos. The MIR was in fourth place, while the ADN — bereft of Banzer as a figurehead and smitten by its record in government — managed only 3.4 per cent of the vote. The system of coalitions that had ruled since 1985, cemented by patronage and graft, no longer attracted voters. By contrast, the MAS, articulating a sense of rejection and protest towards the status quo, proved it was able to bring

---

11 See, for example, Martín Sivak, *Jefazo: Retrato íntimo de Evo Morales* (Buenos Aires: Sudamericana, 2008).

12 This was a point of constant criticism by sectors of the MAS during Morales' first government.

13 In the negotiations surrounding the final approval of a constitutional text, Morales made concessions to the opposition. One of these was the pledge not to seek re-election in 2014.

14 On the erosion of public support for *democracia pactada,* see Pilar Domingo (ed.), *Bolivia: fin de un ciclo y nuevas perspectivas políticas (1993–2003)* (Barcelona: Bellaterra, 2006).

together a disparate collection of social movements and interests around a common project.

The Cochabamba 'water wars' of 1999 and 2000, in which the *cocaleros* of the Chapare had been active participants, had shown the potency of a protest movement that brought together different interests in defiance of the policies of privatisation that had characterised the previous decade. It was the ability of the *cocaleros* and the MAS to widen their original campaign against the policies of US-backed coca eradication and bring together a diverse coalition to oppose the whole neo-liberal scheme that brought it unexpected electoral dividends.[15] Sven Harten, elsewhere in this volume, has described this as bringing together a 'chain of equivalence', an electoral platform that had a common denominator that appealed to a wide range of disparate interests, urban as well as rural and in the eastern lowlands as well as in the western highlands. As well as championing the interests of particular social and ethnic sectors, it resurrected a spirit of nationalism with a much broader appeal across the country.

Privatisation had been sold to Bolivians as a quid pro quo for the modernisation of the country's productive base and the increase in employment this would help generate. In the context of the economic downturn of the late 1990s and the early years of the new millennium, this was shown to be a hollow promise. Both the 'Water War', and subsequently the so-called 'Gas War' of 2003, posed profound questions about who the true beneficiaries of privatisation and neo-liberalism had been.[16] In rallying opinion against neo-liberalism, the MAS accused Bolivia's elites of being more interested in doing the bidding of foreign economic interests than in standing up for those of the majority of the population. Nowhere was this argument more potent than with respect to the semi-privatised gas industry, the source of most of Bolivia's exports. This was widely seen as having been sold off on terms highly disadvantageous to the long-term interests of the Bolivian state. The privatisation of hydrocarbons, backed by international financial institutions like the World Bank as well as local business interests, thus revived old arguments about the failure of elites to stand up for national interests, an argument reminiscent of the 1952 revolution and the nationalisation of the mining industry by the then MNR government. Indeed, notwithstanding economic liberalisation in the 1980s and 1990s, 1952 continued to act as a powerful reference point for those who doubted

15 The Cochabamba Water Wars gave new impetus to activity on the part of a range of different social movements in different parts of the country. See John Crabtree, *Patterns of Protest: Politics and Social Movements in Bolivia* (London: Latin America Bureau, 2005).

16 On both the Water War and the Gas War, as well as other manifestations of protest against globalisation, see Jim Schultz and Melissa Crane Draper (eds.), *Dignity and Defiance: Stories from Bolivia's Challenge to Globalisation* (Pontypool: Merlin Press, 2008).

that privatisation would work to the benefit of all but a tiny minority of the population.

Evo Morales' decision, in May 2006, to send the troops in to proclaim the 're-nationalisation' of the gas industry thus played to deeply-rooted sentiments in public opinion. Although what emerged was far from being a classic nationalisation (more a forcible change of contracts on the part of the international companies involved), it won widespread acceptance among ordinary Bolivians as a symbol of national dignity. Indeed, this was clear at the time of the 2003 'October agenda'. The Mesa government, which took over from Sánchez de Lozada, had little alternative but to agree to holding the 2004 referendum on the future of the hydrocarbons industry. The results of the referendum on hydrocarbons showed quite conclusively the degree of consensus in most parts of the country about the need to re-impose state control over the industry.

Economic nationalism thus provided the political glue required to cement together the diverse groups of interest which underlay the development of the MAS. It appealed to opinion in most sectors of society, urban as well as rural, even winning plaudits in the eastern part of the country. It provided a powerful discourse against the parties of the right which could be portrayed as self-interested and elitist, forcing them to look for other ways of justifying themselves to public opinion. By 2005, therefore, the MAS had built up a powerful presence in the country, taking full advantage of the political weakness of its opponents. Although its support was more solid in rural areas, it had also been able to build up a strong presence in many of Bolivia's main cities, opening up the party to the urban marginalised, lower middle classes and sympathetic city-based intellectuals. In promising to fulfil the October agenda by 're-founding' the country and rewriting its Constitution, it struck a positive note that appealed to a large majority of voters. It had come a long way in a short time from being simply the 'political instrument' of the federation of *cocaleros* in the Cochabamba tropics.

Indigenous politics and social movements

The MAS, however, was more than simply Bolivian nationalism revamped for the new millennium. It stood for the transfer of political power away from elites to those long marginalised in the process of the nation's development, especially its indigenous majority.[17] Through the various social movements that had become increasingly active since the late 1990s, many defining themselves in ethnic terms, the MAS had acquired a strong social base which underpinned

17 James Dunkerley, *Bolivia: Revolution and the Power of History in the Present* (London: Institute for the Study of the Americas, 2007), stresses the 'plebeian' nature of the MAS in defining its revolutionary nature.

its electoral performance. The relationship between the party and these social movements has proved difficult to define, but they represent a bottom-up presence that counteracts some of the more 'top-down' attributes of the MAS government. The party is essentially made up of these social movements and they have proved themselves assertive, not only in defence of their own interests but in ensuring that their representatives are selected when it comes to choosing candidates for elections. Their attitude towards the government differs, but is not just one of uncritical support.[18]

How to define issues of race and class has long been debated in Bolivia, particularly on the left, but, as Albó has argued, it is something of a semantic debate; those who are poor in Bolivia are largely indigenous and those who are indigenous are largely poor.[19] Although the methodology behind the most recent census (2001) has been questioned, most authors agree that Bolivia is one of the few countries of Latin America where the indigenous population is in the majority, not a minority. According to the census findings, 62 per cent of the population identify themselves as indigenous, a large number of them city-dwellers. The distribution of indigenous populations varies considerably, however, between the western highlands and the eastern lowlands. But even in the lowlands, large numbers are of indigenous descent, even though the families of many migrated from the highlands decades earlier.

The resurgence of indigenous politics in Bolivia dates from the 1970s when the *Katarista* movement began to impact on *campesino* politics.[20] The *Kataristas* criticised what they saw as the ethnically homogenising project of the MNR that sought to promote the *mestizo* nation, a project designed fundamentally to co-opt the peasant movement and to incorporate it into the structure of the new state. The promotion of indigenous identities therefore became part of a reassertion of the autonomy of the peasant movement as a whole, particularly in relation to the infamous *Pacto Militar Campesino* (Military-Peasant Pact). Although the *Katarista* movement split and fractured into various different tendencies in the 1980s and 1990s, it popularised new

---

18 For a useful discussion of how the position of protest movements changes when the party that supports them becomes the government, see Maria Teresa Zegada, Yuri Tórrez, and Gloria Cámara, *Movimientos sociales en tiempos de poder: articulaciones y campos de conflicto en el gobierno del MAS* (La Paz: Centro Cuarto Intermedio/Plural, 2008).

19 Xavier Albó, 'The Long Memory of Ethnicity in Bolivia and some Temporary Oscillations', in John Crabtree and Laurence Whitehead (eds.), *Unresolved Tensions: Bolivia Past and Present* (Pittsburgh: University of Pittsburgh Press, 2008), pp. 13–34.

20 See Xavier Albó, 'De MNRistas a Kataristas: campesinado, estado y partidos (1953–1983)', *Historia Boliviana* 5:1 (1985), pp. 87–127, and Esteban Ticona, Gonzalo Rojas and Xavier Albó, *Votos y wiphalas* (La Paz: Fundación Milenio/CIPCA, 1995).

forms of social organisation that differed from the traditional *clasismo* of the left. Its main institutional expression was the CSUTCB which involved not only pro-indigenous groups on the Altiplano, but also those of a more *clasista* inclination, including the *cocaleros* from the Chapare.

Although the *cocaleros* adopted some symbols that were arguably indigenous, their agenda was not one of ethnic affirmation. The coca leaf was more a symbol of national sovereignty than an ethnic rallying cry. Still, the influence of ethnicity was not altogether absent because of the overlap between class and ethnicity, even in the Chapare. But as the MAS advanced, building strength in the Altiplano, it began to incorporate other sectors which brought with them different political preoccupations. This was particularly the case after the 2002 elections when the party won significant support across the Altiplano.[21] But it was in 2005, when the MAS became the new government, that indigenous concerns became central to its identity as a party. Large numbers of people elected to Congress for the MAS were representatives of social movements from the Altiplano and prominent indigenous leaders became cabinet ministers.[22]

The discourse of the MAS came to focus on ethnicity as a claim, but a plurinational and multicultural discourse reflecting the range of different ethnicities to be found in Bolivia. It has thus been able to build up a presence in both the highlands as well as in the lowlands where ethnic consciousness takes different forms. At the same time, it picks up on other traditions and ideological reference points. While, in his inaugural speech of January 2006, Morales gave due weight to indigenous forebears, he also underscored the plurality of the MAS by referring to other non-indigenous iconic martyrs: Che Guevara, Marcelo Quiroga Santa Cruz, the Socialist Party leader, and Luis Espinal, the Jesuit priest, both murdered in 1980. Ideologically speaking, the MAS is a 'broad church'. Its commitment to *indigenismo*, as well as to *clasismo*, was made explicit in the drafting of the new Constitution, one which has enhanced indigenous as well as other social rights relating to a whole range of activities.

---

21 See Roxana Liendo, *Participación Popular y el movimiento campesino Aymara* (La Paz: CIPCE/AIPE/Fundación Tierra, 2009), who emphasises the way in which reforms of the 1990s contributed to the development of an ethnic consciousness among the Aymara people. The MAS's electoral success on the Altiplano contrasted with that of the more narrowly indigenous *Movimiento Indígena Pachakuti* (MIP), whose support was concentrated around Lake Titicaca. The MIP, which gave less importance to electoral politics than the MAS, won 2.1% of the vote in 2005.

22 These included (among others) David Choquehuanca, the foreign minister, and Félix Patzi, the education minister.

Economic policy and social gains

Although it was not clear then, the MAS took office in Bolivia at a time when economic growth was on an upwards trajectory. Helped by strong world demand for Bolivia's main commodity exports, the economy grew by 4.8 per cent in 2006, 4.6 per cent in 2007, and 6.1 per cent in 2008. Even in 2009, the year of the global downturn, GDP expanded by around 3.5 per cent, one of the highest rates anywhere in Latin America. The MAS government's economic policies were outlined in June 2006, when it published its five-year plan for the period 2006–11. The strategy was based on what seemed at the time fairly optimistic assumptions regarding growth and investment. It made explicit the government's concern to translate this growth into creating a fairer and more democratic society in which poverty and inequality would be reduced. It invoked the indigenous idea of the need to 'vivir bien', for people to live well, not just in income terms but in terms of their relations with one another and with the natural environment. It also posited the need for Bolivia to become less dependent on outside influences, in terms of stimulating growth, and to regain dignity as a nation.

In practice, Bolivia's growth rates over the subsequent period had a great deal to do with export-led demand. The country's exports rose from 2.8 billion dollars in 2005 to 6.4 billion in 2008. In large part this was to do with increasing the volumes and price for Bolivian gas exports to Brazil and Argentina, but it was also influenced by the rise in prices for minerals and other commodities. More important from the point of view of social policy, however, was the impact of the gas 'nationalisation' of May 2006, which led to a large increase in tax revenues flowing into the government's coffers. Having suffered a chronic deficit on its fiscal accounts for decades, the colour of the ink changed to black in 2006. Indeed, the government had great difficulty — at least initially — in finding ways in which to spend the increased tax income. There were also moves to increase the amount of revenue generated by the mining industry at this time, although the effects were not nearly so dramatic.

With money to spend, the government introduced a series of new programmes designed to boost welfare and fight poverty. These were mainly either extensions of existing policies or adaptations of the sort of conditional cash transfer (CCT) programmes being implemented in different ways in other parts of Latin America. In the first category was the Renta Dignidad, involving an expansion of the original Bonosol pensions programme introduced in the 1990s. The Renta Dignidad raised the amounts payable to the elderly, reduced the qualification age from 65 to 60 and made payment monthly rather than annual. The programme, financed by gas revenues, proved highly successful in the benefits it brought to families on low incomes, whilst enhancing the status of older people within their families and the wider society. In the second category, two other programmes sought to target specific groups. The so-called Bono Juancito Pinto is a subsidy to families with children of primary school age and paid on condition of school attendance. The second, the Bono Juana Azurduy, is paid to pregnant and nursing mothers and is designed to reduce infant and maternal mortality by encouraging them to take up available health provision, often geared specifically to women of indigenous backgrounds.[23] Although the amounts paid to recipients are modest, they are greatly valued.

The extent to which such policies are tackling the structural roots of poverty in Bolivia is less obvious, as is the extent to which the economic model broke with traditional notions of export-led growth. The pattern of growth is such that it requires particularly high annual growth rates to reduce poverty on a sustainable basis. The take-up of benefits also depends on the ability of schools and health facilities to improve social conditions over the longer term. Both are deficient in rural Bolivia where extreme poverty is concentrated. However, the data available (despite having limitations) suggest that poverty rates have fallen, as has the degree of inequality in Bolivian society. According to the UN, the proportion of the population living in poverty declined from 32.1 per cent in 2004 to 27.8 per cent in 2007, while the country's Gini coefficient (the main measure of income inequality) fell from 0.61 in 2002 (among the highest in the world) to 0.56 in 2007.[24] Using different measures, the National Statistics Institute (INE) reaches roughly similar conclusions. It has yet to be seen whether these trends will continue into the future, but anecdotal evidence would suggest that the availability of social benefits (especially in rural areas) is something that is prized by those who receive them, as are the impacts of other special programmes in the area of rural health. Such feelings translate into votes.

Tackling the right

The results of the 2005 presidential elections were a sobering reminder to the traditional parties of the extent to which they had lost public confidence. Neither Banzer's ADN nor the MIR of Jaime Paz Zamora presented candidates in the elections, while the once mighty MNR polled a paltry 6.5 per cent of the vote. As we have seen, some leading politicians read the runes correctly, seeing in the prefectural elections in the *Media Luna* the best chances of maintaining their political influence. Two electoral coalitions contested the 2005 elections. *Podemos*, which grouped together those on the right behind the candidacy of Jorge Quiroga (the former President, albeit briefly), won 28.6 per cent of the

---

23 It is particularly aimed at reducing infant malnutrition by providing mothers with an allowance to supplement food needs.

24 UN, Comisión Económica para América Latina, *Anuario estadístico de América Latina y el Caribe, 2009* (Santiago de Chile: CEPAL, 2010).

vote, principally in the *Media Luna*. *Unidad Nacional* (UN), a more centrist business-oriented group with the former MIRista Samuel Doria Medina as its presidential candidate, won 7.8 per cent. Apart from achieving a slim majority in the Senate, which could be used to block legislation and appointments, the opposition parties found themselves in too weak a position to influence national politics. However, they were able to put their blocking role to good effect in the Constituent Assembly, elected in July 2006. The MAS failed to achieve the two-thirds majority required to approve its preferred text outright, giving the opposition the power of effective veto.

It was the combination of this power to frustrate the majority will in the Assembly, with a new-found power to mobilise opinion against the government in the *Media Luna*, that gave the right-wing opposition scope for manoeuvre. Faced with a majority constitutional text they refused to ratify, the *Podemos* delegates withdrew from the Assembly, forcing the MAS delegates and their allies to approve a text which could not be ratified by the necessary two-thirds of Assembly members. At much the same time, the civic committees and prefects of the *Media Luna* took matters into their own hands by publishing their de facto 'statutes of autonomy' for each of the four departments and holding their own referendums to approve these statutes. The referendums resulted in well over 80 per cent of voters in the *Media Luna* approving the statutes, radical statements of autonomy that were not far removed from unilateral declarations of independence. The referendum results, and the threat of possible secession behind them, probably represented the high-point of popular support for the right-wing opposition in the *Media Luna*. The initiative had passed from *Podemos* and other parties on the right to *Conalde*, a coordinating mechanism between dissident prefects in the east of the country that was better placed to rally support on the streets.[25]

However, *Conalde* and the civic committees of the *Media Luna* overplayed their hand. In September 2008, they became actively involved in a wave of violence that swept Santa Cruz, Tarija, Beni and Pando in which MAS sympathisers were attacked, government offices ransacked, airports closed and gas installations threatened. A plot was subsequently revealed to launch an armed rebellion against the government in La Paz and to assassinate Morales. The scale of the violence offended many in the *Media Luna*, driving a wedge between more moderate opinion and radical secessionists. A process of international mediation involving neighbouring countries ended up ratifying the territorial integrity of Bolivia, a position that effectively leant support to the government. Meanwhile, bolstered by his ratification in the recall referendum

25 *Conalde* also included the prefect of Chuquisaca, following the forced resignation of the
   MAS prefect originally elected in 2005, over the issue of *capitalía plena*, the pretension of
   Sucre to regain its status as the full capital of Bolivia.

of August 2008, Morales was able to negotiate changes to the constitutional draft with the more moderate members of *Podemos* that would allow this to be put to voters in a referendum. While opinion in Santa Cruz could be galvanised around calls for greater autonomy, the crisis showed that there was no mood for any moves that would threaten the unity of Bolivia as a country. The events of September 2008 — which ended in the killing of a substantial number of *campesinos* in Pando — were to prove a turning point, after which the opposition star began to wane.

The failure of the opposition parties to mount a unified campaign against the MAS was made clear the following year as the date set for presidential elections grew close. In the event, none of the leading figures of the opposition were able to forge a united opposition bloc. Reyes Villa emerged at the last moment as the candidate of a hastily-created right-wing party, the *Plan Progreso para Bolivia* (PPB). Other more capable politicians, such as Quiroga and the former Vice-President Víctor Hugo Cárdenas, were sidelined. In the end, the PPB pitted itself against Doria Medina's *Unidad Nacional*, splitting the opposition vote in Santa Cruz. The scale of the MAS victory in the 2009 elections was thus underscored by the splits and rivalries in the opposition camp, itself a consequence of its failure to articulate a convincing alternative to the MAS during the previous period. Not only did the opposition parties lose their hold over the Senate, but their electoral weakness was even exposed in the *Media Luna*. As we have seen, 51 per cent of the voters in Tarija opted for the MAS, while 45 per cent did so in Pando, 41 per cent in Santa Cruz, and even 38 per cent in the Beni.

As the MAS embarked on its second term in 2010, the political barometer seemed set fair at the national level. The chances of the opposition parties mounting a strong challenge seemed remote. Indeed, the next scheduled elections would not be until 2014. Rather, the focus of opposition would be regional. The victory of incumbent prefects or governors in Santa Cruz, Tarija and the Beni in the April 2010 departmental elections served as a reminder to the MAS that the regional problem is yet unresolved. The civic committees in the lowlands will be looking for an opportunity to flex their muscles once again. Although a formula of autonomies was agreed in the new Constitution, much would depend on how the powers and responsibilities of governors, mayors and indigenous leaders are defined in practice. Despite having a water-tight majority in the legislature, new areas of tension are bound to emerge in the process of implementing the new Constitution and in responding to the demands of the social movements. Although the MAS can derive some satisfaction from the local election results, they showed that electoral validation was not something that could necessarily be taken for granted.

Conclusions

The story of the MAS, since it first emerged as a political party in the mid-1990s, has so far been one of consolidation; it has gone from being the political expression of a narrow interest group, the *cocaleros* of the Chapare, to being the hegemonic force in Bolivian politics. As we have seen, its electoral advance has been both cause and consequence of the development of an organised grass-roots presence throughout the country. The strength of this local organisation, and the party's electoral strength, has been subject to regional variations, but both have grown remarkably in the period under review, strengthening one another. The MAS has been able to appeal to a wide range of interests on the basis of a discourse and a government agenda that has overcome regional particularism and can appeal to the majority of the population.

The success of the MAS has depended on a variety of factors that we have analysed here: its leadership; its ability to take advantage of political opportunities; its ability to project a message that has wide appeal to a range of different voters; its success in government in creating viable policies and then rewarding its supporters; and the failure of opposition parties to identify a rallying cry that can appeal to other than a relatively small proportion of the population. Through its repeated exercises in electoral validation, the MAS has showed itself capable of appealing to the vast majority of the population, whether indigenous or not. The increase in its vote in departments like Tarija, Santa Cruz, Beni and Pando stands as testimony to its ability to go beyond its social, ethnic and geographical 'comfort zone'.

Continued electoral success, of course, is not something that any party can take for granted. A victory such as that of December 2009, when nearly two-thirds of the electorate voted for one party and its candidates, would in any case be something that would be hard to repeat. Indeed, the passage from a period of constant electoral activity to one with fewer electoral contests may bring its own problems. One of the conclusions we have reached here is that the role of Evo Morales has been hugely important in explaining the growth of the MAS. As local elections have shown — and the same is also true in elections to the Chamber of Deputies — his popularity has not automatically transferred to those selected in one way or another to become MAS candidates. Arguably, one of the weaknesses of the party has been its failure to exercise greater control over those that seek electoral office as representatives of social movements. Given the loose structure of the party and its lack of institutional procedures, this may be a problem that will not easily be resolved. As was clear in the local elections of April 2010, other parties will find and be able to exploit spaces where the MAS is found wanting.

The standing of the MAS will also depend on its ability to manage internal conflicts and rivalries. The broad nature of the MAS's support means that conflicts of interest within are never far from the surface. Not all social movements are equally supportive of the MAS and the government, and some may adopt an increasingly critical stance. Up to now, at least, Evo Morales has managed those internal problems deftly, exploiting his undisputed authority as leader. But this may not always be the case, particularly as problems of succession eventually emerge. He has promised to stand aside in the 2014 elections, a pledge that may encourage internal dissent within the MAS.

Nor can it be taken for granted that parties of the right will not find ways of capitalising on discontent with the record of the MAS government. The ongoing debate about regional autonomies is likely to open up spaces for opposition activity. And should the economy go into decline, it is likely to embitter the debate over the way in which the available fiscal resources are divided up between central and other levels of government. During his first administration, Morales was fortunate to inherit a relatively benign economic situation that may well not continue into his second. Problems of economic management could re-emerge, complicating the task of political management. If inflation was to become a major problem once again, for instance, the electoral popularity of the government could suffer.

Although the electoral fortunes of the MAS may fluctuate as time goes by, it still stands out in Latin America as a party that has established itself with a broad following and with an organised base in society. It may be hard to manage and lead, but it stands out as a very different sort of party than those that typify the political scene in most other countries in the region. As such, it stands a good chance of maintaining its political pre-eminence in years to come.

5

THE BOLIVIANISATION OF WASHINGTON-LA PAZ RELATIONS: EVO MORALES' FOREIGN POLICY AGENDA IN HISTORICAL CONTEXT

Martín Sivak

If the spectacle of the bourgeois crowding round the Ambassador and smiling servilely to get a loan is repulsive, looking at the peasant put up flower arches as a testimony of gratitude for the gift of a little school building or a water well is painful. Extreme poverty facilitates colonisation: men in Bolivia cost less. There comes a point where poverty destroys dignity: the Americans have identified this point, and work with it; to their eyes and their pockets, a Bolivian costs less than an Argentine or Chilean.

Sergio Almaraz, *Réquiem para una República* [1]

On 11 September 2008, the US Ambassador to Bolivia, Philip Goldberg, was formally expelled from the country. The rationale given was that Goldberg played an important role in an ill-defined destabilisation plan, concocted in the Eastern department of Santa Cruz de la Sierra, with a well-defined goal: putting an abrupt end to the presidency of Evo Morales. In his summing up of the case, which came from the Presidential Palace the day before, Morales stated, 'The one who conspires against democracy and above all seeks the division of Bolivia is the Ambassador of the United States'.[2] In this argument, the Bolivian leader offered an inversion of an oft-repeated American accusation: it was the Ambassador, not the first Aymara to be elected to presidential office, who was behaving 'against democracy'. The context to these events was widespread internal crisis with daily speculation about the outbreak of civil war. Morales' government was confronting the country's Eastern elites, who were demanding a form of departmental autonomy as their

---

1   Sergio Almaraz Paz, *Réquiem para una república* (La Paz: Los amigos del libro, 1985), p. 28.

2   Mary Vaca, 'Morales expulsa a embajador de EE.UU' (BBC Mundo), 11 September, 2008.

most effective tool for rejecting the administration's agenda. According to the Morales government, the US Embassy was meddling in internal political affairs by supporting these Eastern elites.

Latin American and US audiences offered differing readings of Goldberg's expulsion. By addressing the risk of a right-wing coup in the name of democracy, Morales' speech echoed that of Chilean President Salvador Allende on the eve of his fall in 1973. The 35th anniversary of the coup that overthrew Allende fell on 11 September, while in the US, this very date galvanised all the patriotic pathos that was the subtext to the much decried (in liberal circles) War on Terror. This global war, as defined by George W. Bush, entailed a Bolivian chapter. Without any noticeable success, the State Department attempted to frame Bolivian politics within the War on Terror. In February 2002, Ambassador Manuel Rocha compared the *cocaleros* (Bolivian coca producers) with the Taliban (alleged poppy-seed growers). With this narcoterrorist simile, Rocha attacked Morales' bid for the presidency. In the event, however, he only strengthened Morales' first presidential candidacy by exacerbating anti-US sentiment among voters.

Following the failed attempt to place Bolivia within the framework of the War on Terror, and prior to the expulsion of Goldberg, Morales was elected President of Bolivia in December 2005. His administration was epoch-making in political, economic and social terms. The policies adopted under his tutelage included: the nationalisation of key areas of the economy, such as the hydrocarbons sector; the widely-supported approval of a new Constitution to redefine the Bolivian State as a plurinational entity; a sustained process of social inclusion, encompassing the *campesinos* (peasantry), indigenous peoples, and other popular sectors; and a moderate distribution of public fiscal land along with the end of unproductive large states, among many other reforms. The nationalisations carried out under Morales, with the *basso continuo* of nationalist discourse, reinvigorated an already lively social consensus around the need to exert more sovereignty in foreign policy, particularly with regard to the US. For 50 years, a significant portion of Bolivian society has sustained an anti-American sentiment,[3] driven by continuous US intervention in Bolivian economic and political affairs. As we will see, this deeply rooted anti-Americanism is key to understanding the shift in Bolivian foreign policy towards the US since 2005.

Morales' policy towards the US during his first year in office was a combination of clear ruptures and some continuities. Seven main points

3   Alan McPherson defines anti-Americanism as the 'expression of a disposition against U.S. influence abroad'; see his *Yankee No! Anti-Americanism in U.S.-Latin American Relations* (Cambridge MA: Harvard University Press, 2006), p. 5. In this paper, and in the light of Bolivia-US relations, presence and intervention would replace the idea of influence.

may be identified: first, the Bolivian government rejected further aid from the International Monetary Fund (IMF) and the World Bank, often key vehicles of US influence in Bolivia. Second, the government discarded the Free Trade Area of the Americas (FTAA) initiative, to the dismay of the US State Department, which had used FTAA to enlarge US economic ties with individual countries and weaken the independence of the regional bloc. Third, the Bolivian administration supported the policy of 'social control' to manage coca cultivation, by enforcing a cap of 1,600 square metres per family — which effectively reduced the role of the US in the process of eradication and, in a broad sense, deprived the War on Drugs of any global epic. Fourth, it established a regional alliance with Cuba and Venezuela. Fifth, the Morales administration deprived the US Embassy of any former power it enjoyed to choose or veto any Ministers or Secretaries of State, and to design key public policies, as in the War on Drugs. Sixth, Morales asked that any American citizens wanting to visit Bolivia obtain a compulsory visa, as a way of enforcing reciprocity. Seventh, Morales has begun using the word 'empire' in order to define the US's position in the world, to characterise the motives of its government, and to denounce its gifts of financial aid to Morales' opposition within Bolivia. During the first year of Morales' presidency, such rhetoric was the main source of complaints by US officials.

Despite these ruptures, certain continuities persisted. The Bolivian government still claimed the right to approximately US$120 million annually in American aid.[4] Several programmes channel this money, and the US Embassy has continued to control them, including the ones related to the War on Drugs at the local level. The government made a strong appeal to the US for the continuation of the Andean Trade Promotion and Drug Eradication Act (ATPDEA), which bestows preferential tariffs on Bolivian goods entering the US and is granted in exchange for the successful realisation of goals in the War on Drugs. After Goldberg's expulsion, however, the US government withdrew the ATPDEA privilege and included Bolivia in the list of countries that do not meet the standards of a good Drugs Warrior.

This paper aims to examine the patterns of changes in US-Bolivian relations during the Morales presidency, by examining the overall period from the 1952 Revolution up to the expulsion of the American Ambassador in 2008. The historical perspective highlights the preeminence of American grand narratives framing Washington-La Paz relations as part of the US's own agenda (particularly the War against Communism, War on Drugs and War on Terror) during the period 1952–2005. This time-frame witnessed what this essay will term the 'Americanisation' of Bolivian-US diplomatic relations. Despite

4   An estimate made by Evo Morales himself, since there are no official or reliable data available.

certain tensions and conflicts, most Bolivian governments willingly accepted the US narratives during 1952–2005. But, if Americanisation was dominant in Bolivian-US relations, there were also significant upsurges of anti-Americanism within Bolivian popular sectors. The 'Anti-Yankee imperialist' stance of the Pulacayo Thesis, defended by the miners' union in 1946, would become an important reference for those sectors over the next 30 years.

In the years 2002–5, the loss of momentum of the regional neo-liberal consensus combined with the emergence in Bolivia of a radical political cycle with an ethno-cultural accent. This radical cycle enjoyed a triumphal beginning in 2000 with the Water War waged in Cochabamba. The cycle reached a peak with the 'Gas War' in October 2003. Thousands of people protested and marched from El Alto to La Paz against the exportation of gas to the US via Chile and forced the resignation of the President, Gonzalo Sánchez de Lozada. From this uprising, the so-called 'October agenda' (ultimately entailing nationalisation of hydrocarbons and the summoning of a Constitutional Assembly) was born. This radical cycle introduced, in a new key, the notion of national sovereignty and the ideal of national control of national resources, which were to be crucial in the redefinition of the relationship with the US. The Morales administration has established a new internal agenda, strongly driven by these two wars (especially the Gas War), and by the *cocaleros*' active rejection of US intervention through the War on Drugs and the eradication of coca crops since the early 1980s.

In terms of historical periodisation, the novelty is striking; before the radical cycle began in 2000, wars identified by the US alone drove bilateral relations. From the Bolivian perspective, the shift apparent since 2005 was the result not of any new doctrine in foreign relations devised by the Morales administration, but of a deeper historical process which resulted in the empowerment of domestic actors formerly excluded from both State management and foreign policy. This interpretation of US-Bolivian relations is what this essay identifies as the new phase experienced under Morales, of the 'Bolivianisation' of bilateral relations.

Simultaneously, foreign policy has been 'Bolivianised' in the way the Morales administration understands the US's new intervention in the country. This is not through the rationale of the War against Communism, War on Terror, or the War on Drugs but, rather, the Bolivianised perspective views US intervention as resulting from the internal dynamic of the country, specifically the conflict between the Eastern elites and the national government. In Bolivian official discourse, the US is included in a broad coalition led by the Eastern elites that are not saving Bolivia from Communism or terrorism, but from the MAS government agenda. The evidence of the alliance between the US State Department and the right-wing regional elites, as will be shown hereafter, is partially convincing, sometimes vague, and suggestive of conspiracy theory. But what is impressive is the capacity of the government to create a narrative that enjoys a broad social consensus in Bolivia, in which the US is seen as intervening at the heart of national politics.

The War against Communism, 1952–82

Throughout the three decades following the National Revolution headed by the *Movimiento Nacionalista Revolucionario* (MNR) in 1952, the War against Communism acted as the main framework for relations between Bolivia and the US. Neither democracy nor modernisation theory drove the American agenda, though both were used as effective discursive means in obstructing Soviet or Cuban influence. Affluent American aid was the most effective way to sustain the war against Communism; the recipients were the MNR and the Army.

After the Second World War, the US's main concern in regard to Bolivia was the MNR and its political projection. The State Department, in a confidential document circulated to other governments, characterised the party as anti-Semitic, hostile to democracy, with fascist-oriented programmes, connections with Nazi groups in Argentina and a recipient of Axis financial support during the Second World War.[5] A less demonising portrait of the MNR would define the Movement as reformist, nationalist and opposed to the oligarchy of the tin barons (all but one of them national), the owners of Bolivia's most important natural resource. And indeed, according to a 1950 American Embassy report titled 'Survey of Communism in Bolivia', the Army and the MNR were the major domestic forces limiting the 'chances for a full development of a Communist movement'.[6] By this point there were said to be no more than 150 fully indoctrinated Communists in Bolivia. After the April Revolution, the State Department asked the Embassy in La Paz to determine who was in charge, to measure the Communist influence, and to assess plans for nationalisation by finding out if the country would become another Iran (in reference to the oil nationalisation led by Mohammad Mosaddeq).[7]

---

5   Cole Blaiser, 'The United States and the Revolution', in James M. Malloy and Richard Thorn (eds.), *Beyond the Revolution: Bolivia since 1952* (Pittsburgh: University of Pittsburgh Press, 1971), pp. 60–1.

6   'Survey of Communism in Bolivia', 29 March 1950, NA 724.001-3-3050.

7   Kenneth Lehman, 'Braked but not Broken: The United States and Revolutionaries in Mexico and Bolivia', in Merilee S. Grindle and Pilar Domingo (eds.), *Proclaiming Revolution. Bolivia in Comparative Perspective* (Cambridge MA, and London: David Rockefeller Center for Latin American Studies and Institute of Latin American Studies, 2003), pp. 91–113. Mosaddeq was overthrown a year later in a coup in which the CIA was involved. That coup

The MNR programme, which included nationalisation of the mines, an agrarian reform and universal suffrage, was neither less nor more radical than those of Mossaddeq or Jacobo Arbenz, the Guatemalan President overthrown in 1954 in a coup with large US involvement. Why did the US not respond by sponsoring a coup in Bolivia, as it had in Guatemala? Among other reasons, Lavaud enumerates: the geographical distance (much greater than for Central America); the lack of significant American interests in the country; the nationalist ideology of the MNR; its electoral legitimacy (the Movement won the 1951 election); and the ability of its leaders to guarantee that tin exportation would continue and that tin companies would receive indemnisation.[8] In the event, far from backing a coup, the US provided economic assistance and political support to the MNR government, on the assumption that the State Department could re-direct and de-radicalise the Revolution. Indeed, Blaiser asserts that the Bolivian Revolution was the only 'genuine social revolution to which the United States provided early and sustained support'.[9] During the 1952–64 MNR administrations, the US gave more per capita assistance to Bolivia than to any other Latin American country. It also encouraged the 1956 stabilisation programme that started a half-century cycle of IMF influence in the design of Bolivian economic policies and began to fund and rebuild the Bolivian Army, weakened after the Chaco War (1932–5) and the 1952 Revolution.

From the MNR point of view, the explanation for the strategic alliance with the US was vital economic assistance to finance the State, and international support and backing for Bolivia's main foreign policy concern: access to the Pacific Ocean, lost in a war with Chile in 1879–84.[10] Such an alliance with the US would be helpful for the signing of long-term tin contracts and, in the long run, the newly nationalised tin mines would give the government greater independence.[11] In its 'initial radicalism' (1952–6), as defined by Whitehead,[12] the MNR, led by Paz Estenssoro, was able to satisfy internal diverse tendencies, including conservative nationalists, right-wing groups and the majority of the radical *Central Obrera Boliviana* (COB, the major trades union federation)

inaugurated the denationalisation of the oil industry in Iran. See Ervand Abrahamian, '1953 coup in Iran', *Science and Society* 65:2 (Summer 2001), p. 211.

8   Jean-Pierre Lavaud, *El embrollo boliviano. Turbulencias sociales y desplazamientos políticos (1952–1982)* (La Paz: IEA-CESU-HISBOL, 1988), p. 354.

9   Blaiser, 'The United States and the Revolution', in Malloy and Thorn (eds.), p. 53.

10 For the US's role, see Jorge Gumucio Granier, *Estados Unidos y el mar boliviano* (Bolivia: Plural, 2005), specifically chapter 12.

11 Blaiser, 'The United States and the Revolution', p. 107.

12 Laurence Whitehead, 'The Bolivian National Revolution: A Comparison', in Grindle and Domingo (eds.), *Proclaiming Revolution*, pp. 25–53, see pp. 27–9.

beyond the MNR alliance with Washington. The dilemma posed by *Le Monde* — 'The Bolivian Revolution between Wall Street and Trotsky' — did not work within the government coalition, but did reflect the conflict between the radical anti-capitalist and anti-yankee Pulacayo thesis and the course of the MNR government.[13] The achievement of the MNR, then, was to embrace US aid (not exactly Wall Street) while maintaining a nationalist rhetoric.

During his second and third terms as President (1960–4), Víctor Paz Estenssoro understood the Alliance for Progress as the best means for a long-term economic development plan, the main goal of his administration. Modernisation, as a new faith, could enjoy a broader social consensus and justify US aid. Paz Estenssoro needed a new social alliance for his national development project, which included sectors threatened by the 'initial radicalism' of the Revolution, such as medium-scale mine owners, the Pro Santa Cruz Committee, the Catholic Church and the conservative press.[14] Estenssoro demonstrated his skills as an astute negotiator in dealing with Washington. In December 1960, he used Khrushchev's offer to Bolivia of US$150 million in direct assistance to reinforce US commitment to Bolivia.[15] The Kennedy administration increased its aid to Bolivia by 600 per cent between 1960 and 1964.[16] In November 1963, Estenssoro made the first official visit of a Bolivian President to the White House. Kennedy, just days before his assassination, said that Bolivia was an example of what the Alliance for Progress could accomplish.[17] Michael Latham states that Bolivia in fact became a showcase for the Alliance for Progress. The ideological subtext of this Kennedy administration plan was the notion that a modernisation shock was all that was needed to halt Soviet and Cuban influence. By promoting the benefits of modernisation, the Alliance emphasised America's transformative power while legitimising the direct intervention of the US.[18]

In November 1964 Paz was overthrown in a coup led by his Vice-President, René Barrientos. This general embodied a new trend in the Bolivian Army: officers trained in the US and shaped in the war against Communism.[19]

---

13 Quoted in S. Sándor John, *Bolivia's Radical Tradition: Permanent Revolution in the Andes* (Tucson: University of Arizona Press, 2009), p. 193.

14 Whitehead, 'The Bolivian National Revolution', p. 38.

15 Kenneth Lehman, *Bolivia and the United States: A Limited Partnership* (Athens: University of Georgia Press, 1999) p. 134.

16 Lehman, *Bolivia and the United States*, p. 136.

17 Ibid. p. 137

18 Michael E. Latham, *Modernization as Ideology: American Social Science and "Nation Building" in the Kennedy era* (Chapel Hill: University of North Carolina Press, 2000).

19 René Zavaleta Mercado offers a thorough characterisation of Barrientos; see *50 años de historia de Bolivia* (La Paz : Los amigos del libro, 1998).

Washington did nothing to stop Barrientos' coup, and indeed (according to James Dunkerley) the CIA oversaw it.[20] The coup must be interpreted in the dim light of the militarisation of US foreign policy towards Latin America after the Cuban Revolution. Under Barrientos' presidency (1964–9), US aid came in the new form of loans as opposed to donations, which had been pre-eminent during the 1950s. North American military aid was maintained and, indeed, came to represent more than a third of the Bolivian military budget. One of the most salient episodes of US influence in this period was the capture and murder of Ernesto 'Che' Guevara on Bolivian soil. Several publications have offered proof of the involvement of the CIA in that particular counter-insurgency operation;[21] it was, however, exceptional for the American military to be physically present in the country.

Far from enjoying universal acceptance, American influence created resistance within the Army. A national-leftist branch took power in 1969, after Barrientos' death in a helicopter accident, and inaugurated the first serious challenge since the Revolution against US policy towards Bolivia. Coetaneous with the Peruvian nationalist experience of General Juan Velasco Alvarado (1968–75), this Bolivian process (1969–71) was led by two Nasserist generals, Alfredo Ovando and Juan José Torres. Nationalisations and decisions unfriendly to American interests followed in due course (such as that of the American Matilde Corporation), an agreement with Unions that replaced Congress by the *Asamblea Popular* (a Parliament led by the COB, where unionised miners were hegemonic). Torres closed an American military base called Guantanamito, expelled the Peace Corps (having accused them of encouraging the sterilisation of women in the country), signed commercial agreements with the Soviet Union, revealed his intentions of establishing diplomatic ties with Cuba and claimed that Bolivia should join the Non-Aligned Movement.

The Torres administration sealed a conflictive alliance with the *Asamblea Popular*, defined by Zavaleta Mercado as a soviet organization and the most advanced state experience of the working class in Latin America.[22] Some of the 'Anti-American' decisions made by Torres, such as the expulsion of the Peace Corps, were the result of an agenda established by the unions represented in the *Asamblea Popular*. The US responded first with an economic blockade that included the suspension of World Bank and Inter-American Development Bank loans, a decision that *The Washington Post* called the most open action ever by a treasury secretary to manipulate international aid with political

20   James Dunkerley, *Rebellion in the veins, Political Struggle in Bolivia, 1952–1982* (London: Verso, 1984), p. 115.

21   Carlos Soria published the hitherto best-researched interpretation of Guevara's Bolivian experience in the four volumes of *El Che en Bolivia* (La Paz: CEDOIN, 1996).

22   René Zavaleta Mercado, *El poder dual* (La Paz: Los amigos del libro, 1987), pp. 120, 139.

goals.[23] Second, the US formed part of a broader alliance, which also included Paz Estenssoro's branch of the MNR, the Santa Cruz elite, the vast majority of officers in the Army and the military dictatorships of Argentina and Brazil. All these actors contributed to the August 1971 coup that overthrew Torres' government. Declassified documents released by the US State Department in 2010 show how the Nixon administration gave nearly half a million dollars — 'coup money' to use the US Ambassador in La Paz's terminology — to support the plots of politicians and military officers against Torres.[24]

The new President, Colonel Hugo Banzer Suárez, was a former pupil of the School of the Americas. His commitment to the US is described in a confidential document prepared for the visit of Henry Kissinger to Santa Cruz in 1976: 'He knows and likes the US and he has gone out of his way on many occasions to demonstrate his adherence to US leadership in this hemisphere and in the world'.[25] The Banzer coup buried one of the most significant projects which aimed to establish in Bolivia a sustainable national-left administration hostile to the US. To some extent, then, the coup made a reality the 1950 US memo which claimed that the military and the MNR were crucial for stopping Communism. And subsequent American support for the Banzer regime was extraordinary. According to Dunkerley, from the coup until mid-1973 Bolivia became 'the most critical strategic redoubt' for US interests in the southern cone.[26] Between 1942 and 1970, Bolivia received US$6.7 million from the US for 'Administration and Government', but in the first 16 months of the Banzer administration, it received US$32 million under the same heading. Moreover, the military grants for 1973 and 1974 were three times 'as big as any previously made by the US to any Latin American country'.[27]

During Banzer's dictatorship (1971–8), narcotics became a new issue in bilateral relations. Nevertheless, this new concern remained secondary to the main priority, that of the War against Communism. Kissinger's visit to Bolivia in 1976 sought to seal the alliance with the *Banzerato* and to start a 'systematic' fight against narcotics. Documents relating to his visit, declassified by the US, suggest some suspicion surrounding Banzer's fight against drugs, but they praised his commitment to the War against Communism and his identification with US global leadership.[28]

23 James Dunkerley, *Rebellion in the veins*, p. 185.

24 Robert P. Baird, "Exclusive: the US paid money to support Hugo Banzer's 1971 coup in Bolivia", Digital Emunction (blog), 30 May 2010.

25 Martín Sivak, *El dictador elegido. Biografía no autorizada de Hugo Banzer Suárez* (La Paz: Plural, 2001), p. 359.

26 James Dunkerley, *Rebellion in the veins*, p. 205.

27 Ibid.

28 Martín Sivak, *El dictador elegido*, pp. 361–6.

When Jimmy Carter came into office in January 1977, the defence of Human Rights was the main stated goal in foreign policy for the new Democratic administration.[29] Concerned also about the legitimacy crisis that the US was experiencing because of American-backed dictatorial regimes, Carter called for a democratisation of the region. In the Bolivian case, some pressure was put on Banzer (although internal discontent was the main cause of his regime's disintegration in 1978). After Ronald Reagan's inauguration in 1981, the US administration ceased to mention human rights abuses in Bolivia, but did complain about narcotics. The peak of the conflict came during the regime of Luis García Meza (1980–1), with the striking case of a group of officials taking power in order to gain elbow-room for unabashed drugs trafficking.[30] Despite his strong anti-communist credentials, García Meza was not able to persuade the Reagan administration that he was the ultimate warrior in the War against Communism; the strong evidence of his relationship with drugs-trafficking interests made this barely feasible. Washington withdrew its Ambassador, suspended aid and asked for a return to civilian rule.[31] The key factor in the US repudiation of Meza was not democratisation, but the War on Drugs.

García Meza's fall marked a transition in the theatre of American narratives: exit the War against Communism, enter the War on Drugs. The War against Communism was the umbrella under which the US's significant aid to Bolivia operated, marking bilateral relations throughout the period 1952–82. Although MNR leaders like Paz Estenssorro did not adopt a Cold War discourse, as did Barrientos or Banzer, Bolivian governments during 1952–82 were unable to use US aid to establish more economic and political independence from Washington, as initially foreseen by the MNR. On the contrary, the Americanisation of this period lay in the capacity of the Cold War narrative to shape bilateral relations and to deepen Bolivian dependency upon the US.

The War on Drugs, 1980s–c. 2000 and neo-liberalism

The particularity of the period which began in the early 1980s and ran broadly until the turn of the century was the overlapping of a main US priority — the War on Drugs — with a Neoliberal agenda, backed by the US but also adopted by the mainstream Bolivian political parties (and legitimised by their voters). This overlap meant that US aid in the War on Drugs would be tied to Bolivian government collaboration in that war, which would also eventually help win

29 Odd Arne Westad, *The Global Cold War* (Cambridge: Cambridge University Press, 2005), p. 260.

30 See Gregorio Selser, *El cuartelazo de los coca dólares* (Mexico City: Editorial Mex Sur, 1982).

31 Raúl Barrios Morón, *Bolivia y Estados Unidos: Democracia, derechos humanos y narcotráfico (1980–1982)* (La Paz: FLACSO/HISBOL, 1989), p. 67.

US support (or not) in funding decisions for multilateral credits or loans given by the IMF and the World Bank: financial aid that was key for the Bolivian government to carry out the Neoliberal agenda. In short, these two funding mechanisms marked the bilateral relationship and deepened Americanisation and dependency.

Democratic Popular Unity (UDP), the left-wing alliance that ruled the country from 1982, collapsed when a serious economic crisis provoked hyperinflation of more than 10,350 per cent during 1984–5.[32] In a dramatic sequence of events, the three-times President, Victor Paz Estenssoro, appeared helmeted in the governmental palace on 29 August 1985 and made a speech in which he announced, 'Bolivia is dying on us' ('*Bolivia se nos muere*'). The lawyer and leader of the 1952 Revolution and the MNR became the doctor of the Republic, his diagnosis provoked by hyperinflation, street protests and a serious political crisis. The remedy, presented by Estenssoro as the only one likely to work, was Supreme Executive Order 21060. This decree reduced the fiscal deficit, froze salaries, liberalised markets, adjusted the State's reach and size and inaugurated the process of privatisation of State companies. Dunkerley has remarked that the 20th century thus ended in Bolivia not only with the collapse of mining and of the price of tin in international markets, but also with the conversion of the MNR from a nationalist party into a liberal one.[33]

An influential advisor behind Paz's dramatic speech was Harvard rising star and 'shock treatment' guru, Jeffrey Sachs. 'You have a miserable, poor economy with hyperinflation', Sachs told Paz Estenssoro. 'If you are brave, if you do everything right, you will end up with a miserable, poor economy with stable prices'.[34] In his book, *The End of Poverty*, Sachs confesses that before he was hired he did not know exactly where Bolivia was in South America.[35] But he was right in his modest forecast to Paz Estenssoro. Although Executive Order 21060 halted hyperinflation, the harsh social consequences included an unemployment rate of 25 per cent. As Pilar Domingo states, there is general consensus that the Order did not reduce poverty and income inequalities in any structural way. Rather, it led to a deterioration of labour conditions and to a re-concentration of land holdings.[36] In a paper describing his intervention

32 Juan Cariaga, *Estabilización y Desarrollo. Importantes Lecciones del Programa Económico de Bolivia* (La Paz: Los Amigos del Libro, 1996), p. 238.

33 James Dunkerley, 'The Origins of the Bolivian Revolution in the Twentieth Century: Some Reflections', in Merilee and Domingo (eds.), *Proclaiming Revolution*, pp. 135–63, see p. 141.

34 Lehman, *Bolivia and the United States*, p. 197.

35 Jeffrey D. Sachs, *The End of Poverty. Economic Possibilities of Our Time* (Harmondsworth: Penguin, 2005), p. 92.

36 Pilar Domingo, 'Democracy and New Social Forces in Bolivia', *Social Forces* 83:4 (June 2005), pp. 1,727–45.

in the Bolivian crisis as adviser to the MNR, Sachs underlines that the first reason for Bolivian hyperinflation was the cutting-off of international loans. He consequently designed a stabilisation plan which deepened the Bolivian economy's dependence on the IMF, World Bank and US government.[37] And in exchange for financial aid, La Paz was obliged both to accomplish the US's anti-drugs goals and to adjust to its economic model.

The resulting New Economic Policy (NEP) was, according to the US and the Bolivian government, quite apt for the 'modernisation' the country required. If the former modernisation of the Alliance for Progress sought development through industrialisation and infrastructure, the new era required a small State that allowed for markets to rule the economy. This new State should be strong enough, nevertheless, to fight drug lords and to guarantee the new economic and political model. The new agenda of the War on Drugs came at a moment when the MNR was reducing the national State due to neo-liberal reforms and when it could no longer invoke the Soviet and Cuban threat to bargain better agreements with the US (as Paz Estenssoro had done in the times of Khrushchev and Kennedy). The pragmatism of the MNR and the need for American support meant that the coexistence of decree 21060 with the War on Drugs raised much less resistance among what was left of the party of the 1952 Revolution. A 'pacted democracy' was established, and worked for almost 20 years. This pact between three mainstream political parties — Banzer's Nationalist Democratic Action (ADN), the Revolutionary Left Movement (MIR), and the MNR — upheld Executive Order 21060 and strengthened the relationship with the US. In the short term, the economy was de-nationalised through capitalisations (the Bolivian model for privatisation, whereby the state kept 51 per cent of the state companies but private firms retained decision-making control), the IMF and the World Bank increased their influence and the country experienced a de-Bolivianisation (and a contrasting Americanisation) of its security and defence policies.

After Reagan identified drug trafficking as a threat to US national security, the War on Drugs thus became the new priority in bilateral relationships. Reagan's rhetoric, reiterated during the Presidency of George Bush Senior, was directed at Republican voters — typically concerned about higher crime rates[38] — and opened up the possibility of displacing the war to the overseas front, for instance, to Bolivia, where drugs were produced. This internal and external dimension to the War on Drugs permitted increased budgets, troop mobilisations and intervention in foreign countries. Reagan's discourse had direct

---

37 Jeffrey Sachs, 'The Bolivian Hyperinflation and Stabilization', *American Economic Review* 77:2 (1987) pp. 279–83.

38 William N. Elwood, *Rhetoric in the War on Drugs. The Triumphs and Tragedies of Public Relations* (Westport CO: Praeger, 1994), p. 11.

repercussions for Bolivia's War on Drugs. In June 1986, Congress convinced Reagan to suspend US$7.2 million of aid to the country. Paz Estenssoro then agreed to an exceptional US-Bolivian military exercise called Operation Blast Furnace. More than 160 US and Bolivian military troops acted jointly during ten days using six US Black Hawk helicopters. The American Embassy stated that the ultimate goal of Operation Blast Furnace was to lower the market price of the coca leaf. By destroying cocaine laboratories, they hoped to reduce the demand for raw coca. According to Malamud Goti, however, Operation Blast Furnace was a failure because no major dealer was arrested and larger laboratories were found already dismantled.[39] But the Operation nevertheless had broader implications. It expressed the MNR's fear of further sanctions that, in Lehman's words, 'could foreclose bilateral assistance, endanger crucial credits from multilateral lending agencies, end IMF assistance to keep the country's economy stable, and again stamp Bolivia as a renegade nation'.[40] As stated, the dynamic of the relationship — not always amicable — tied the continuation of US aid to the achievement of the goals of the War on Drugs.

This context notwithstanding, the growing demand for cocaine in Europe and the US (where North Americans snorted US$28 billion a year by the late 1980s), coupled with the economic crisis in Bolivia, triggered a boom in coca production in the country. According to the State Department, the area devoted to coca cultivation increased from 35,000 hectares in 1980, to 55,400 in 1989. The US made no distinction between cocaine and the coca leaf, despite the deeply-rooted tradition of cultivation and consumption of coca among the Bolivian indigenous and popular sectors. American misconceptions regarding the coca leaf were not new, of course. At the beginning of the 20th century, a US Ambassador imagined that coca was the source of Bolivia's problems and, by way of remedy, proposed 'plain American chewing gum for everyone', donated by US gum companies and distributed by the Embassy.[41] By the late 1980s, with the gum solution discarded, George Bush launched his 'Andean initiative', which gave Bolivia US$830 million of the US$2.2 billon aid distributed to the region. Bolivia was at this time, as Gamarra states, a laboratory for the US anti-drugs war. Included as it was within the Democratic Alliance for Progress, the country became a showcase in this war. Bush justified the presence of American troops on Bolivian soil in explicit terms: 'The logic is simple. The fastest and cheapest way to eradicate narcotics is at its source. We need to finish off the plantations where they grow and eliminate the laboratories'.[42]

39 Jaime Malamud Goti, *Smoke and Mirrors: The Paradox of the Drug Wars* (Boulder CO: Westview Press, 1992), p. 30.

40 Lehman, *Bolivia and the United States*, p. 200.

41 Ibid., p. 191.

42 Cited in Alex Contreras, *La marcha histórica* (Cochabamba: CEDIB, 1994), p. 46.

The militarisation of the War on Drugs was thus a consequence of US assistance. According to Waltraud Queiser Morales, between 50 and 70 per cent of almost US$100 million earmarked for 1990 was potentially designated for military assistance and 'militarised' police-related activities, and only between 30 and 50 per cent for actual economic and alternative development.[43] This militarisation brought with it an increase in human rights abuses.[44] In addition, with the US's powerful capacity to influence political parties in Bolivia, the government approved a new Law: Law 1008 criminalised coca production outside restricted areas and beyond limited yields and established the basis for forced eradication.[45] Hence, the MNR and its allies took a significant step towards the legalisation of the War on Drugs as designed by the US. Indeed, one of the main legacies of the fourth and last Paz Estenssoro administration was the implementation of a long-term relationship with the US, where the war on drugs was confessedly central.[46]

The US Embassy strengthened its position as a key institution in Bolivian democracy. It was referred to simply as 'the Embassy' and, by 1989, was the second largest in Latin America. Ambassador Robert Gelbard, who presented his credentials in 1988, made his considerable influence with the Bolivian government visible with a high profile in the press. In public statements, Gelbard offered opinions on Bolivian political parties, advised the government about state policies, accused Bolivian public servants (both current and retired) of involvement in the drugs trade and, with joking unselfconsciousness, claimed that the Bolivian Ambassador in Washington was intervening in the internal affairs of the US. In his visits to Washington, Gelbard requested that the Bolivian police group in charge of the drugs fight (the *Unidad Móvil de Patrullaje Rural*, or UMOPAR) and the Drugs Enforcement Agency (DEA) be replaced with American troops.[47] Publicly he called for a militarisation of the drugs war as waged in the country.

As part of a new policy to increase its internal power, the Embassy decided to reject visa requests to visit the US made by different Bolivian congressmen, senators and trade union leaders. The politicians denied visas in this way suffered public stigmatisation and their political careers were put in jeopardy.

43 Waltraud Queiser Morales, 'Militarising the Drug War in Bolivia', *Third World Quarterly* 12:2 (1992), p. 362.

44 As Dunkerley pointed out, approximately 70 *cocaleros* were killed after the recovery of democracy, *Bolivia: Revolution and the Power of History in the Present*, p. 30.

45 Forrest Hylton and Sinclair Thomson, *Revolutionary Horizons. Past and Present in Bolivian Politics* (New York: Verso, 2007) p. 97.

46 Eduardo Gamarra, *Entre la coca y la democracia: La cooperación entre Estados Unidos y Bolivia en la lucha contra el narcotráfico* (La Paz: Ildis, 1993) p. 69.

47 Ibid., p. 84.

Visa denial thus became a new frontier in the political turf war. The 1989–93 MIR government, under the presidency of Jaime Paz Zamora, failed in its weak attempt to *de-cocainise* the bilateral relationship with the US; and, after leaving office, many members of this political party were put on trial accused of links with narcotics. Also used to put pressure on the weakened Bolivian State was the annual 'certification' process. The US government gave certification to those countries that were 'fully committed to the War on Drugs' and, according to Bolivian press reports, the La Paz government made huge efforts to obtain this certification.

The main reaction to the growing influence of the US erupted in the territory where the American presence was both most visible and least desired: the Chapare. In this region, resistance to the eradication of coca favoured the rise of a strong *cocalero* movement drawing on a centuries-old relationship with the coca leaf (which is also the most profitable crop)[48] and profound anti-American feeling. The dynamic of demand-production-eradication-repression-resistance was a constant throughout this period. The Chapare began to be thought of in terms of a setting which synthesised but also catalysed the tensions of the larger society. The valleys were, once again in Bolivian history, the epitome and battlefield of Andean peoples' struggles.

In 1994, the *cocaleros* reached La Paz following a 23-day walk from the Chapare.[49] Debunking the Bolivian government's claim that they were a phantom movement, or at most only small groups, the march greatly increased the visibility of the *cocalero* movement among Bolivians and projected on a national scale a demand until then restricted to the Chapare and Yungas regions. During the walk, the political rhetoric of their songs and slogans and the speech of one of their leaders — a young Evo Morales — were openly confrontational. On some city walls, *cocaleros* graffitied the slogan '*Gringos, erradiquen sus narices*' ('Yankees, eradicate your noses'), demonstrating their desire to target the US government and draw a line under the war on drugs unleashed in their country.

The War on Drugs and the Neoliberal agenda, then, dominated Washington-La Paz relations to the turn of the century. This credo provoked considerable consensus among a significant part of the population that supported, or at least voted for, the parties of the 'pacted democracy'. But discontent and anti-US sentiment was stronger in the countryside, specifically the Chapare and Yungas, showing a shift in the main anti-American sector. The miners and the COB, much weaker after Executive Order 21060, were displaced by the *cocaleros*, who would now play a key role in the redefinition of US-Bolivian relations.

48 Alison Spedding describes the economic profitability of coca in *Kawsachun coca: Economía campesina cocalera en los Yungas y el Chapare* (La Paz: PIEB, 2005).

49 See Contreras, *La marcha histórica*.

The War on Terror from 2001

The War on Terror did not strictly replace the War on Drugs, in the sense that Bolivia received neither more nor less US assistance according to its accomplishments in this latest war. The former appears to be an erratic attempt to reproduce within the region a universal war that was not, however, internalised by any South American government. The exception is Colombia, which through Plan Colombia receives more US assistance than any other Latin American country. To an extent, the label of narco-terrorism the US applied to the Colombian FARC (*Fuerzas Armadas Revolucionarias de Colombia*) would similarly be employed with the *cocaleros*, and particularly Evo Morales, in Bolivia.

The War on Terror was launched in Bolivia when the 'pacted democracy', along with the political consensus around Order 21060, experienced a crisis of legitimacy. A turning point was the 'Water War' in Cochabamba in 2000, when a broad coalition of factory workers, students, *cocaleros*, green activists, and unaffiliated *cochabambinos* protested against an increase in water rates by the Aguas del Tunari company, a subsidiary of the US-based multinational Bechtel. First, the *Coordinadora del Agua* coalition put a stop to the increase in prices and then, in April 2000, achieved the expulsion of Aguas del Tunari. It was replaced by a collective called SEMAPA, which stands for self-managed enterprise.[50] In the following months, blockades in the Highlands, led by the radical Aymara Felipe Quispe, and the mobilisation of *cocalero* unions fortified the anti-neo-liberal agenda and weakened the government of former dictator Hugo Banzer.

The 2002 election marked the immediate decline of 'pacted democracy', the discredit of the neo-liberal model and the weakening of the alliance with the US, whose Embassy indulged in a series of manoeuvres designed to manipulate the results of the elections and to strengthen the American favourite, Gonzalo Sánchez de Lozada of the MNR. The US Ambassador Manuel Rocha's comparison of the *cocaleros* with the Taliban at the beginning of the campaign showed how he misread Bolivian politics by thinking that the War on Terror could play a role within the electoral campaign. Four days before the general election, Rocha encouraged voters not to choose Morales. In the Chapare, he declared, 'I want to remind Bolivians that if they choose the person that wants Bolivia to become a cocaine exporter, the results will jeopardise American aid to Bolivia'.[51] But Rocha's speech only served to boost Morales in the polls.

---

50 Hylton and Thomson, *Revolutionary Horizons*, p. 104. See A. García Linera, R. Gutiérrez, R. Prada and L. Tapia, *El retorno de la Bolivia Plebeya* (La Paz: La muela del diablo, 2000).

51 'El embajador Rocha pide a los electores que no voten por Evo', *La Prensa* (Bolivia), 27 June 2002.

According to two post-electoral surveys, the two main candidates lost around 3.5 per cent of the vote due to the speech, while 14 per cent of those who voted for Morales did so in a reaction against Rocha's words.[52] Morales commented ironically that Rocha was his campaign chief and that he would like to pay the Ambassador for his services, but that the MAS had no money. The MAS released an effective campaign advertisement: 'Fellow Bolivian, you decide who's in charge: Rocha or the voice of the people. We are the people. We are MAS [also a play on the Spanish *más*, i.e., 'we are more']. Let's vote for ourselves on June 30'.[53]

Carlos Mesa, Sánchez de Lozada's candidate for Vice-President, explained that Ambassador Rocha acted as a member of 'our campaign team as he gave suggestions, set strategies, and coined some of the master-slogans of the campaign'. According to Mesa, Rocha was very much concerned from the beginning about the growth of support for Morales, while other presidential candidates were not. Mesa admitted that he knew Rocha's speech was discussed and agreed upon by the heads of Sánchez de Lozada's campaign. Their strategy, according to Mesa, was that Rocha's speech would give more votes to Morales and that ultimately he would defeat Manfred Reyes Villa of *Nueva Fuerza Republicana*, who was first or second in the polls. Therefore, according to their calculations, Sánchez de Lozada's victory would be all but guaranteed, due to their assumption that all political parties in Congress would vote against Morales. In short, the strategy was to avoid a run-off between Sánchez de Lozada and Manfred Reyes Villa, where the Embassy's favourite candidate would most definitely lose.[54] In the event, Sánchez de Lozada obtained 22.5 per cent of the vote, followed by Morales, who won almost 21 per cent and just 720 more votes than Reyes Villa. Thus, when the Congress had to make a choice between the two candidates with the most votes, Morales ended up competing against Sánchez de Lozada.

The US Embassy then strongly encouraged all the traditional political parties to sign a broad agreement against Morales, according to three top politicians involved in the negotiations.[55] The Embassy was convinced that, by encouraging the democratisation of these political parties, it would be possible to counter-balance Morales and the MAS in the coming years. Documents

52 Fernando Molina, *Bajo el signo del cambio. Análisis de tres procesos electorales (2002, 2005 and 2006)* (La Paz: Eureka, 2006), p. 23.

53 Pablo Stefanoni and Hervé do Alto, *Evo Morales, de la coca al palacio. Una oportunidad para la izquierda indígena* (La Paz, Malatesta, 2006), p. 78.

54 Interview with Carlos Mesa (ex-President of Bolivia), La Paz, December 2006.

55 Interviews with Carlos Mesa (La Paz, December 2006), Oscar Eid, top campaign strategist to Paz Zamora (La Paz, May 2007), Ricardo Paz, top campaign strategist to Reyes Villa (La Paz, December 2006).

declassified by the US government include remarkable references to Morales after the 2002 election. He is referred to as the 'illegal coca agitator': 'illegal' because the US claimed that most of the coca harvests were destined for the narcotics trade, and 'agitator' because the US sought to stigmatise Morales' role as union leader and to emphasise his active role in the blockade of roads and streets.[56] These depictions situate Morales at the margins of acceptable political behavior and, moreover, the rule of law. The documents reflect Washington's aim to halt Morales' political rise:

> A planned USAID [United States Agency for International Development] political party reform project aims at implementing an existing Bolivian law that would make internal party procedures more democratic and transparent. The project should dovetail with the MNR's inclusiveness plank and, over the long run, help build moderate, pro-democracy political parties that can serve as a counter-weight to the radical MAS or its successor … Our long term goal is for citizens not to channel their political message through street protest.[57]

The Embassy's strategy failed in the medium run. First, Evo Morales became the main leader of the opposition, combining street protest with a robust parliamentary brigade. Second, Sánchez de Lozada resigned in October 2003 after a wave of protests against the sale of gas to the US via Chile, which ended in 67 deaths and hundreds of wounded. In his first speech following his resignation, in Washington DC, Sánchez de Lozada spoke about Bolivian politics in the language of the War on Terror, saying that Bolivian radicals would likely take power 'by no democratic means and they will transform the country in a sort of Afghanistan that exports cocaine'.[58] In Bolivia, Sánchez de Lozada's resignation invigorated the October agenda (for nationalisation of hydrocarbons and a Constituent Assembly), which signalled the peak of a radical cycle marked by both national-popular and ethnic demands. Thirdly, all the proposed USAID 'counter-balancing' measures, and the strengthening of democratic political parties, failed in the 2005 general election. The three political parties that had defeated Morales in the 2002 Congressional vote received a total of just 7 per cent of the popular vote in 2005. Furthermore, Morales won the election with 53.7 per cent — at that time the largest victory since the return to democracy in 1982 — installing the least US-friendly government in Bolivian history. On 18 December, Election Day, he ended

---

56　Ministerio de Relaciones Exteriores de Bolivia-Centro de Documentación. Documentos desclasificados del Departamento de Estado. Document Number: 2002LAPAZ02723.

57　Ibid.

58　Cited in Martín Sivak, *Evo Morales. The extraordinary rise of the first indigenous president of Bolivia* (New York: Palgrave, 2010), p. 103.

his first speech as elected President by shouting '*Causachun coca, wañuchun yanquis*' ('Long live coca, death to the Yankees').[59] The formula had been coined by the *cocaleros*' union. It is rooted in a rejection of US intervention in the eradication of the coca leaf over the past 20 years.

The War on Terror reflects US misunderstanding of the radical cycle that commenced in 2000. The US obsession with Evo Morales, as reflected in the documents cited and in Rocha's public speeches, illustrates the belief that by stopping his career or political projection, using the narco-terrorist frame or strengthening the traditional and dying parties, social unrest would be contained. Interestingly enough, Morales was not the leader of the Water and Gas wars, despite his participation, and he did not initiate or own the national sovereignty discourse — though he did make it central to his successful 2005 presidential campaign.

Building a Bolivian narrative

Evo Morales and the Bolivianisation of La Paz-Washington Relations

'In the world there are large and small countries, rich countries and poor countries, but we are equal in one thing, which is our right to dignity and sovereignty'. Thus spoke Morales in his inaugural speech as President on 22 January 2006.[60] The idea expressed here, which reflects the spirit of the radical cycle vis-à-vis the US and the transnational companies, summarised the Morales administration's foreign policy-making in regard to the US. With some concessions (if compared to the radical voices of October 2003), Morales inaugurated a new era in relations with the US that represented a re-reading of the radical cycle and of his own experience as leader of the *cocaleros* in rejecting the War on Drugs on the US's terms. The outcome has been the Bolivianisation of La Paz-Washington relations.

The US was a rather passive actor in the earliest stage of Morales' presidency. In contrast to its role in the 2002 campaign, the US Embassy decided to avoid any public comment during the 2005 election. During informal conversations with top MAS candidates, US officials repeatedly asked whether Bolivia would become a satellite of Venezuela if Morales won the election.[61] But following his inauguration, President Bush called his Bolivian peer to congratulate him on his electoral victory. The US then made a number of recommendations to the

59 Pablo Stefanoni, Eduardo Febbro, 'Como arrasar sin dar más vueltas', Página 12 (Argentina), 19 Dec. 2005.

60 Evo Morales, *La revolución democrática y cultural. Diez discursos de Evo* (La Paz: Malatesta, Movimiento al Socialismo, 2006), p. 41.

61 Interview with Walter Chávez (Evo Morales' former senior advisor and chief of campaign), La Paz, Dec. 2006.

new government. Among the first was to encourage an FTAA agreement: 'It's the best way to have a good relationship with the US', an American official told Pablo Solón, one of Morales' top foreign policy advisers.[62] The new Bolivian government, however, refused to join the FTAA. The other suggestion, made directly to Morales by the American Ambassador David Greenlee, related to the appointment of Bolivian officials. In a meeting, he mentioned his disapproval of the proposed appointments of Juan Ramón Quintana and Alex Contreras due to their alleged 'anti-US' backgrounds.[63] In Contreras' case, the reason given was his close relationship with the *cocaleros'* unions while he was a journalist based in Cochabamba. In regard to Quintana, he played a vital role in the 2005 electoral campaign, gathering information and denouncing a US undercover mission on Bolivian soil to seize and deactivate 25 Chinese-fabricated missiles belonging to the Bolivian Army, similar to the ones used by the Iraqi resistance and the Taliban. By showing dissatisfaction with Contreras and Quintana, the Ambassador was reproducing a practice common to the era of consensus based around Executive Order 21060: US proposal or disapproval of appointments of certain public servants. But again, Morales promptly gave Quintana and Contreras key positions — minister of the presidency and presidential spokesman respectively. In this way, he emphasised that the Bolivian government would not follow unprompted American tips in building up the new administration. In the same vein, the President designated as anti-drugs czar the *cocalero* unionist Felipe Cáceres, who took over coordination of the supervision of coca production by the peasant unions. Just weeks later, the US revealed that it would cut back military support for that year by 96 per cent (from $1,700,000 to $70,000) in response to the Bolivian Congress's refusal to grant immunity to US soldiers arriving in the country.

During the first semester of 2006, the government debated what tone to adopt towards the US. More prone to confrontation, Morales cited two events to justify his preferred approach. First, in March 2006, an incident occurred in which a US citizen set off a bomb, killing two people and sparking a sharp presidential response: 'Is the US government in a fight against terrorism or are they sending North Americans here to create terrorism in Bolivia?'.[64] The Embassy had known about this citizen's entry and had failed to notify Morales, although it did apologise afterwards. The government also denounced a group of Marines that entered Bolivia in the guise of students to perform covert operations.[65] The President tried his best to contain himself when dealing

62 Interview with Pablo Solón, La Paz, Dec. 2006.

63 Interviews with Evo Morales, Juan Ramón Quintana (Presidency Minister), and Alex
     Contreras (spokesman) in June 2006, Nov. 2006 and April 2007.

64 Pablo Stefanoni, 'Falsa alarma con dos muertos', *Página 12* (Argentina), 23 March 2006.

65 Pablo Stefanoni, 'Estudiantes disfrazados de marines', *Pagina 12* (Argentina), 22 June 2006.

with the US because Bolivia was trying to get an extension of the ATPDEA. Assuming the role of liaison with the Embassy, Vice-President Alvaro García Linera did not encourage confrontation with the US, during internal debates, partly for practical reasons involving trade negotiations, but partly from the theoretical rationale of not believing in 'imperialism' as an explanatory category (despite saying that Lenin was one of the authors he re-read during the first term in office). In his view, the interference, manipulation and subordination to which other countries subject Bolivia is due rather (or at least in part) to local intermediaries who should be removed.[66]

Hoping to reach a rapprochement of sorts, García Linera organised a trip to the US with the salient objective of obtaining the expansion of the ATPDEA and of once again refusing a commercial relationship with the US based on the FTAA. In his meetings with State Department top officials, García Linera was systematically asked about the relationship between his government and Cuba and Venezuela. Nicholas Burns — Under Secretary of State for Political Affairs, the Department of State's third ranking official — told him in a private meeting, 'None of Mr Bush's comments regarding Bolivia can be compared with Mr Morales' "*Causachun coca, wañuchun yanquis!*"'.[67] This, then, marked the formalisation of US concerns regarding the President's 'rhetoric'. The latter word was the one used most frequently by State Department officials in La Paz and Washington to summarise Morales' references to 'empire', 'imperialism' and the US. Testifying to the influence exercised by presidential discourse, foreign policy and Bolivia's relationship with the US became highly galvanised by Morales' 'rhetoric'.

In these early days, the second main US concern was Morales' alliance with Venezuela and Cuba. These new priorities show how certain US preoccupations in the region, like the nationalisation of foreign firms, statisation of companies, or the so-called populisms, were displaced, at least as figures of speech, by concerns about 'rhetoric' and international allies. In reality, in the first stage of the MAS government, Cuba contributed with eye surgery and literacy programmes and grants for Bolivians to study on the island. Venezuela announced that it would invest $1.5 billon in the hydrocarbon sector, buy Bolivian bonds and offer loans to industrialise the coca-leaf. In addition, Caracas lent Morales helicopters for his domestic trips and planes for his international tours. Venezuela and Cuba also gave advice to the Bolivian government on security and intelligence topics. In regional terms, Bolivia joined the *Alternativa Bolivariana para América Latina y el Caribe* (ALBA), of which Venezuela and Cuba were already members. ALBA is a regional association that challenges equivalent organisations like the FTAA, backed by Washington. In general,

66   Interview with Alvaro García Linera, La Paz, Dec. 2006.

67   Interview with one of the members of the Bolivian delegation, La Paz, April 2007.

this alliance was read as evidence that Morales was dominated by Castro and Chávez. The right-wing opposition party Podemos used *'Digale no a Chávez'* ('Say no to Chávez') as a slogan in the June 2006 electoral campaign for the Constituent Assembly.

This interpretation of Morales' alliance probably underestimated him, while overemphasising any power that Chávez wielded over the country. In contrast with Chávez' anti-US discourse, that of Morales is rooted in the strong *cocalero* tradition of rejecting US intervention in Bolivian domestic affairs. Chávez, for his part, radicalised his antagonism with the US after the Venezuelan coup of 2002. In addition, his anti-US discourse was launched from the State and the government and has not had a social and territorial grounding, as with the Bolivian case. In Bolivia, moreover, anti-US sentiment is not restricted to the *cocaleros*. Rather, in the western part of the country, the nationalist vein coupled with the rejection of US intervention and anti-imperialist sentiment have a long tradition. Nevertheless, Chávez and Morales constitute part of a diverse and heterogeneous turn to the left in South American politics at the beginning of the 21st century, of which a critical stance towards the US is one of the main features. The larger processes of social unrest have worked upon these post-neo-liberal projects along with the radicalisation of demands from formerly marginal groups aiming to establish new agendas. In the Bolivian case, a new agenda, constructed outside State institutions, as shown in the Water and Gas Wars, eventually won large electoral support. The October agenda became State policy under Morales' government.

In the economic field, the Morales administration initially rejected IMF and World Bank aid and loans. While preparing the government's Economic Plan, the Planification minister Carlos Villegas informed the IMF and the World Bank that the new plan would be elaborated by the Treasury Minister and the Central Bank without consulting them. During the first year of Morales' administration, the World Bank halved Bolivia's annual budget to $35 million and the IMF stopped lending money to the country.[68] Yet during his first presidency, albeit by alternative means, Morales' administration accomplished goals in accord with IMF and World Bank indications for the region — namely a fiscal surplus, low deficit, and low inflation.

With regard to coca, Morales encouraged *cocaleros* to enforce 'social control' of coca cultivation, marking a rupture with the policies of the War on Drugs. He emphasised the importance of keeping to one *cato* (1,600 metres square) per family and not provoking a cultivation boom, because this would decrease the product's value. In addition, this 'social control' would reduce external pressure for eradication. The new policy illustrates the role of non-state actors in the redefinition of bilateral relations. The *cocaleros*, given their condition as

68   Interview with Carlos Villegas (Planification Minister), La Paz, June 2006.

targets in the drug war, had already developed an agenda in the 1990s linking the defence of valuable natural resources (coca) to the question of national sovereignty vis-à-vis foreign intervention.

The new state policy empowered the *cocaleros* while reducing the eradication policies, but it did not end all coordinated work between La Paz and Washington.[69] According to the Washington Office on Latin America (WOLA), US-Bolivian cooperation on coca reduction and drug interdiction has continued and Bolivia has actively pursued counter-drugs coordination with its neighbours and the international community.[70] At the same time, the government persisted in its aim of obtaining the 'certification' the US granted to countries that accomplished goals in the war on drugs. In other words, compliance with the external mechanism to punish or reward Bolivian performance was still in working order during Morales' presidency.

On 31 December 2006, Morales signed a Supreme Decree that requested a compulsory visa for American citizens wishing to enter Bolivia. This Supreme Decree, framed in the so-called diplomacy of reciprocity based on Aymara communal practices, symbolised the turning point in US-Bolivian relations. Although the number of Americans who visit Bolivia is not significant, the Decree reflects La Paz's attempt to establish the notion of reciprocity with the US. During the first two years of Morales' administration, at least five members of the MAS government have had visa problems, including the substitute senator Leonilda Zurita. And Morales himself was not allowed to enter the US because, according to a *60 Minutes* survey, he was included on a list of terrorists.[71] The first American visa issued to him was on the occasion of the United Nations' annual inauguration meeting in New York in September 2006.[72]

From an early date, the extradition from the US of former President Sánchez de Lozada was a top priority for Morales' administration. The Bolivian Courts accused de Lozada of 'genocide' because of his alleged responsibility for the deaths of 67 Bolivian citizens during the 'Gas War' of 2003. This uprising was to shape Morales' administration's approach to the nationalisation of gas and oil. It also reinforced the political necessity of securing justice for

69 Interview with Alfredo Rada (government minister), La Paz, May 2007.

70 Kathryn Ledebur and John Walsh, 'Change for the Better: The Chance to Recast U.S-Bolivian Relations', Washington Office on Latin America/Andean Information Network, 23 Jan. 2009, and Kathryn Ledebur and John Walsh, 'Obama's Bolivia ATPDEA Decision: Blast from the Past or Wave of the Future?', Washington Office on Latin America/Andean Information Network, 11 Aug. 2009. Both pieces are available at www.wola.org

71 Daniel Schorn, 'Unlikely terrorists on No Fly list', CBS news, 10 June 2007.

72 As the visa was only valid for a couple of weeks, President Morales said 'they thought that I would stay in office for a short time'; interview with Evo Morales, New York, Sept. 2007.

the killings by promoting a trial of the former President and members of his cabinet. The extradition request eventually affected relations with the US. After escaping from Bolivia, Sánchez de Lozada flew to Miami and made a home in Washington DC. When Morales chose Sacha Llorenti as his first ambassador to the US, he was instructed to bring back Sánchez de Lozada as a main diplomatic priority. Llorenti having declined the position for personal reasons, the journalist and editor Gustavo Guzmán was appointed. Apart from Sánchez de Lozada's extradition, his new goals included issues such as coca and bilateral trade.[73] In numerous speeches, Morales claimed that by delaying an answer on the Sánchez de Lozada case, the US was protecting a person responsible for a massacre. Morales was thus framing US actions within Bolivian politics: by contrast, Washington was defending and protecting a former ally. This case, then, can be read as an early instance of the Bolivianisation of bilateral relations. It also stresses the notion of reciprocity: for years, the US requested (and obtained) the extradition of Bolivian citizens accused of drugs trafficking; now, La Paz was claiming the same right. Interestingly enough, the last extradition agreement between Bolivia and the US was signed in 1995, during Sánchez de Lozada's first term and in the context of the 'War on Drugs'. As of June 2010, the US government still had not answered the extradition request formally presented by Bolivia.

The United States and Bolivia's 'Fertile Crescent'

After 2005, the radicalisation of the conflict between Morales' government and the *Media Luna* — the 'fertile crescent', the rich departments of the Eastern lowlands, whose main demand on the national stage was for autonomy from the central government — deepened the tensions between La Paz and Washington. Indeed, in the view of Morales' administration, this regional conflict, with the traditional Bolivian party system exhausted, turned out to be the vehicle for new US intervention in the country and for effective opposition to the policies of La Paz. For the first time, then, it was an internal and deeply-rooted conflict in Bolivia that gave leverage to US actions, further 'Bolivianising' bilateral relations.

By June 2007, Morales had re-launched his verbal confrontation with the US, in the context of governmental difficulties in the Constitutional Assembly and arguments with the province of Santa Cruz and the *Media Luna*. La Paz stated that the American Embassy was funding the opposition. To back these charges, the government presented as evidence two documents declassified by the State Department. One, dated February 2007, claimed that the US's main concern was the 'erosion' of democracy:

> The United States' primary challenge in Bolivia is to support democracy
> actively in a country with a history of political unrest. To help meet

73   Interview with Gustavo Guzmán, La Paz, May 2007.

these challenges, partnerships will be developed with regional and local governments and non-governmental organizations (NGOs), the private sector, and other non-executive branch entities to prevent further erosion of democracy...[74]

According to a second US document, USAID would play a key role in this task: 'USAID is focusing assistance to Bolivia on programs that strengthen vibrant and effective democracies, including the support of counterweights to one-party control...'.[75] 'One-party control', of course, referred to MAS, seeking to portray it as an authoritarian organisation, while failing to mention that the weakness of the political opposition was provoked by the collapse of traditional political parties in the 2005 presidential election. The new political parties were as yet unable to consolidate themselves as serious national options.

In September, the government announced that Bolivia would initiate diplomatic ties with Iran, a country accused by the Bush administration of being the 'best ally of Terrorism'. It also formally asked the US to give a detailed description of American aid to Bolivia. Furthermore, in a speech at the United Nations, Morales proposed moving the UN headquarters to a country where no visa was required. He claimed that he and his ministers, parliamentarians and 'indigenous brothers' suffered mistreatment every time they entered the US. A day after the speech, Iran's head of state Mahmoud Ahmadinejad arrived in La Paz for the signing of an economic agreement with the Bolivian government and Morales publicly addressed him as *compañero revolucionario*. The US Ambassador Philip Goldberg's reaction was the harshest from the American Embassy since Morales' inauguration. He stated facetiously that he would not be surprised if Morales' next request was for the transfer elsewhere of Disney World. Morales responded by barring Goldberg from the Palacio Quemado (the Bolivian Palace of Government). On 12 October 2007, in a rally with indigenous groups, Morales ended a speech in Chimoré (in the Chapare) with the shout, '*Causachun coca, wañuchun yanquis!*'.[76] It was the first time that Morales had uttered the slogan publicly since his arrival in the Palacio Quemado.

In early 2008, the deterioration in Bolivian-US relations continued, as the internal conflict in the country worsened. A new case was revealed by ABC News in February, which strained bilateral relations even further: on 5 November

---

74 Congressional Budget Justification, Foreign Operations, FY 2008, p. 602.

75 Testimony of Adolfo A. Franco, Assistant Administrator, Bureau for Latin America and the Caribbean, United States Agency for International Development, before the Committee on International Relations, US House of Representatives, Wednesday, 21 June 2006.

76 'Evo prohibe a Philip Goldberg entrar al Palacio', *La Razón* (La Paz), 13 October 2007.

2007, Fulbright scholar John Alexander van Schaick went for an orientation meeting at the US Embassy in La Paz before starting his research project. He told ABC that, during his one-on-one security briefing, the Assistant Regional Security Advisor Vincent Cooper had asked him to provide information on any Cubans and Venezuelans working in Bolivia he might encounter during his year of fieldwork. According to Peace Corps volunteers and staff, Cooper also instructed 30 new volunteers to do the same, with respect to Cuban nationals.[77] The episode demonstrated the deep US concern about the alliance between Bolivia, Cuba and Venezuela and that the political will existed to use resources to control (and hopefully undermine) this regional agreement. After the publication of the *ABC* story, the Morales administration placed espionage charges against a US official, marking the first time in history that the Bolivian government had charged a US Embassy official with a criminal offence.[78] Following a meeting in La Paz, officials from both countries declared their intentions to improve relations and US representatives announced that Vincent Cooper would not return to the Embassy in Bolivia.

This incident was the last to occur before the most significant escalation of the internal conflict between the Eastern elites of Bolivia and the central government. From this point, Morales deepened his anti-US rhetoric by denouncing secret meetings and agreements between Ambassador Goldberg and leaders from the east. His claims were not always backed with evidence, though in some cases the government presented pictures and footage of Goldberg entering unofficial meetings with important figures of the regional opposition — illustrating the difficulty of demonstrating a political conspiracy.[79] The Eastern elites did not in fact need US help — they were strong enough to destabilise the government by themselves. But US diplomacy needed these elites if Washington was to have a say in Bolivian internal affairs.

This local elite, highly territorialised in the four Eastern departments of the country, and therefore lacking an inclusive national project, was able to become a serious opponent to Morales' administration. On 4 May 2008, a referendum organised in Santa Cruz without legal fiat from the central government produced a vote of 85 per cent in support of autonomy. Consensus on such support from the central government also proved high in the departments of Beni, Pando and Tarija, despite the abstention of around 40 per cent of the electorate. On 10 August, Morales obtained 67.5 per cent of the votes in a separate recall referendum that ratified his mandate and also those of all governors of Eastern Bolivia. During the campaign, the fact that the President could not land in

77 Jean Friedman-Rudovsky and Brian Ross, 'Exclusive: Peace Corps, Fulbright Scholar asked to spy on Cubans, Venezuelans', ABC News, 8 Feb. 2008.

78 Ibid.

79 'Canciller prohíbe a Goldberg reunirse con la oposición', ANF (La Paz), 26 Aug. 2008.

some airports in the east of the country due to rallies and protests against him strengthened the perception of the government's incapacity to control areas of the national territory.

The August recall referendum, a defeat for the opposition due to strong support for Morales, did not resolve the crisis as the government had expected. Indeed, by the beginning of September the conflict reached a peak. On 10 September, anti-government protesters stormed public buildings in the east of the country, while military troops were deployed to guard gas pipelines to guarantee exports to Brazil and Argentina. A day later, nine of Morales' peasant supporters were killed by officials or hit men of the local government in Pando, one of the departments of the Eastern alliance against the MAS administration. Two members of the opposition also died in the confrontations. Leopoldo Fernández, the governor of Pando, was later imprisoned for his alleged responsibility for the so-called Pando Massacre. Hours after the carnage, Morales called for the expulsion of the US Ambassador Goldberg, citing the latter's participation in what he defined as a civic coup. In his farewell speech in the Embassy gardens, Goldberg categorised his expulsion as completely unjustified and asserted that there would be significant consequences.[80]

In Venezuela, Hugo Chávez supported Morales' decision by giving US Ambassador Patrick Duddy 72 hours to leave Caracas, telling him to 'Go to hell 100 times'.[81] Immediately afterwards, Honduran President Manuel Zelaya refused to accept the credentials of a new US Ambassador. In this conflictive context of US-Latin American relations, the Presidents of the region, under the umbrella of UNASUR (a regional organisation of which all South American countries are members) held an emergency meeting in Santiago de Chile to analyse the turmoil in Bolivia. The international press pointed to catastrophic scenarios that underlined the serious possibility of civil war in Bolivia, or of the secession of the Eastern provinces. During the UNASUR meeting, which close allies of Washington like President Alvaro Uribe of Colombia attended, the Presidents signed a document that gave clear support to the Bolivian government, announcing that they would not recognise any government that took power as the result of a civic coup.[82] Despite US attempts to send envoys to the meeting, the Latin American Presidents, partly pressured by Morales and Chávez, did not accept any US participation.[83] Yet Morales had come to Santiago denouncing a civil-military coup with US participation. He asked UNASUR to take an even tougher stance towards Washington, but his request went unheard.

80 'El embajador Goldberg se va', PAT (Bolivia), 14 Sept. 2008.

81 'Chávez acts over US-Bolivia row', BBC, 12 Sept. 2008.

82 The document was published by BBC Mundo (16 Sept. 2008).

83 Interviews with senior advisers of the Bolivian Foreign Ministry (New York, Sept. 2008).

The US responded to the expulsion of its Ambassador and its exclusion from the UNASUR meeting on 16 September by announcing Bolivia's 'decertification'. In a telling political use of the certification process in the war on drugs, the Bush administration stated that Bolivia had 'failed demonstrably during the previous 12 months' to meet its 'obligations under international counternarcotics agreements'.[84] Ten days later, the administration announced that Bolivia was ineligible for benefits under the Andean Trade Promotion and Drug Eradication Act (ATPDEA), asserting that 'Bolivia's demonstrable failure to cooperate in counternarcotics efforts over the past 12 months indicates that Bolivia is not meeting important criteria' to qualify for tariff preferences.[85] In short, Goldberg's promises of punishment came true. Morales responded by expelling the DEA from Bolivia.

In testimony before the Committee on Foreign Affairs Subcommittee on the Western Hemisphere, Kathryn Ledebur, who has been researching and reporting on the effects of US foreign policy in Bolivia for nearly 20 years, stated that by labelling Bolivia a 'demonstrable failure' in drugs control, the administration perpetuated serious distortions of the record.[86] With demand for cocaine remaining stable in the US in recent years and rising elsewhere, coca growing has been on the rise in the three major Andean producing countries: Colombia, Peru and Bolivia. According to Ledebur, the United Nations Office on Drugs and Crime indicates a net 16 per cent increase from 2006 to 2007 in the land area under coca cultivation in the Andes, led by a 27 per cent jump in Colombia. By comparison, the increases reported for Peru (4 per cent) and Bolivia (5 per cent) were relatively small. Overall, Colombia accounted for 85 per cent of the net 24,700 hectares increase region-wide, while Peru accounted for 9 per cent and Bolivia for 6 per cent. And yet Colombia and Peru, allies of the Bush administration, did not receive the decertification that punished Bolivia.[87]

84 Kathryn Ledebur and John Walsh, 'Decertifying Bolivia: Bush administration "fails demonstrably" to make its case', Washington Office on Latin America/Andean Information Network, 4 Nov. 2008.

85 Ibid.

86 Testimony of Kathryn Ledebur, House Committee on Foreign Affairs Subcommittee on the Western Hemisphere, 3 March 2009.

87 As Ledebur states, US and UN figures for the increase of coca cultivation vary significantly. 'The 1% increase reported by UNODC for 2009 contrasts sharply with the 2010 U.S. International Narcotics Control Strategy report, which cited a 9.38% increase from 32,000 to 35,000 hectares for 2009, which they inexplicably rounded up to 10%'; Kathryn Ledebur, 'The UNODC Coca Cultivation Study for Bolivia Shows Minimal Increase in Coca Crop: Sharply Contrasts with U.S. Statistics', Andean Information Network, 23 June 2010.

Decertification represented the US attempt to reframe US-Bolivian relations within the War on Drugs, following the failure to demonise Morales in the War on Terror in 2002. In 2009, the Bush administration tried to portray Morales as a partner of the drugs traffickers, in the same way other US administrations had linked Morales and the *cocaleros* during the '80s and '90s. In this case, so the story went, a partner of drugs traffickers was leading the country into a catastrophic civil war.

Coda: Morales and Obama

The last year of Morales' first term coincided with the first year of the Obama administration, but despite a promising beginning, bilateral relations did not improve. Barack Obama and Evo Morales met for the first time in Trinidad and Tobago, at the Summit of the Americas in April 2009. In a meeting attended by all the Presidents, Morales addressed the alleged coup of September 2008, situating the conflict and US- Bolivian relations in the day that Goldberg was expelled. In addition, he asked Obama publicly to repudiate an assassination plot against him.[88] Obama answered in a press conference, 'Now, specifically on the Bolivia issue, I just want to make absolutely clear that I am absolutely opposed and condemn any efforts at violent overthrows of democratically elected governments, wherever it happens in the hemisphere. That is not the policy of our government. That is not how the American people expect their government to conduct themselves. And so I want to be as clear as possible on that'.[89]

In May 2009, Secretary of State Hillary Clinton criticised the Bush administration's policies with respect to Morales and Chávez, 'The prior administration tried to isolate them, tried to support opposition to them, tried to turn them into international pariahs. It didn't work'. According to Clinton, that policy had allowed China, Iran and Russia to increase their presence in the hemisphere. 'If you look at the gains particularly in Latin America that Iran is making and China is making, it is quite disturbing. They are building very strong economic and political connections with a lot of these leaders'.[90]

During the Trinidad and Tobago summit Morales said that the main difference between the US President and George W. Bush is that Obama listened to the other Presidents as if they were peers. But after the coup against Manuel Zelaya in June 2009, he started to connect events in Honduras and Bolivia. 'What they could not do in Bolivia in 2008 they did in Honduras

88 Frank Bajak, 'Bolivia's Morales: US conspiring against him', Associated Press, 18 April 2009.

89 'Obama offers olive branch to Bolivia', *USA Today*, 19 April 2009.

90 'China, Iran's gains in Latam "disturbing": Clinton', Reuters, 1 May 2009.

one year later', he said. By the broad 'they' here, he meant the 'Empire'.[91] By August, Morales was beginning to downgrade his expectations concerning Barack Obama's policies in Latin America. All soft diplomacy to normalise relations and designate new Ambassadors was frozen in September 2009. The first significant decision made by the democratic administration in relation to Bolivia was to maintain the decertification of the government in the fight against drug trafficking, along with other countries such as Venezuela — a direct continuation of Bush administration policies.

Conclusion

The Water and Gas Wars in Bolivia proved to be driving forces in the country's radical cycle. They were highly influential, along with the anti-US stance of the *cocaleros*, in the way Evo Morales' administration interpreted and redefined La Paz-Washington relations. These conflicts, targeting enemies both domestic (the executors of Presidential Decree 21060) and international (transnational capital and companies), gave the rhetoric of war a central place in the political discourse of securing sovereignty over national resources. During the last decade, these domestic conflicts have fuelled the prospect of a civil war. This prospect was especially acute in October 2003, with the appearance in El Alto of the slogan 'Civil War Now', and during the conflict between Morales' administration and the *Media Luna*. The word *war* has thus become a hallmark of the political culture in popular sectors, and an essential backdrop for Morales' foreign policy towards the US.

Yet before the radical cycle of the 20th century, *war* had a different connotation in Bolivia, shaped by two bloody conflicts against neighbouring countries. According to at least one main strain in the nationalist tradition, the War of the Pacific of 1879–84, and even more so the Chaco War of 1932–5, provoked the building of forms of national consciousness in Bolivia. These wars also contributed to the construction of an external enemy that would continue to appropriate Bolivian soil, as did Chile in the 19th century, or the natural resources under that soil, as was the case with the transnational companies at the dawn of the 20th. The Pacific War deeply shaped Bolivia's foreign policy. For more than 100 years, La Paz has reiterated to the international community a main priority: direct access to the Pacific Ocean.

Morales' administration modified this priority by introducing a new agenda in foreign affairs and by establishing a new framework for relations with the US. By invoking notions of sovereignty, dignity and reciprocity, his administration was determined to reduce US influence and intervention, particularly in all

91   Interview with Evo Morales, New York, Sept. 2009.

issues related to economic and narco-trafficking policies. The (not entirely cut) US aid flowing to Bolivia helps to underscore the limits (and main features) of the new La Paz-Washington bilateral relations. But the resulting Bolivianisation countered the hitherto dominant US narratives centred on successive 'wars' — against Communism, Drugs and Terror. Accused at different times of being a left-wing radical, a partner of narco-traffickers and a terrorist, Morales may thus be seen as a survivor of the three main wars the US has waged on Bolivian soil since the 1950s. The Bolivianisation of bilateral relations displaces these American narratives. US intervention is thus forced to come to terms not only with the changed war on drugs disputed on Bolivian turf, but centrally with the harsh conflict that opposes the MAS administration and the Eastern elites. Bolivianisation illustrates the US's inability to generate new narrative agencies after the failed attempt to capitalise on the War on Terror. The continental erosion of legitimacy of free market policies was a blow against the verisimilitude of any new overarching American narrative. Bolivia for the first time seemed able to offer a counter narrative of sovereignty.

The Bolivianisation of bilateral relations was also a consequence of the regionalisation of Bolivian politics. The empowerment of the already-strong Eastern elites displaced the waning political parties and channelled discontent with Morales' agenda, provoking the major conflict of his first presidency. The power of these elites is not, as the President suggested, based primarily on US support. The regionalisation of Bolivian politics — the central domestic topic in the last decade — redefines new internal political alliances, forcing the US to participate, and even to be seen as participating, in the regional conflict. Goldberg was expelled from the Palacio Quemado and gave his farewell speech from the gardens of the US residence. The new conflict was a long distance from the State Department Building in Washington, and close to Santa Cruz de la Sierra, just 1,000 kilometres from the US diplomatic legation in La Paz.

6

PACHAKUTI IN BOLIVIA, 2008–10:
A PERSONAL DIARY

James Dunkerley

7 February 2009
What's the problem?

Evo Morales officially inaugurates the new Constitution (CPE) approved in the referendum of 25 January by an overall national majority of 61 per cent. But within the four of the country's nine departments that are known as the '*Media Luna*' (Pando; Beni; Santa Cruz; Tarija), it is the opponents of the CPE who win handily. Chief among their many objections is the continued retention of the bulk of oil and gas revenues by the central state. This has been a core national controversy for the better part of a decade, but the issue of collective and private property — and the allied matter of social unity and diversity within the republic — goes back much further. Perhaps it is not surprising that the President, whose *Movimiento al Socialismo* (MAS) administration has just completed three extraordinarily 'eventful' and conflictive years in office, inveighs against the political elite in those regions, 'They wanted to quarter Bolivia, just like four horses pulled Túpaq Katari to pieces'.[1]

Such a pungent evocation of the indigenous uprising of 1781 is given extra force by the fact that Morales has not sworn to uphold the CPE on the crucifix, bible, or indeed any Christian artefact or text. The fourth of the new charter's 411 articles now states, 'The State respects and guarantees freedom of religion and spiritual beliefs, in accordance with their respective cosmovisions. The State is independent of religion'.

No wonder the Church hierarchy has been conspicuous in its opposition; this is far worse than the 1906 amendment to the 1880 Constitution that

---

1 *La Razón*, 8 Feb. 2009. Evo continued, 'De la rebelión de nuestros antepasados a la revolución democrática cultural; de la revolución democrática cultural a la refundación de Bolivia; de la refundación de Bolivia — que es mi pedido con respeto — a la reconciliación de los originarios milenarios con los originarios contemporaneos, respetando la igualdad.'

formally separated Church and State in 19th-century liberal style and to so little tangible effect.

Morales' speech starkly highlights the importance of both continuity and rupture. Here is a charter for political change, and that change is itself expressly related to a past of continuous (albeit often contested) unfreedom for the bulk of the population. In a sense all new Constitutions should be about change.[2] But this is Bolivia's 17th or 18th charter — depending on how you weigh the amendments — and such an abundance of paper has itself long been associated with political instability. After the Revolution of April 1952, the ruling *Movimiento Nacionalista Revolucionario* (MNR) so disparaged the vacuities of constitutionalism that it tarried nine years before drafting a charter.

Of course, one might note that in 1787–8 over a third of those citizens of the USA who were consulted on the Constitution — drafted not just in private but in secret — voted against it (and nowhere was that opposition more entrenched than in New York; Madison had seriously to help out Jay and Hamilton with 85 pro-constitutional Federalist papers in six months). Equally, we need to recall the fuss amongst the European political elite over the opposition by the French and Dutch electorates in 2005 to the new Constitution for the EU, and the similar vote in Ireland in 2008 — a vote that, it was promised, would be re-held (and, by very strong implication, reversed). Voters in the UK were not offered such an option.

Perhaps rupture and instability are not always quite so contrary to democracy? Certainly, in addition to countless strikes, roadblocks (*bloqueos*) and even more comprehensive besieging (*cercos*) of urban centres, the Bolivian electorate has been to the polls at least once a year since 2002 and in some years (2004; 2006; 2008) and in some places twice.[3] It is not unreasonable to term this experience one of 'plebiscitary democracy', provided one accepts the concomitant value of the classical allusion as well as the inferred disparagement from the perspective of Eurocentric liberal constitutionalism.

Since the Constituent Assembly (CA) was elected in July 2006 and installed the following month, there has been an extraordinary expansion of the political arena, taking in not only revived conflicts between the established powers of the state (executive, legislature, judiciary) but also between each and all of these and the CA, and those institutions in turn with the regional authorities, the social movements and even the trade unions who once so dominated the

---

2   Luis Tapia, 'Constitution and Constitutional Reform in Bolivia', in John Crabtree and Laurence Whitehead (eds.), *Unresolved Tensions: Bolivia Past and Present* (Pittsburgh: University of Pittsburgh Press, 2008), pp. 160–71.

3   An outline chronology for 2000–5 may be found in James Dunkerley, 'Evo Morales, Alvaro García Linera and the Third Bolivian Revolution', in same author, *Bolivia: Revolution and the Power of History in the Present*, pp. 1–56.

political scene. The security forces have been far from absent, but they no longer constitute a leading player. As George Gray Molina puts it:

> A typical political negotiation is a three-act drama. First, there are shows of strength from social and regional movements on the streets, followed by forced negotiation and then continued postponement of substantive agreements on the issues of the day (land, autonomies, constitution, and inter-governmental relations, among others). The consequences of this process include both a devaluation of democratic procedures and a weakening of public debate on policy issues.[4]

It was in this mode that the CA remained bitterly divided over the degree of its sovereign powers, over whether it would make decisions on the basis of a simple majority or by two-thirds of the delegates. Eventually moving its formally prolonged and literally embattled proceedings from Sucre to Oruro, the MAS majority approved in December 2007 a document with almost all the CA opposition boycotting the session. It was in the self-same mode that in October 2008, after a horrible provincial massacre and international intervention (excluding the USA), the government and opposition in congress agreed bilaterally to renegotiate more than 100 articles of the MAS text and to submit the revised draft to a popular vote in the January 2009 referendum.

Perhaps most notable among those changes to the Oruro draft was the withdrawal of Morales' claim to the right of two further presidential terms — something at the core of the Venezuelan campaign of Hugo Chávez, who, from as early as June 2006, had been urging Bolivians (in a TV broadcast from Tiahuanaco) to adopt the Venezuelan Constitution as their ideal template. Whatever one might feel about the over-heated and under-informed debates about the 'new Latin American left', such 'Bolivarianism' undoubtedly strikes a chord. Morales is after all intent upon keeping the republic named after Simón Bolívar; he wants to refound it, not establish Qullasuyo or some other pre-Columbian polity.

But, in the event, the parallels with Venezuela have proved to be limited. Article 1 of the Bolivian Constitution of 2008–9 — please draw breath — states:

> Bolivia se constituye en un Estado Unitario Social de Derecho Plurinacional Comunitario, libre, independiente, soberano, democrático, intercultural, descentralizado y con autonomías. Bolivia se funda en pluralidad y el pluralismo político, económico, jurídico, cultural y linguistico, dentro del proceso integrador del país.

---

4   'Bolivia's Long and Winding Road', *Inter-American Dialogue,* Working Paper, July 2008, p. 7.

This string of adjectives is quite un-Venezuelan and certainly reflects more than serial risk- aversion by a committee. It is a rhetorical effort to 'square the circle' of longstanding conflicts, leavening through aggregate syllables and often contradictory terminology any ideological, regional or social differences deriving from the past.

The predominance of 'pluralism' might seem altogether too insistent to be convincing and it might be worth remembering, on the 150th anniversary of the publication of *Origin of the Species,* that Darwin was furiously opposed to the 'pluralism' of Louis Agassiz, whose racist defence of slavery was founded upon polygenism — the belief that species were derived from separate origins and endowed with unequal attributes.[5] Equally, as Xavier Albó has several times commented, the revised Constitution of 1994 also began describing Bolivia as *'multiétnico y pluricultural'*, and then proceeded to endorse the *'tierra comunitaria de origen'* as a principal attribute of indigenous peoples.[6] Perhaps rather less has changed than is being touted?

This is very recent and very *political* — scarcely 'history' at all, even if we allow for 'quick' events. It forms part of a contemporary pattern of what Vice-President Alvaro García Linera has dubbed *'el empate catastrófico'*, which has certainly been at play since October 2003 (the 'Gas War'), and probably since January 2000 (the 'Water War'), with strong referents cast back to August 1985 (Decree 21060 and 'neoliberal' stabilisation), October 1982 (the ending of military rule), and April 1952 (the National Revolution) as the more recent public historical 'moments'.

Who, in such circumstances, would lay odds on political quietude and social contentment descending on Bolivia in 2009? Who, responding to intuition or even the more contested evidence of the past, would wager against the recrudescence of social conflict? It has been widely and seriously argued by historians as well as by Evo Morales that this 'reality' has much deeper and more telling 'roots' or origins, be they empirico-objective, imagined, 'remembered' or evoked.

We should interrogate those possibilities as much to avoid teleological determinisms as for the purpose of calibrating the particular pattern of rupture and continuity in this Andean republic. In a recent critical survey of the developing historiography of the Latin American public sphere, Pablo Piccato enjoins us to be much more careful about teleologies related to 'modernisation',

---

5   Adrian Desmond and James Moore, *Darwin's Sacred Cause: Race, Slavery and the Quest for Human Origins* (London: Allen Lane, 2009).

6   Xavier Albó, '25 años de democracia, participación campesino — indígena y cambios reales en la sociedad', in same author (ed.), *25 años construyendo Democracia* (La Paz: Vicepresidencia de la Republica, 2008), pp. 39–58, see p. 50.

coming forward, so to speak, from the intellectuals in the 19th century.[7] So should we be cautious about too readily 'reading tradition backwards' and doing so with schematic linearity.

This is a distinct tension, highlighted by Olivia Harris when she noted that, 'Andean cultures harness the powers of the past ... remnants of bygone eras are put to work for the living and for the reproduction of the world'. And yet, 'All too often the nature of Indian identity in the 20th Century has been read back onto the historical past'.[8]

Brooke Larson likewise cautions against over-stressing colonial legacies, sensitising us to the circumstantial or conjunctural importance of recourse being made to the past:

> In moments of political crisis and rupture, local indigenous peoples might
> tap into those long-term historical memories, or they might conjure Inca
> or Andean utopias, as armament in local struggles for land and justice.[9]

In a dense and often complex book about the recent period, Raquel Gutiérrez claims that,

> [in 2000–5] ... a space-time of *Pachakuti* opened up; that is, a social
> situation of inversion was configured, upturning all that which had
> hitherto been thought of as everyday normality.

We'll definitely need to think more deeply about this term, but Gutiérrez assuredly doesn't see it as an immanent property. It comes and it goes — 'the rhythms of *Pachakuti* are to be found when they are produced'.[10] This may seem blindingly obvious, but I do prefer it to the more poetic declamation of René Zavaleta Mercado (whom both Gutiérrez and I greatly admire), 'Bolivia, effectively, is conflict, and it can only be resolved in terms of conflict and catastrophe ... that is the natural form of the nation'.[11] On such a premise, we

---

7   *Public Sphere in Latin America: A map of the historiography*, ms. New York, p. 15.

8   Brooke Larson and Olivia Harris (eds.), *Ethnicity, Markets, and Migration in the Andes. At the Crossroads of History and Anthropology* (Durham NC: Duke University Press, 1995), pp. 322, 353.

9   *Trials of Nation Making. Liberalism, Race, and Ethnicity in the Andes, 1810–1910* (Cambridge: Cambridge University Press, 2004), p. 5.

10 *Los Ritmos del Pachakuti. Movilización y Levantamiento Indígena-Popular en Bolivia (2000–2005)* (La Paz: 2008), pp. 17, 313. Likewise, Gutiérrez recognises that, 'el conjunto de luchas anticapitalistas y antiestatales no propuso de forma sintética ... ningún *sistema sustituto* al orden de explotación' (p. 312).

11 *La formación de la conciencia nacional* (1967; Cochabamba: Los Amigos del Libro, 1990), p. 167. Zavaleta was a Romantic as well as a Marxist, and it is not untypical of his writing

will always find what we go back to look for and we can only expect trouble up ahead. That's a problem.

In fact, the circumstances of the latest Bolivian Constitution could hardly be more distinct than those of the first, in 1826. In August 1825 the country's first Constituent Assembly (there have been nine in all, amongst 62 heads of state) met in the city of Chuquisaca to draw up a charter for the newly independent Audiencia de Charcas. What did they write? Not a word. They asked the Liberator Simón Bolívar — ah, these Venezuelan generals! — to do the job for them. And when, the following year, he completed the text, he circulated it throughout South America, proclaiming that in it were combined 'all the advantages of federalism, all the strength of centralised government, all the stability of monarchical regimes'.[12] Just a bit like the current melange, in fact, except that the first contradictory confection was drafted in a wholly different manner ...

We need to break from a strictly constitutional focus. Only die-hard lawyers believe the charter to be anything other than one more input, an independent variable. It is highly important in times of democracy and due process, but no more of a driver than other factors. It is appellable in conditions of what I have — probably too tamely — termed a 'rogatory culture', but it is also so often avoided, evaded, manipulated and transgressed as to provide more of an ideational siting than a reliable guide to public conduct, still less a practical guarantee of rights.

Here, historians will likely part company with other social scientists, for whom institutional architecture and modal patterns are both cause and effect in the short- to medium-term. They have, quite understandably, been having an exciting but often troublesome time with the Bolivia of the late 20th and early 21st century. In their analytical repertoire 'plebiscitary democracy' is terminologically bracketed alongside explanations based on deficient party cohesion, misguided electoral design and the longitudinal imbalances between parliamentarianism and presidentialism, the patrimonial antecedents of power structures, 'anti-systemic populism' and the less predictable, more energetic, analysis of 'deliberative democracy' and popular participation.[13] Only the recidivist iconoclasts come out openly and declare Bolivia (left-wing, right-

that this long essay begins with a quote from Disraeli, just as his other writing on the military took de Tocqueville seriously.

12   Letter to Colombia, 3 Aug. 1826, in Vicente Lecuna and Harold Bierck (eds.), *Selected Writings of Bolívar* 2 vols. (New York: 1951), vol. 2, p. 627.

13   For examples of high-quality political science appraisal of the contemporary scene in the region, see S. Mainwaring and T. Scully (eds.), *Building Democratic Institutions. Party Systems in Latin America* (Stanford: Stanford University Press, 1995); Joe Foweraker, Todd Landman and Neil Harvey, *Governing Latin America* (Oxford: Polity, 2003).

wing and plumb-centre) as 'conservative', but even those armed with a phalanx of matrices and regressions deem the country damnably well inoculated against the zeitgeist.[14]

As a general rule, right-thinking progressive supporters of the rule of statutory law — like George Gray, Eduardo Gamarra, Jorge Lazarte and Carlos Toranzos — have tried to mask their dismay, whilst proponents of a 'new indigenous politics' and those opposed to 'neo-liberalism' — say, Donna Lee Van Cott, Ben Kohl and Linda Farthing as well as Raquel Gutiérrez — see many fewer problems and much more substantial progress in the human condition.[15]

What both sides lack, however, is a significant concern with the *historicity* of where Bolivia now stands and where she might be 'going'. They share a strictly subordinate interest in what we might call the 'sedimented' features of the present, discernible in and recoverable from a past beyond living memory (1985; 1982; 1952 at a receding pinch; and the Chaco War of 1932–5 as rapidly approaching a purely monumentalised incarnation).

I myself am certainly guilty on this count. In finding 'Three Revolutions' (2000–9 and on-going; 1952; and 1809–41), I narrowly and pedantically stuck to the existence (nigh-on) of 'Bolivia', making the denominated republic the prerequisite and formalistically ruling out of serious consideration the prior Audiencia de Charcas, which, of course, is scarcely less 'Bolivian', by virtue of predating the name when it occupied the same natural and social *space*. If we are indeed to take the dialectic of *space-time* seriously, then we cannot sensibly

---

14 H.C.F. Mansilla, *El carácter conservador de la nación boliviana* (Santa Cruz: El País, 2004). Felipe Mansilla can spend too much time winding up the left as a spectator sport, but he has studied his Kant as well as Habermas, reads (Alcides) Arguedas intelligently and needs to be addressed directly.

15 Perhaps I should note that I know all those named personally and have what I believe the friendliest of relations with them. Gray (ed.), *El Estado del estado en Bolivia. Informe Nacional sobre Desarrollo Humano 2007* (La Paz: Programa de las Naciones Unidas para el Desarrollo, 2007) and 'State-Society Relations in Bolivia: The Strength of Weakness', in Crabtree and Whitehead (eds.), *Unresolved Tensions*, pp. 109–24. In addition to Gamarra's chapter in Mainwaring and Scully, see his evidently exasperated editorial in the *Miami Herald*, 17 June 2008 (and the point-by-point rebuttal by the Andean Information Centre on 23 June); Carlos Toranzo Roca, *Rostros de la democracia: una mirada mestiza,* (La Paz: Plural, 2006), and 'Let the Mestizos Stand Up and Be Counted', in Crabtree and Whitehead (eds.), *Unresolved Tensions*, pp. 35–50; Jorge Lazarte Rojas, *Entre los espectros del pasado y las incertidumbres del futuro* (La Paz: Plural, 2005); Donna Lee Van Cott, *Radical Democracy in the Andes* (Cambridge: Cambridge University Press, 2008); Benjamin Kohl and Linda Farthing, *Impasse in Bolivia: Neoliberal Hegemony and Popular Resistance* (London: Zed, 2006).

start our stories in 1825. We ought also to be actively 'translating' words and names across time.

That clumsiness encouraged Sian Lazar, reviewing *Revolutionary Horizons* by Forrest Hylton and Sinclair Thomson, to attribute to me an argument that independence was 'more revolutionary' than 1781, which wasn't my aim at all.[16] It is an interesting (rather unfashionable) position, but I simply wanted to distinguish the Aymara-Spanish conflict as strictly pre-Bolivian and for the purpose of underlining Evo Morales' variegated use of history — *evoking* 1781 whilst *upholding* the construction of 1825, which was the very antithesis of Túpaq Katari's objectives. It is precisely this contradictory combination that marks Morales out from both *Katarista* left (Felipe Quispe) and the *criollo* right of the post-1952 parties.

12 February 2009
'Chaos, rudis indigestaque moles'[17]

Twenty five years ago today Verso published *Rebellion in the Veins*, for which, surely unknowingly, I filched a determinist title (from Gregorio Iriarte, still going strong ...) and in the Foreword tried my own squaring of the circle:

> The newspapers trot out the mathematics of disorder — all of it fifth-hand and incorrect — but do not pose the question that if disorder is so prevalent might it not be order itself? Could there not be system in the chaos? Should it not be understood less as interruption than as continuity?[18]

Rupture and continuity. Conjoined. Pretty close to Zavaleta's 'Bolivia is conflict' riff. But then I was following a Marxist-Leninist track. Which is why Lazar makes a fair thematic and generational distinction with the work of Hylton and Sinclair, who do not share the superannuated denigration of the rural/agricultural/peasantry/indigenous, still somehow consigned to rhetorical allusion with a 'sack of potatoes'.[19]

---

16 *Revolutionary Horizons. Past and Present in Bolivian Politics* (New York: Verso, 2007), reviewed by Sian Lazar in *A Contracorriente*, 6:1 (Fall 2008), pp. 362–7. In a supportive piece Lazar asks whether 1781 was more 'revolt' than 'revolution' — a rather traditional distinction but worth considering — and questions the prominence of indigeneity with the current experience of Zavaleta's 'national-popular' axis.

17 'Chaos, a rough and unordered mess'. Ovid, *Metamorphoses*, 1:7.

18 James Dunkerley, *Rebellion in the Veins. Political Struggle in Bolivia, 1952–1982* (London: Verso, 1984), p. xi.

19 This reference, from *The Eighteenth Brumaire of Louis Bonaparte*, has always been exploited a little unfairly since it is abstracted from a passage with essentially quantitative objectives in mind: 'A small holding, a peasant and his family; alongside them another small holding,

Now, we must accept that things, as John Coatsworth puts it,

> we thought we knew a quarter century ago [are] upside down. Marxists
> have discovered that capitalism can generate sustained economic growth
> and improvements in living standards. Dependency scholars turned up
> the data that show that sustained economic growth can be positively,
> not negatively, correlated with the growth of external trade and foreign
> investment. Modernisationists have discovered the significance of
> inequality and exclusion, and the institutions that sustain them, as
> obstacles to economic growth.[20]

Sic transit gloria mundi. But the world changes pretty radically in shorter cycles
too. Looking over my notes for the last nine months, I can see how difficult it
is to keep pace with Bolivia, even from quite close up.

3 February 2008
Quickstep and jump-start

Sinclair Thomson writes to ask if I'd be interested in giving a presentation to
the New York Latin American History Workshop next year. We agree that I'll
address 'continuity and rupture' in Bolivia, but as soon as I send the email, I
realise how a neat idea is going to present a horrible practical problem. Bolivia
is in total meltdown right now, and I'll be in really hot water if I try to go
back much before 1809. How on earth am I going to make a plausible case for
the salience of a prolonged past of domination amidst a present of continual
contestation and crisis?

another peasant and another family. A few score more of these make up a village, and a few
score of villages make up a Department. In this way, the great mass of the French nation
is formed by simple addition of homologous magnitudes, much as potatoes in a sack form
a sack of potatoes'. Yet Marx and Engels never really had any time for the revolutionary
potential of the rural masses, perhaps because the widespread European failures of 1848
followed the traumatic experience of the Irish Famine. In the *Manifesto of the Communist
Party*, they averred, 'The lower middle class, the small manufacturer, the shopkeeper,
the artisan, the peasant, all these fight against the bourgeoisie, to save from extinction
their existence as fractions of the middle class. They are therefore not revolutionary, but
conservative. Nay more, they are reactionary, for they try to roll back the wheel of history':
Karl Marx and Friedrich Engels, *Selected Works of Karl Marx and Frederick Engels* (London:
Lawrence and Wishart, 1968), pp. 172, 44. Strangely, though, it is almost always the *French*
peasants that dominate their vision, even when writing on Ireland: Karl Marx and Friedrich
Engels, *On Ireland. Karl Marx and Friedrich Engels* (London: Lawrence and Wishart, 1971),
pp. 146–7.

20 'Inequality, Institutions and Economic Growth in Latin America', *Journal of Latin American
Studies* 40:3 (Aug. 2008), pp. 545–69, see p. 546.

Normally political conflict comes to a halt in February on account of Carnival. It is as if all other ruptures within civil society will cede to this marvellous symbolic display that combines pre-Columbian myth, such as the plagues of Huari, with a strong indigenous presence in dances dedicated to representing syncretic experiences, like the abortive flight of Chiru-Chiru the thief, which relates to events on the Carnival Saturday of 1789. And that is just in Oruro, where the processions dedicated to the Virgen del Socavón and the Diablada give proper prominence to the telluric and mystical qualities of a world in which mining has predominated for half a millennium. There are distinct stories, rituals and ancillary customs in the carnivals of La Paz (Jisk'a Anata), Cochabamba (Jaihuayco), Tarija (where the markedly *criollo* dances show similarities with Asturias, although the region has a generally Andalucian connection), and now more than ever, Santa Cruz, where the Queens, their election and coronation rule above all else, beauty being harnessed over recent decades to floats promoting regional identity.

Anthropologists have debated just how and why some of these dances developed, and how directly we should see them — and particularly the 'Dance of the Conquest' depicting Pizarro and Atahuallpa — as representing an indigenous trauma resulting from the Conquest and colonial dominion.[21] Andrew Canessa has recently reminded us that even the Tinku, which has a substantial extra-carnival existence and hardly any Hispanic reference beyond the leather helmets, is a real as well as ritual fight all about intra-Ayllu energies and can only be conducted between groups eligible to inter-marry.[22] In the communities themselves, police officers are required to invigilate the combat, and they struggle to keep serious injuries down — a rather unusual variation of the state-civil society interface.

None the less, the carnivals in Bolivia do, for the most part, symbolically turn the 'world upside down', as Henry Devine declared in the midst of the English Revolution.[23] They certainly empower the non-Hispanic account of

21 See Manuel Burga, *Nacimiento de una utopía. Muerte y resurrección de los Incas* (Lima: 1988); Nathan Wachtel, *Vision of the Vanquished. The Spanish Conquest of Peru through Indian Eyes* (Hassocks: Harvester Press, 1977); Jesús Lara, *La literatura de los Quechuas* (La Paz: 1985); and the discussion in Olivia Harris, '"The Coming of the White People". Reflections on the Mythologisation of History in Latin America', *Bulletin of Latin American Research*, 14:1 (Jan. 1995), pp. 9–24.

22 'Forgetting the Revolution and Remembering the War: Memory and Violence in Highland Bolivia', *History Workshop Journal* 68 (Autumn 2009), pp. 173–98.

23 'I may peradventure to many seem guilty of that crime which was laid against the Apostle. To turn the world upside down, and to set that in the bottom which others make the top of the building', Christopher Hill, *The World Turned Upside Down. Radical Ideas during the English Revolution* (Harmondsworth: Penguin, 1972), frontispiece.

the past, the sound of the hundreds of the bands, richness of the colour of the costumes and mesmeric movement of thousands of dancers giving the lie to suspicion that this is no more than twee folklore and cheapskate cooptation. There is no other time or place that provides such material and sensory evidence for René Zavaleta's assertion that Bolivia is a 'multicoloured social formation' ('*una formación abigarrada*'), wherein the mixture of primary hues reflects the coexistence of different epochs.[24]

It is also worth remembering Bakhtin's de- and re-construction of 16th-century rituals through Rabelais' *Gargantua and Pantagruel,* where he finds more than a mere crowd: 'Here, in the town square, a special form of free and familiar contact reigned among people who were usually divided by the barriers of caste, property, profession and age'. The time and space are unique, the transmigration of body and soul further sanctioned through masks and costume.[25] In the first half of the 20th century these often emulated European fashion — '*terroristas*' and '*fascistas*' may be seen cavorting amongst the streamers in the La Paz streets of the 1920s — but all that has now gone.

If carnival may fairly be said to produce a heightened sense of individual sensuality and collective unity, as well as the discharging of religious obligations, it is a process that has grown considerably in recent decades, particularly in La Paz, still the epicentre of political conflict. In the 1930s, after the Chaco War, the *Fiesta del Gran Poder* became established in the Chijini neighbourhood as a semi-subversive act of veneration to Christ's incarnation as the second person in the Trinity. Now the June parade, centred on the *Morenada*, has spread into the city centre and dwarfed the event's devotional attributes. At core it remains resolutely *mestizo/cholo* — more syncretic than dichotomous, and more urban than rural, but still a temporal and behavioural moment favouring the autochthonous.

Much more 'pluri-multi' in both aspirational and institutional aspects is the *Entrada Universitaria* of July. Founded in 1988 and officially supported by the Alcaldía from 2000, this competition between faculty-based dance groups energetically promotes the diversity of national folklore. It supplements the traditional *diabladas, caporales, morenadas, cuecas* and the Afro-Bolivian *saya* with the war-dance of the Toba Indians from the lowlands of the *oriente*. Some marvellous syncopated jump-dancing gives authority and centrality to those marginal 'feathered indians' who 150 years ago had been depicted as 'wild, undomesticated, and part of nature' by Bolivia's foundational artist, Melchor

24 'Las masas en noviembre', in René Zavaleta Mercado (ed.), *Bolivia hoy* (Mexico City: Siglo Veintiuno, 1983), p. 17.

25 Mikhail Bakhtin, *Rabelais and his World* (1941; Indiana: 1993), p. 10.

María Mercado.[26] Against the run of play, then, clothing is less subtracted than added.

Here the energy and beauty of youth provide a more consciously representational spectacle, something that, in keeping with its lifespan, *seems* to be part of the post-military democratic era. This is not Rio, but at 12,000 feet above sea-level, the proud display of underwear is quite brazen enough to qualify as rule-breaking of fully carnivalesque dimension.

If today's students are just as likely to strip off as dress up, the key denominator is still costume. Remember the fuss about Evo Morales' serially displayed striped jumper on his world tour of January 2006? What was that all about? For Alma Guillermoprieto it was quintessentially non-carnivalesque: 'the poor man's native costume world-wide, one could say'. In a flight of fancy, perhaps only to be found in the fashion pages, Imogen Fox of *The Guardian* hazarded an analogy with Liz Hurley on the grounds that both she and Evo were celebrities unafraid to be photographed many times in the same kit — 'it bestows on the wearer a certain credibility ... [they] acquire a "significant look"'. Fox went on, rather patronisingly, to deplore the fact that, 'sadly Bolivia is outside the usual fashion circuit'.[27] But, of course, Bolivia has *haute couture* as part of its tradition as well as the imported variety. Once Morales took office, he cast aside the man-made fibres of Everyman and shifted between the shirt-sleeve-and–jerkin sartorial populism adopted by Chávez and, courtesy of the talented designer Beatriz Canedo Patiño, 'couture leather jackets trimmed with Indian embroidery — they are much more elegant than the fussy suits and long strips of cloth roped around the neck of the Western business costume'.[28]

There is surely much more connecting the epoch of celebrity culture with the era of sumptuary law than we like to admit. At Chuquisaca (today Sucre) in 1540 the Pizarro brothers put clothes at the centre of their gift to Kuysara in thanks for his role in securing the surrender of the lords of that region: 'he was given clothing — a cape of green velvet with its shirt also of green

26 This depiction of 'the Tobas' is inspired by Seemin Qayum's wonderful discussion of Mercado's corpus of work — including, of course, a depiction of Carnival entitled 'El Mundo al Revés' — and its telling comparison with that of the *refined* European traveller Alcides d'Orbigny. That analysis is seriously in need of publication and a wider audience, but I fear that the need to reproduce Mercado's extraordinary pictures in colour may be holding back this vital project. The picture referred to here is entitled 'Women Bathing', its wild pubic zones and phallic palm trees projecting — even to the knowingly contaminated eye — a masculine sexuality 'that is rooted, solid and stable, while feminine sexuality is unstable, mobile and elusive'. *Creole Imaginings: Race, Space and Gender in the Making of Republican Bolivia*, PhD, Goldsmiths College, University of London, 2002, p. 118.

27   *The Guardian*, 13 Jan. 2006.

28   Alma Guillermoprieto, 'A New Bolivia?', *New York Review of Books*, 10 Aug. 2006.

velvet with golden trimming ... and a red hat, then in fashion, as well as a large trunk of knives'.[29] Nearly 250 years later, when Spanish power was under sharp challenge in La Paz, the besieged Spanish officer Ledo described the two emissaries sent by Túpaq Katari as especially elegant, each 'with his undershirt of silk and the outer of velvet trimmed with fine gold'.[30]

These may not be the determining or defining elements in what Armando Méndez Morales calls an enduring lack of hegemony in Bolivia, but neither are they inconsequential to that plausible proposition.[31] Perhaps there was no time since the reforms of Viceroy Toledo in the 1570s that the indigenous people of this part of the world had been more exposed to external forces than in the 19th century, and yet,

> Neither the turn away from colonial-tributary traditions to liberal
> free-trade doctrines around mid-century, nor the emerging "civilizing"
> discourses at the end of the 19th century, succeeded in binding indigenous
> cultural values or identities to the discursive domain of the nation-state in
> the greater Andean region.[32]

And, of course, we need to be sceptical about all those university-led disciplinary boundaries that discourage us from thinking sensibly about the connection between clothes and dance, on the one hand, and raw economic forces on the other. What was Karl Marx doing in the British Museum in the 1850s if not discovering that,

> 'Money' comes to signify not merely some scrap of paper or metal, but
> rather an entire system of social relationships based on certain rules and
> laws, and involving certain types of politics, culture, even personality ...[33]

29 Quoted in Tristan Platt, Thérèse Bouysse-Cassagne and Olivia Harris, *Qaraqara-Charka. Mallku, Inka y Rey en la provincia de Charcas (siglos xv–xvii)* (La Paz: Plural/Fundación Cultural del Banco Central de Bolivia, 2006), p. 124.

30 Quoted in María Eugenia del Valle de Siles, *Testimonios del Cerco de La Paz: el campo contra la ciudad, 1781* (La Paz: Última Hora, 1980), p. 165.

31 *La Razón*, 1 Feb. 2009.

32 Larson, *Trials of Nation Making*, p. 11. Of course, these are two-way processes, as shown by Greg Grandin for the case of Guatemala: 'Along with other highland communities, Quezaltenango K'iché political participation contributed to the failure of the first postindependence liberal regime (1821–38), the defeat of a highland separatist movement (1838–40), the endurance of Rafael Carrera's long conservative rule (1840–65), the establishment of the liberal coffee estate (1871), and both the triumph *and* defeat of Guatemala's democratic revolution (1944–54)': *The Blood of Guatemala. A History of Race and Nation* (Durham NC: Duke University Press, 2000), p. 14.

33 Martin Nicolaus, 'Foreword' to Karl Marx, *Grundrisse: Foundations of the Critique of Political Economy* (Harmondworth: Penguin, 1973), p. 14.

But what goes up also comes down. And now, in 2008, it appears to be money that's threatening carnival, at least in Oruro. The Asociación de Conjuntos del Folklore de Oruro (ACFO) seemed to have overplayed its hand in laying down the rules for rehearsal. Formed under the aegis of the MNR in 1963, the ACFO is a quite formidable part of that institutional architecture Evo Morales refers to as the 'democratic cultural revolution'. Last year it sold the TV rights for covering the procession for only $18,000 and the advertising for Bs.490,000; but, together with other fees, royalties and sundry income, it clears $8 million in the four days of carnival. But it also has to deal with 49 troupes, thousands of dancers and, even more of a challenge, the bands (mostly brass) that accompany them. This does not exactly require hegemony, but it does depend on careful consultation and tactful negotiation. They certainly overstepped the mark in demanding limited, unadorned and unaccompanied, dry, 'professional' rehearsals. It has taken a threatened national boycott, including that by sponsors, to restore creative insobriety.

4 May 2008
Downside-up. Republican time and change

The referendum on autonomy in Santa Cruz is backed by 86 per cent of voters in the department. Such is the level of antagonism with the government in La Paz that what are administrative changes which fall well below the level of decentralisation in the world's 11 federal systems and even states such as Spain have come to be seen by many as preliminary to separatism. The Organisation of American States is warning of an 'explosion'. Is this the end of the Bolivia constituted in August 1825? We surely have to look forward as well as back.

In an especially suggestive essay on theorising political temporality, Kimberly Hutchings distinguishes between *chronos*, associated with the inevitable birth-life cycles of individuals, and *kairos*, 'associated with the transformational time of action, in which the certainty of death and decay is challenged'. Perhaps if we were pinning these approaches to schools of political thought, we would tag the first as 'realist' and the second as 'idealist'. But Hutchings doesn't want to go that route. She forms part of that increasingly influential strand of political thought in the UK which concentrates on reviewing the classical and Renaissance tradition of republicanism:

> Politics, as opposed to nature, is the sphere of re-shaped nature, emerging
> out of the potential of *kairos* ... For Machiavelli, the struggle between
> fortune and *virtú* is not capable of being won by one side or another.
> The most virtuous leader is liable to come unstuck through bad luck,
> the most profound bad luck may still be countered and even exploited
> by the 'virtuous' leader. For this reason, the combination of *chronos* and
> *kairos* in Machiavelli's thinking about the temporality of politics results

in a cyclical understanding of politics as the rise and fall of power. In contrast, according to the Romantic theories of history ... political time is structured in relation to a specific end, which can be understood in positive or negative terms. Instead of the Machiavellian struggle and its cyclical implications for the understanding of politics, here we find an eschatological temporal trajectory, which may provide grounds for either hope or despair.[34]

Let's not get too worried by the theory. We can think 1781 as well as 2008 and we should definitely consider the idea of *Pachakuti*, which is not just about backwards and forwards, but both of these understood as *cycle*, albeit one of unpredictable and indeterminate qualities. What better illustration of such a republican matrix of fortune and *virtú* than the (reported) statement of 1795, of the leader of a local insurrection to overthrow an illegitimate *cacique* in Jesús de Machaca,

> The present was now another time (*ya era otro tiempo el presente*) and the cacique, his number two, as well as the priest had to stay silent and comply with whatever the community decided.[35]

The words in italics (rendered in the present tense) were adopted as the title of an essay by Forrest Hylton and Sinclair Thomson, which introduces us to four 'moments' — not a continuous experience — of indigenous insurgency. We are drawn away from seamless continuity towards a process marked by intermittent events.

The richness of *Pachakuti* resides precisely in its amalgamation of *chronos* and *kairos*. According to Olivia Harris and Therese Bouysse-Cassagne, the term conjoins words that variously signify time/earth/place/moment (*pacha*) and change/shift/cycle/alternation (*kuti*). So the term could indeed apply to political transformation as well as to conflicts between the moieties of an *ayllu* or the more *chronos*-related phenomena of seasonal cycles, gender relations, interaction

---

34 'Dream or Nightmare? Thinking the Future of World Politics', in Gideon Baker and Jens Bartelson (eds.), *The Future of Political Community* (Abingdon: Routledge, 2009), ch. 1; see also Kimberly Hutchings, *Time and World Politics: Thinking the Present* (Manchester: Manchester University Press, 2008).

35 Quoted in Forrest Hylton, Félix Patzi, Sergio Serulnikov and Sinclair Thomson, *Ya es otro tiempo el presente. Cuatro momentos de insurgencia indígena* (La Paz: Muela del Diablo, 2003), p. 5. Raquel Gutiérrez, *Los Ritmos del Pachakuti*, p. 128, expressly dissents from the idea of *pachakuti* representing an era when/where '*sólo reinasen los indios ...*', which, without any precise reference, she attributes to this volume. She is surely right to insist on a fuller meaning to the term than this, but her attribution of a 'thinner' one to this text is unwarranted.

between the natural elements and related metaphysical associations.[36] This need not envelop a simple indigenous-European dichotomy — the *'guerra de los tiempos'* during the early phase covered by the authors' *Qaraqara-Charka* is an inter-Inca conflict and Harris, particularly, has inveighed against a hubristic assignment of total temporal rupture to the Conquest. However, it does stand in contrast to the convictions of Juan de Matienzo, a judge in Chuquisaca who in 1567 looked simply to *chronos* moving forward to eradicate memory of the pre-Hispanic order. For Matienzo, according to Sabine MacCormack,

> What made this enterprise [Spanish government of Peru] feasible, at least on paper, was, *inter alia*, the passage of time: a new generation of Andean people was replacing those who had witnessed or participated in 'how the Incas governed'. If memory was a social and political force, so was forgetting.[37]

And when MacCormack notes of the Incas, 'no one whether of Andean, Spanish or Creole origin was able to forget them, and they are not forgotten now', she is only signalling an elementary fact. As Thomas Abercrombie has shown so richly for K'ulta, there are 'myriad ways of construing and using the past' in the present, and not least among them are non-Inca Andean myths, genealogies and rituals.[38]

This is so often missed in the simple and compelling socio-imperial dichotomy between Spanish Emperor and Quechua Inca. *Qaraqara-Charka* treats the Spanish Conquest as part of a process and so does not begin in 1520, reviving discussion of Max Uhle's neglected periodisation of the pre-Columbian era in which continuity and rupture are treated as 'horizons' and 'intervals'.

Uhle was an archaeologist studying an illiterate civilisation, but one can evidently find written sources for the Andes from the end of the first third of the 16th century. (Indeed, given the current prognosis of the electronically-driven disappearance of handwriting and the physical book within the next decades, perhaps we should set aside the hoary old oral-documentary duel as a looming anachronism?). With the Toledan reforms of the 1570s another 'horizon' opens after a 30-year 'interval' formed by the warring Pizarro and

---

36 'Pacha: en torno al pensamiento aymara', in Thérèse Bouysse-Cassagne, Olivia Harris, Tristan Platt and V. Cereceda, *Tres reflexiones sobre el pensamiento andino* (La Paz: Hisbol, 1987), pp. 18, 31.

37 *On the Wings of Time. Rome, the Incas, Spain, and Peru* (Princeton: Princeton University Press, 2007), p. 20.

38 *Pathways of Memory and Power: Ethnography and History among an Andean People* (Madison WI: University of Wisconsin Press, 1998), p. 319.

Almagro clans. Toledo mediates even as he assiduously dominates. Now the paperwork begins in earnest.

Talk of intra-colonial cycles, stages and periodisation is still very much the property of specialists. It should be appreciated far more widely, even if there are few ruptures of the order registered in Europe (and from the mid-18th century, North America). Unable to call upon new coeval oral sources, we might be tempted to over-rate the documentary accounts, especially those relating to the well-preserved sphere of the law. Some 'un-triangulated' legal studies of Spanish America are so mesmerised by the formalism of their subject that they offer, less a reliable guide to local conditions, than insight into the colonial imagination, first in Spain and then among the early republican elites. Yet, when looked at close-up, especially through the medium of indigenous language, one finds marked and fascinating changes as, for instance, in the language employed in the wills of ordinary folk.[39]

What all of this must lead us towards is a pluralism of object as well as of method. If the people of Pocobaya studied by Canessa 'remember' the 1952 Revolution as far more important than Independence from Spain, 'which did little more than transfer power from one white elite to another', they also recall the 'war' between the moieties of the *ayllu* as, in turn, far more important than 1952.[40] Coming, figuratively, in the other direction is Filemón Escobar. Highly influential in the foundation of the MAS a decade ago, he had progressively abandoned the Trotskyist critique of 1952, replacing the supremacist teleology of the permanent revolution (how much more Romantic — in Hutchings' reading — can you get than that variant of Marxism?) with a cultural politics of complementarity, *yaqaña ayni* or mutual respect.[41]

According to José Luis Roca, who should know since he belongs to it, during the 1990s the contemporary elite of Santa Cruz, 'simply *forgot* about any ideals of decentralisation'.[42] Indeed, since the late 1950s, when (MNR-led) mass mobilisation forced an 11 per cent departmental royalty on oil production out of (MNR-controlled) La Paz, Santa Cruz had been relatively

39 Caterina Pizzigoni, *Testaments of Toluca* (Stanford: Stanford University Press, 2007), p. 3.

40 'Forgetting the Revolution and Remembering the War', pp. 8, 10.

41 'El reto del respeto recíproco: *jaqi wakini uñjitata*, implica aceptar, en la lógica del parentesco, junto al monteismo el animismo; junto al individualismo el comunalismo; junto al intercambio la reciprocidad; junto al derecho positivo el derecho consuetudinario; junto a la propiedad privada la propiedad pública y la propiedad comunitaria y, a saber, en su complementaridad mutual', *De la Revolución al Pachakuti: el aprendizaje de respeto recíproco entre blancos e indianos* (La Paz: Garza Azul, 2008).

42 'Regionalism Revisited', in John Crabtree and Laurence Whitehead (eds.), *Unresolved Tensions: Bolivia Past and Present* (Pittsburgh: University of Pittsburgh Press, 2008), pp. 65–82, see p. 76.

quiescent over autonomy, especially under the dictatorship (1971–8) of Hugo Banzer (a *cruceño*), when the extensive foreign loans to the private sector were underwritten by the central state.

As Roca argues, since independence the *de facto* balance of power had quite favoured the departments, simply by virtue of the institutional weakness and impossible geography of a republic that was truly an imagined/invented community. Even today Bolivia — the size of France, Spain and Germany combined — possesses a mere 110 border posts, each with an average garrison of three police officers.[43]

Moreover, as has been persuasively shown by Rossana Barragán, Santa Cruz had benefited especially from transfers and subsidies from central government for nearly a century before it gained the oil royalty. The decision after oil nationalisation in 1937 to treat hydrocarbons differently to minerals (for which all fiscal receipts were deemed 'national' and remitted exclusively to the treasury) greatly favoured the region, which was receiving two-thirds of all oil taxes on the eve of the 1952 Revolution.[44]

Today, with natural gas the strategic commodity, it is Tarija that stands to benefit most, but Santa Cruz continues to lead the political charge and can call upon an intermittent but robust rhetorical tradition descending from the Federal Revolution of 1876.

As with Sucre's demand for full capital status, one can readily spot deep socio-cultural resentment with the MAS programme masquerading beneath the pieties of provincial identity politics and, in the case of Sucre, collapsed dignity. Here is a real power issue as well as a constitutional impasse, and both have been exacerbated by the fact that the MAS fell aggressively upon the semi-occluded sectional interests when it was itself all set to concede the sense and propriety of decentralisation. Perhaps that willingness to be goaded has been its single greatest miscalculation since taking office (although it was one shared by the 2003–5 administration of Carlos Mesa, who is today loathed by *Cambas* even more than Evo Morales is because of his disdain for the distempered vulgarities of the provincial *caudillos*, caballing Croats, and outright chancers who head up what passes for an oligarchy in Santa Cruz).

Juan Ramón Quintana, the minister of the presidency, is surely right when he says that this group has 'no project at all' for national development. Every

<hr />

43 *Council on Hemispheric Affairs*, 18 Oct. 2006. This weakness is not merely 'outward-looking'. When the MAS government was preparing the 'Juancito Pinto' programme whereby each of 1.2 million children who attend school received Bs.200, the ministry discovered 90 'phantom schools', prompting Morales to declare, 'We've really got to know how many schools we have in the country', *Bolivia Information Bulletin*, March 2007.

44 Rossana Barragán and José Luis Roca, *Regiones y poder constituyente en Bolivia. Una historia de pactos y disputas* (La Paz: 2005).

time it ups the ante and lets loose the thugs of the *Unión Juvenil Cruceña* on the (substantial) population of Andean migrants in the city and its environs, it conspicuously lacks an end-game, exhibits no sense of strategy or even any serviceable short-term proposition beyond those proffered by the inevitable string of mediators (increasingly drawn from abroad — were it not for Lula's working knowledge of the behavioural tics of this species in its Brazilian setting, things would be a great deal worse).

Nonetheless, the political arrivistes of Santa Cruz are still only the effect of a deeper problem. This was lucidly outlined 35 years ago by the geographer Valerie Fifer:

> In seeking political separation in 1825 from *both* Peru and Argentina,
> Bolivia was obliged by the application of the principle of *uti possidetis de
> jure 1810* to accept a singularly inappropriate distribution of territory
> — one whose frontiers, though ill-defined, reflected patterns of internal
> administrative convenience rather than those which would be required for
> successful participation in overseas trade.[45]

Roca perceives the problem to possess even deeper roots:

> The strong personality of Bolivia's regions is derived from the fact that it
> is the only country in Latin America where the political/administrative
> structure designed by the Bourbon kings in the 18th century remains
> intact. The republic was organised on the model announced in 1782 in the
> Ordinance on Intendancies of the Viceroyalty of Rio de la Plata.[46]

Such an effort to sustain — even enforce — territorial continuity has itself produced attempted ruptures (the 1876 and 1891 federal revolts in Santa Cruz; the Federal War of 1898–9 between Sucre and La Paz, which battled against a southern centralism and, upon victory, imposed a northern variant of the same, not the promised decentralisation). It has also, however, engendered a thoroughly unproductive flip-flopping pattern, whereby, on the one hand, no national treasury existed before 1872 and, on the other, no town mayor was elected between 1938 and 1983 and no departmental prefect between 1825 and 2006.[47]

---

45 *Bolivia: Land, Location and Politics* (Cambridge: Cambridge University Press, 1972), p. 3.

46 'Regionalism Revisited', p. 70. Roca's magisterial account of this process in the 19th century is given in *Ni con Lima ni con Buenos Aires. La formación de un estado nacional en Charcas* (La Paz: Plural, 2007).

47 Roca, 'Regionalism Revisited', p. 75, and Rossana Barragán, 'Oppressed or Privileged Regions? Some Historical Reflections on the Use of State Resources', in John Crabtree and Laurence Whitehead (eds.), *Unresolved Tensions: Bolivia Past and Present* (Pittsburgh: University of Pittsburgh Press, 2008), pp. 83–103, see pp. 90, 102.

Perhaps, given the almost entirely post-colonial duration of the problem, it is no great surprise that it was from Spain — albeit the democratic member of the EU that had in 2004 supplanted Castilian hegemony with some fine constitutional fudges in favour of elective regionalism — that the departments of Bolivia derived their decentralist inspiration.

24 May 2008
Racist humiliation and violence in Sucre

A crowd comprised mostly of youths — many of them by no means 'white' — detain and beat a group of *campesinos* who had come to Sucre to support the (now cancelled) visit of Evo Morales. Abused as '*indios*', the captured men are forced to their knees and made to watch their ponchos being burnt in a ritual form. Perhaps it is because of the immediacy of images taken on mobile phones, maybe it is because one had — amidst all that talk of multiculturalism — forgotten the depth and power of racist sentiment, but the scene is unusually shocking. As a European, I find myself thinking of not dissimilar images of Bosnian Moslems held by Serbian forces and I wonder whether we might in months to come be talking of Chuquisaca in the same fashion as Srebrenica.

Even the army high command is outraged by the city authorities, who seem actively to have planned this event, because they force the (unarmed and largely indigenous) conscripts to march under the departmental flag of Chuquisaca. This seems like an enforced rolling back not just of 2005, or even of 1952, but of the liberal post-colonialism that in 1899 saw the transfer of Bolivia's government from Sucre, the 'white city', to La Paz, still organised along sharply hierarchical ethnic lines but also more dependent upon inter-racial cohabitation. Not for nothing that Xavier Albó reminds us of the primacy of ethnicity:

> This ... is the oldest and most enduring conditioning factor affecting both politics and social forces in Bolivia. Neither biological *mestizaje* during the colonial period nor the subsequent period of cultural *mestizaje*, which after 1952 became the ideological backdrop of Bolivian national identity, has managed to replace it — as the re-emergence of ethnic politics from the 1960s makes plain.[48]

Juan Ramón Quintana, a historian and an ex-army officer as well as a minister, tells me that an indigenous *cerco* in response to such provocations is Evo's worst nightmare. He's not at all sure that the authority of the presidency will be able to halt escalation into outright physical conflict. I am reminded of the response

---

48 'The "Long Memory" of Ethnicity in Bolivia and some Temporary Oscillations', in John Crabtree and Laurence Whitehead (eds.), *Unresolved Tensions: Bolivia Past and Present* (Pittsburgh: University of Pittsburgh Press, 2008), pp. 13–34, see p. 30.

of the radical Achacachi leader Felipe Quispe, 'El Mallku', to the journalist Amalia Pando when she asked him why he had taken up guerrilla warfare in the 1980s, 'So that my daughter would not become your servant'. There's a lot at stake here.

It's 150 years almost to the day since the Lincoln-Douglas debates opened in Illinois, but in Sucre it seems that Douglas would still find ready audience:

> I am opposed to negro citizenship in any and every form ... I am in favor
> of confining citizenship to white men, men of European birth and descent,
> instead of conferring it upon negroes, Indians, and other inferior races.

9 June 2008
Crowds besiege the US embassy demanding the extradition of Gonzalo Sánchez de Lozada

A real sense of crisis in the acceleration of public clashes, the quickening of longstanding demands, and the consequences at stake. The ex-President — still called 'Goni' but much less often than before and scarcely ever with any affection, even by his erstwhile allies — is charged with 'genocide' for the three-score deaths in the repression of October 2003. He is now in the USA, where he grew up, and Washington shows absolutely no sign of allowing the request made by La Paz, despite the strong *prima facie* case for direct responsibility for the killings. One thinks of comparisons — not least, Colonel Luis Arce Gómez, the minister of the interior in the dictatorship of 1980–1, whose many victims numbered fewer than in October 2003 and yet who was readily extradited to the USA because of the cocaine connection.

October 2003 forms part of a sad calendar of massacres, executions and infamous killings that litter Bolivian history and may now be added to. But what is so strange in this case is, less Sánchez's status as a civilian (most of the authors down the ages have been soldiers even when they are on the left), but his prior commitment to a formally inclusionary politics. Indeed, whatever anybody may say after the start of his second term in 2002, before that his political profile at home and in the region was precisely that of a populist neoliberal and architect of the 1994 *Ley de Participación Popular* (LPP).

That is surely important. Even under the present moral weight of the campaign for justice, can we really accept that every social ill is to be ascribed to a catch-all, homogenised, uniformly anti-popular 'entity' known as neo-liberalism? The issue is more complicated than that. The debates on indigenous involvement in colonial and early-republican markets (not to mention those since the return of democratic government), the symbolic importance of 'money' from the 16th century onwards, and the whole gamut of themes raised by Filemón Escobar as being open to reciprocity, all show a much more complex, interactive dynamic.

In the early 1840s the programme of (largely plebeian) British Chartism overlapped significantly with that of the (predominantly bourgeois) Anti-Corn Law League. The claim that free trade means lower prices for the poor is not always untrue; nor even when it is untrue, is it always an intended lie. John Coatsworth has helped us to rethink old certainties in this regard. Perhaps, along with Argentina and Brazil, Bolivia is the country where there has been greatest support for currency stabilisation, precisely because of the dreadful experience of hyper-inflation in the early 1980s, when the poor were subjected to the withering tax levied by ever-escalating prices. And yet nobody was more closely associated with halting that inflation than Gonzalo Sánchez de Lozada. If 'neoliberalism' is some kind of ideology underpinned by practical policy instruments, then currency stabilisation would, in my view, be the least unpopular of those instruments, even when, as Xavier Albó says of Decree 21060, it closed down in a single day (29 August 1985) an entire politico-economic paradigm — the state-centred system of 1952.[49]

What people often forget about '1952' is '1956', when, in the first IMF programme for the western hemisphere, a good deal of unpalatable conditionality (including the full restoration of the military) was effectively made digestible to ordinary folk by the taming of inflation. The miners struck and parts of the MNR threatened open revolt, but the deal stuck and the government settled in. Likewise in 1985–6, when severe deflation was made even worse by the closure of the tin industry, a series of trade union mobilisations gained sympathy but no politically decisive support from the wider population. The government once more settled in, together with a paradigm that would go challenged but intact for 20 years.

In both 1956 and 1985 'shock treatment' was unpopular but tolerated. In both cases, however, no serious follow-through with further free-market and investment-friendly policies was possible without risk to the entire compact on price stabilisation. The moral economy of a mixed subsistence-mercantile system with a scattering of industrial enclaves can only take so much unilateral intervention.

To be honest, I'm not sure how fully it was thought through or how much it simply derived from some sort of 'hegemonic instinct', but I am convinced that Sánchez de Lozada's second strategic move, in 1993–7, sought to test the limits of economic tolerance amongst the Bolivian poor. According to Olivia Harris,

> ... the commonplace idea that Andean peasants were and are resistant
> to participation in commercial circuits cannot be sustained ... [their
> resistance is] not to markets as such. Rather, it has been to certain forms

49 Ibid., p. 25.

of coercion by which they were forced to hand over their surplus, to offer their labor and produce at disadvantageous or unjust rates, or to sell or give up land vital for the reproduction of their agriculture.[50]

We can see this directly in the abortive effort to impose Bolívar's Trujillo decrees 'privatising' land at the birth of the republic, in the successful resistance to Melgarejo's assaults on the communities of the northern *Altiplano* during the 1860s, in the need for the creole elite to suspend the more organised liberal campaign against collective property enshrined in the *Ley de Ex-vinculación* of 1874, and in the serious qualifications to that statute when it was finally operationalised a decade later. We can also see it, with direct regard to land, in the 1996 agrarian reform law (*Ley INRA*), when the Sánchez de Lozada team sought energetically to give primacy to the *ayllu* (whereas the 1953 agrarian reform only recognised rural '*sindicatos*').

But how do we deal with the wider political economy, state property and public goods up for grabs in the 1990s? Here, I think, lies the crux of the matter — land was not the *prima facie* issue, but a land-linked moral economy had come to prevail over simple market calculus. Bolivia remains exceptionally poor and exceptionally unequal — according to the UN Development Programme, in 2003 its Gini coefficient was 60.1, the worst in the western hemisphere by a country mile — millions of people earn very little indeed and own even less property. That is why such great importance is ascribed not just to the fact but also to the symbolic universe of collective ownership. This is the authentic 'imagined community' in Bolivia; this is why — cut the tax-take, royalties, franchises, contracts and buy-backs any way you like — nationalisation is such a trump card. And so, of course, it is why privatisation is the Achilles heel of neo-liberalism as well as of liberalism in that country.

Sánchez de Lozada certainly knew that much. In 1994 his team implemented a public policy package, the *Plan de Todos*, that sought simultaneously to alleviate the most extreme poverty, to fund an unprecedented pensions programme, and to sell off 'only' half the stock of the leading state corporations in a mixed enterprise — some would say a scam; many might now think of it as a derivative before its day — called 'capitalisation'. As in 1985, it was denounced by elite as well as popular sectors, but it was not broadly understood and so sales (and even some payments) advanced, initially without great opposition.

However, that delayed response — a delay that would close with the 'Water War' of January 2000 — owed much to the 'ancillary' policy of the *Ley de Participación Popular*, also introduced in 1994 by Goni, whose economic liberalism was unembarrassed by deep social prejudice and who had enticed the Aymara intellectual leader Víctor Hugo Cárdenas to serve as his Vice-President.

---

50 Larson and Harris (eds.), *Ethnicity, Markets, and Migration in the Andes*, p. 352.

The LPP was, in fact, the vital element, the catalyst that helped to unlock, first, popular caution over macro-economic adventure and, secondly, the 'catastrophic stalemate' over regionalism. Initially, the LPP seemed a safe circumvention of both dangers since, in a breathtaking innovation, it re-routed the bulk of public sector spending from the treasury to 311 municipalities, each now provided with a (sometimes sizeable) budget, a democratic decision-making structure and provisions for oversight. Hitherto, the only true comparisons in terms of governance were the Toledan reforms of the 1570s, those of the Bourbons in the 1770s and 1780s, the Constitution of 1826, and the 1953–6 package of agrarian reform and universal suffrage.

In saying this, I am taking a distinctly minority position, and it is one uncomfortably close to the claims made at the time by the Sánchez de Lozada administration. However, I think the radicalism lay in the consequences, not in the intent. Most commentators have, quite understandably, taken the line that the LPP may have been chronologically new but it was not substantively radical. For Zizek, of course, multiculturalism is merely the cultural logic of multinational capitalism; and Charlie Hale has made a strong case for its elite co-optation and general political 'defusing' in Guatemala.[51] In the case of Bolivia, Nancy Postero, who has studied the experience of Santa Cruz particularly closely, argues that the LPP did permit indigenous self-organisation, but only in 'authorised' ways 'that reflect the logic of neoliberalism — transparency, efficiency, and rational participation'.[52]

All well and good, as is the quite common observation that the NGOs went overboard with a policy that was both locally popular and right up their ideational and ethical street. But, of course, 'transparency, efficiency and rational participation' are not by any means exclusively 'neoliberal' qualities, nor indeed have they consistently formed part of its repertoire. The LPP was not a cast-iron prospectus for tidy demobilisation or safe co-optation; it opened up dangerous cross-over territory. It gave people enough taste for, and enough experience of, self-management, public debate and home-based confidence in a wider world to counter any constrictive top-down qualities to which its designers may have aspired and which its detractors have identified (sometimes by ideological default, sometimes through serious real-time observation).

The LPP also contributed to the destruction of *Capitalización* by catalysing older cultural and political currents. Sánchez de Lozada may have thought that he could pull off the 'Toledan trick' of taking with one hand (tribute, the *mita*)

51   Charles Hale, 'Does Multiculturalism Menace? Governance, Cultural Rights and the Politics of Identity in Guatemala', *Journal of Latin American Studies* 34:3 (Aug. 2002), pp. 485–524.

52   For a fuller and fairer account than my drastic synopsis here can provide, see *Now we are citizens: indigenous politics in postmulticultural Bolivia* (Stanford: Stanford University Press, 2007).

and giving with the other (self-management through the *república de indios*), but his sequencing, which had started so well, came horribly unstuck. And once he had effectively placed himself in the role of Melgarejo by 'selling' water and gas, then, *almost* inevitably — I'm hardly well-placed to adopt 'logics' in the present discussion — so too did he become the author of massacres.

One may, then, talk of the 'Wars', of Evo's election, and of all that has followed as some form of 'backlash', but one probably ought not to. Why not? Because it wasn't a pre-ordained reflex, it wasn't a purely dichotomised or unilateral phenomenon and — at least until the killings of October 2003 — it wasn't a simple case of popular objection and outrage at a single travesty. 'Backlash' organicises and moralises a complex process that assuredly ended up as one of organic morality and may well be defended politically in those terms, but is not best understood in that language.

Sian Lazar has shown for El Alto that the sentiment against privatisation had built up over several years and derived from a number of local campaigns founded on essentially post-1952 corporate social groupings, like neighbourhood associations and street vendors' guilds.[53] The crowd on the street is almost invariably angry and vulnerable but, as Charles Tilly showed, it reaches its final encounter with the tanks (or the cavalry) through a variety of routes. On 10 April 1848 Feargus O'Connor avoided a mass effusion of Chartist blood on the banks of the Thames because that most ardent of speechifiers possessed a calm distrust of destiny. On 15 October 2003 the chirpy cosmopolitan Gonzalo Sánchez de Lozada ran out of patience with a game of cat-and-mouse he had been playing with the locals for nigh-on two decades. Many died as a consequence, but it is entirely possible that still more lives would have been lost since had that occurrence not brought Bolivians to a dreadful sense of the risks at hand.

11 September 2008
Massacre in Pando

Clearly, I was too sanguine. Today is the 35th anniversary of Pinochet's coup in Chile against the *Unidad Popular* headed by Salvador Allende (an anniversary that has been dwarfed in international memory by 9/11, but which retains a considerable salience within Latin America). The news states that dozens of pro-MAS marchers have been shot down by vigilantes under the orders of the prefect. Both sides seem to have had guns; many of those who died appear to have been chased into a river. I am hearing some dark rumours about the

---

53 Sian Lazar, *El Alto, rebel city: self and citizenship in Andean Bolivia* (Durham NC: Duke University Press, 2008).

role of minister Quintana as an agent provocateur — that sounds like the 'disinformation' so prevalent in the dark days of the early 1970s.

All this is surely connected with yesterday's declaration of US Ambassador Goldberg as persona non grata? Something serious seems to be happening behind the scenes. Rubén Costas, the prefect of Santa Cruz who has called the President 'murderous ... a true criminal' and who is now all but in open revolt, was visited by four US Congressmen in mid-August and then by Goldberg himself at the end of the month, during the departmental strike to enforce its autonomy.

If Goldberg 'miscalculated' in making that visit, then he really ought to be fired for such crassly public ineptitude. As so often with his predecessors, he slipped sedulously into a pro-consular role, which is pretty easy in Bolivia, where policy is so often made on the hoof. Conspiracy theories always abound, but the potential for cock-up is also substantial and I'm initially inclined to see this as a 'mishap' resulting from hubris. Diplomats find it difficult here at the best of times, and it is doubly hard for them to get their heads around the fact that Evo Morales is such an inveterate traveller, whilst Foreign Minister Choquehuanca seems to take an interest in his job on few occasions only.

On the other hand, Tom Shannon, the extremely savvy and cool-tempered head of Latin America at the State Department, was in La Paz in late July, so we should not rule out a change in policy. Of course, in a US election year — and especially this one — one cannot talk of 'settled policy'; nor can they sensibly be thinking of a re-run of the abortive coup attempt in Venezuela in April 2002.

Evo has done generally well 'internationalising' the refoundation of Bolivia. He surely is the best known Bolivian ever, other than Bolívar himself? That is a signal achievement. But he's not sure-footed tactically and has a short fuse. Normally, I would think it wise for him to follow the advice of that great stoic Billy Joel — 'Never get in a pissing war with people who order ink by the barrel' — yet it's particularly hard to see how he could have avoided this particular fight. Once signals like Goldberg's start emanating from Washington, the ultras of the *Media Luna* will feel fully free to behave as they have done in Pando.

When have Bolivia's relations with the USA been so poor? Possibly in 1944–6, when the Villarroel government was backed by the MNR and in alliance with the Argentine military lodge to which Perón belonged. That ended very badly indeed, with a State Department publication itemising the regime's crimes (certainly a couple of especially serious ones) and ideological misdemeanours (many more than you could shake a stick at) being followed within weeks by a revolt and the lynching of Villarroel in the Plaza Murillo.

Of course, Evo has a particular problem because, by virtue of being a representative of the *cocaleros*, he has long been at the heart of Washington's prime policy concern with this country — narcotics. If ever a commodity had a 'cycle' (and here the term *Pachakuti* would serve quite well) and was over-politicised, then it's cocaine from the 1980s onwards. (Although as Paul Gootenberg shows, there is far longer history, replete with Mafiosi marginalia as well as the US Feds' absorbing attention to the bustling underworld of chemistry).[54]

The expulsion of a foreign ambassador from Bolivia is an extraordinary sight. The only precedents I can instantly think of are the German minister, given his marching orders in 1942 (as the result of an adroit MI6 sting in what has become known as the 'Belmonte Letter'), and the British envoy, summarily dismissed by President Belzu in 1854 (possibly under the anti-British influence of General Francisco Burdett O'Connor, Bolívar's Chief of Staff and Feargus' older brother).[55]

After 1952 the MNR wisely took the adroit lead of Pepe Figueres in Costa Rica rather than that offered by Perón (whose famous 1946 run-in with Spruille Braden had preceded Washington's campaign against Villarroel): they almost always sucked up to the US. It is hard to imagine that this wasn't the result of the hard-earned lesson of the 1940s, and it may have given them the edge over Arbenz and the Guatemalan reformists, or was that difference more to do with logistical distance, the sharpness of corporate interests and the visibility of the deterrent effect in Central America?

Thereafter, Washington never had a major problem with Bolivia. (Or if it did, it was with over-enthusiastic and unreliable allies, like René Barrientos.) Until, that is, the right-wing generals got into the cocaine trade and thought that they could run a regime on the proceeds while parroting anti-communist rhetoric to keep the *gringos* off their case. But even the Cold War had its limits. Reagan quickly cut them out; they couldn't help him in Central America, killed people in the open — Bolivia has a modest history of 'disappearances' by the sad standards of the Southern Cone — and could readily be expended in the name of right-thinking even-handedness.

Most Bolivian cocaine now comes to Europe. Moreover, Morales has robustly upheld the standard — of the post-dictatorial Presidents, only Banzer dissented — Bolivian distinction between the traditionally cultivated and

54 *Andean Cocaine: the making of a global drug* (Chapel Hill: University of North Carolina Press, 2009).

55 The 1854 expulsion gave rise to the enjoyable legend that Queen Victoria imperiously ordered Bolivia to be erased from her globe when informed that no gunboat could deliver the requisite penalty through cannonade (which, of course, it could easily have done since Bolivia then did have a coastline — and even some maritime settlements — and British warships were happily undertaking target practice on the Nicaraguan/Miskito shore in the 1850s).

consumed coca leaf and the chemically-processed drug of cocaine. This is a tricky area because it's downright disingenuous to pretend that all permitted coca production goes to chewing or that any 'excess' is successfully withheld by the state from *narcotráfico*. On the other hand, US policy has been single-mindedly focused on eradication and interdiction, abetted by a public theatre of conditionality (aid and tariff suspensions in exchange for compliance in meeting eradication targets) that seems as much designed to humiliate La Paz as to stoke up righteousness on Capitol Hill.[56]

The short story is that Evo has played hardball quite well. He has made eradication a domestic matter, with targets negotiated between the government and the *cocaleros*. He has delivered on interdiction, with seizures rising, albeit in the wake of increased production of leaf (and some, at least, of cocaine). He has held the army in line even as he has been quite rude about the American government in public.

This sounds quite like Chávez. But it is so only in a shallow sense. The big difference between the Presidents is that Morales is the direct political product — some would even say the creature — of the coca-growers. The political capital of the MAS government depends crucially upon that alliance, which has become a core emblem of the wider cultural chasm over economic comportment and power. Evo may enjoy the rudeness for its own sake, but in these exchanges he is tracing the external lineaments of an emphatically *moral* economy. No other issue has drawn Washington — quite heedlessly it would seem, although Sánchez de Lozada told them repeatedly to leave well alone — so deeply into the historic Bolivian mire.

How much easier it would have been — as with silver, rubber, tin, oil, gas — if it were only the external price that was at stake, rather than physical power over land and its produce. Somebody in the State Department should read *Ethnicity, Markets, and Migration* before they draft the next strategic position-paper.

In 1826 Simón Bolívar identified the US (which he called the Republic of the North) and Brazil as natural outliers to — and potential enemies of — the great Spanish American Confederation that he dreamed of. Now, though, Bolivia, which was born in repudiation of Peru and Argentina and still has to settle accounts with Chile for the loss of the sea, seems strongly drawn to an alliance with Brazil. There have been phases of anti-imperialist/anti-American sentiment in Latin America before — the 1850s, 1890s, the 1920s, even the 1950s — but they provided no enduring basis of political development. Why

---

56   Maybe it is the sheer asymmetry that makes US policy so rigid and unresponsive? After all, Washington was equally unbending over the price it paid for Bolivian tin in the late 1940s and early 1950s, seemingly oblivious of the political cost.

should the recent experience offer an exception? There are reasons, but they need to be subjected to a sceptical eye.

Today, the USA is Bolivia's second-largest export market, but one-third of those exports are subject to drug-related conditionality (ATPDEA). Bolivia never had that much to do with Brazil before gas — it lost a short-lived 'Rubber War' in the 1890s, but that had nothing to do with popular economics and everything to do with robber barons. Now it sells Brasilia 28 million cubic meters of natural gas a day, which makes it the country's largest trade. People have been calling Brazil the 'country of the future' for decades but, notwithstanding the fact that it would turn Bolivia's traditional matrices upside-down, that's surely what it now represents for the Andean republic.

8 October 2008
Bond and Che

So far as I know, with the release of the latest James Bond, *Quantum of Solace*, and *Che, Part Two*, Bolivia has been featured in mainstream movies for the first time since *Butch Cassidy and the Sundance Kid* (George Roy Hill, 1969) and so is represented at both ends of the cultural spectrum from blockbuster to art-house cinema. Of course, the broadsheet press, still smarting (like the rest of us) from George Soros' Quantum Fund, has been sniffy about the Bond (although there has been a little extra interest *de haut en bas* with the arrival of the severely enigmatic Daniel Craig as the latest 007).

However, it is in the cultural pages of *La Razón* that I learn — from Fernando Mayorga of all people — that there has been a radical discontinuity in that this is the first in an evergreen series where the MI6 operative fails to self-identify discursively as 'Bond, James Bond'.[57] Can't say I noticed amidst all the hullabaloo caused by shooting in Panama the scenes set in Haiti and in Antofagasta (Bolivia up to 1879, after the War of the Pacific part of Chile) those purporting to be Bolivia. The Chilean locals seem to have been most exercised by the notion of getting paid to be Bolivians (the world turned upside down indeed). But Hollywood logistics have rarely been trumped by high-mindedness. Besides, it seems to me that the theme of dastardly resource robbery — in this telling case, that of water — abetted by corruption with a background of unresolved military repression is pretty progressive for any Bond pic. Perhaps the production team knew their way around recent Bolivian political history rather better than most? Poor Gemma Arterton — whose immortal line, 'We're teachers on sabbatical and need a room for the night', deserves an, er, Academy Award of some sort — expires through the nastiest of carbon imprints: a total coating of bitumen, in a low-grade echo of the

57   Mayorga outed himself as a fan in *La Razón*, 29 Nov. 2008.

auriferous assassination in *Goldfinger*. At the end there are more big bangs than I recall as normal and there is even a suspicion that the exploited masses are on the march to provide a social seal to the dramatic denouement.

Quite the reverse, in fact, to the ending of *Che*, where it is precisely the caution and distrust — rarely outright fear — of the rural poor that catalyse the CIA's strategy and enable the Bolivian troops to run Guevara to ground with relative ease. Most of the critics rate both parts highly — the first, which opened in the UK on the 50th anniversary of the fall of Batista, covers the Cuban campaign from the arrival of the *Granma* until the capture of Havana, but reaches its apogee in the battle for Santa Clara commanded by Che. Equally, there has been as much praise for the performance of Benicio del Toro (who made his movie debut in *Licence to Kill*) as for Soderbergh's direction — which is particularly assured, given his relative lack of experience in action films.

Both parts are, in fact, war films, with far more politics than is usual — the docu-drama scenes at the UN are remarkable — but without the depth of characterisation in, say, *Saving Private Ryan*. Maybe there were simply too many beards as well as too much shooting? Perhaps both lead and director were well advised to avoid 'understanding' Che because he's already been analysed up hill and down dale but little depicted as a soldier? Colin Robinson, who first published the English edition of the *Motorcycle Diaries*, tells me that after the test showing of *Part One* in Manhattan Soderbergh cut the scene where Guevara delivers the coup de grâce after the execution of two errant guerrillas because he no longer felt it necessary to protect himself against charges of excessive sympathy for his subject.

There's also the problem of the comparison with Gael García Bernal's idealist proto-icon in *Motorcycle Diaries*. That raised the optimism of the will. Here, time and time again in *Part Two*, it's the pessimism of the intelligence (literally and metaphorically). In Cuba Castro had demoted Guevara from a command after an operational failure before he won acclaim at Santa Clara; here the price is much higher. Perhaps we forget — we may even forgive — the poor record of generalship when it is set against the radicalism of the ideas, the personal courage and charisma and the extraordinary impact of a sacrifice at once modern and ancient (not for nothing the continued allusions to Jesus Christ)?

5 November 2008
Barack Obama wins the election

The election because it is so manifestly a world event. Already, a day later, the amount of commentary is exceeded only by the pictorial coverage. All this has evidently required the felling of entire forests, but we're not hearing much from the usual Cassandras and Jeremiahs, perhaps because the prolonged campaign(s) have exhausted their stocks of bromide. However, I see that out there on the West Coast Judith Butler is doing a pretty good imitation of Cotton Mather, issuing instruction as to imminent political disappointment. I know that it's an inside job and involves no heavy lifting, but it must be mighty hard being a deconstructionist. The rest of the world is going to enjoy its wish-fulfilment for as long as it can — certainly until 20 January. Get real, Judith — enjoy the dreaming.

Obama has signalled next to nothing on Latin America, beyond a speech on Cuba in May, when he referred to the Bush policy as a 'humanitarian and strategic blunder', promising to review trade and travel restrictions. He's also identified the formidable legal activist Cecilia Muñoz, born in Michigan of parents from La Paz, as director of inter-governmental affairs in the White House. That might help a little bit. But the inertial forces will be formidable, all hopes will indeed have to be tempered and real energy will have to be invested in *working intelligently* to make 'the change' practical beyond the borders of the USA.

Bolivia is not well placed to do this. The professional diplomatic corps is only a few dozen strong, its cosmopolitan elite deeply suspicious of the government in La Paz (and now probably of the one about to be inaugurated in Washington), and the intellectuals around the MAS possessed of a distinctly mixed skills-set. I like and admire Gustavo Guzmán, the brave crusading journalist who has just been expelled as ambassador in DC in response to the Goldberg affair, but I really don't think it's clever to have heads of mission who can't speak the local language. Chávez can do his naughty boy thing, for the most part because Venezuela has a real state apparatus to mop up after him. Evo has to borrow helicopters to get around his own country… . It's time to think big and act small at the same time.

22 December 2008
La Reina Hispanoamericana 2008 is arrested in Jalisco

That's 23 year-old Laura Elena Zuniga, Miss Sinaloa, who has just been duly dethroned from the presumably greater title (above) by Promociones Gloria of Santa Cruz. Laura was detained with her boyfriend, Angel Orlando García, a boss in the Juárez Cartel, together with six bodyguards in two trucks, which also contained two rifles, three pistols, 633 rounds of ammunition, 16 cell-phones and $53,000 in cash. Over a dozen Mexican lawyers have already offered their services on a *pro bono* basis. Looks like Laura might need them since, when detained, she was asked where she was off to in such style, and replied, 'to Colombia and Bolivia, shopping…'.[58] Since when was Bolivia an

---

58 *La Razón*, 27 Dec. 2008; *The Observer*, 28 Dec. 2008.

international shopping centre, except for you-know-what? Not even for striped jumpers… But hold up. Perhaps Laura has a deeper historical consciousness than you might expect from an alleged *narcotraficante* moll? Four hundred years ago, anybody in their right acquisitive mind would have been heading off to Potosí, the largest and richest city in the western hemisphere.

Alma Guillermoprieto obviously enjoyed the mineral metaphor when, in her NYRB piece on Evo, she declared that Potosí's silver 'made the Spanish Golden Age possible'.[59] Guamán Poma, writing when the Hill/Mountain was at its zenith, properly projected its precious output in terms of global power:

> Potosí. By the said mine Castile exists. Rome is Rome, the pope is
> pope, and the King is the monarch of the world. Holy mother church is
> defended, and our holy faith guarded by the four kings of the Indies and
> by the Inca Emperor. Now the power is with the pope of Rome and our
> lord King don Phelipe the third.[60]

According to Herb Klein, who has spent a lot of time on the sums, in the first 90 years of its exploitation, between 1550 and 1640, Potosí produced 5 million marks (230 grams each) of silver. That is 500,000 more marks than the mine yielded over the entire rest of the colony, from 1650 through to 1810.[61]

And, of course, it also powered up the imagination. In *Don Quixote*, published in 1615, Cervantes makes one reference to the regular contemporary saying, '*vale un Potosí*', simply to express wondrous wealth, but in a later chapter he depicts the flight of a unicorn between Paris and Potosí taking place in a wink of an eye … a space-time journey between the two magical citadels of the world.

When Evo Morales came to office, Potosí was the poorest department in Bolivia, itself the poorest country in South America. How are the mighty fallen. But the process did take several centuries and the mint that converted all that metal into money is beautifully preserved. This is now a venerable UNESCO world cultural site. It's all done and dusted. If you are prepared to countenance the existence of economic cycles, they should surely be long-term and slow-burning.

But let's look at Iceland — why not practise a little 'most dissimilar systems' theorising? In 2005 the *Human Development Index* put Iceland at number 1 in the world. It was the kind of place that fuelled neo-liberal dreams — a perfect offshore, white settler, social democratic laboratory for hyper-capitalist experimentation. The complete antithesis to that Andean land of indigenous tradition and truculent refusal of progress.

---

59 *New York Review of Books*, 10 Aug. 2006.

60 *Nueva Corónica*, p. 1057, quoted in MacCormack, *On the Wings of Time*, p. 233.

61 *A Concise History of Bolivia* (New York: Cambridge University Press, 2003), pp. 271–2.

When, the other day, all the phantom money that the entrepreneurs of Reykjavik had conjured up disappeared in a Surtsey-like eruption, the good Icelanders, who mostly seemed to have gone along with the script, staged a proper riot — their first since 1949.

Now, Bolivia is richer than Iceland. It's probably not cheaper and is still rather more boisterous. But you can still go shopping there. In fact, the French and Russians are fixing to do just that. They want to buy lithium, which is being widely touted as 'the mineral of the future' because it is the core ingredient in the batteries that power the electric vehicles which the world will need to deal with global warming and the depletion in fossil fuels. So, Potosí is all set to make a comeback on the world-stage because half of the world's reserves of lithium are located at the department's Salar de Uyuni.

In an era of marauding mercantile magic, we may well want to check those figures, as they say in the trade, against delivery. Moreover, Bolivia, like its antecedent societies of Alto Perú, Charcas and Kollasuyo, is scarcely unaware of the dark fates that accompany great fortune. This time, Evo is determined, the riches of the land will benefit those who live and work on it before anybody else. We shall see. But it does rather look like 'back to the future'.

7 April 2009
José Luis Roca dies

I am back in 'real time'. The talk to the New York Latin American History Workshop went OK, I feel, but since they distribute the paper beforehand, I couldn't see the point of simply reading a small segment and so, in my first-ever (and greatly assisted) PowerPoint presentation, I showed some photos to illustrate the events mentioned in the diary. The one that struck the audience most was of *campesinos* from Achacachi beheading dogs used to symbolise the *Comité Cívico* of Chuquisaca in May 2008. There was mention of the use of dead dogs by Sendero Luminoso, but nobody seemed to know if a dead dog had particular connotations in Andean culture.

When I get back to the Butler Library at Columbia I see a message in my email inbox: 'News from my Dad' from Marcela Roca (who was brought up in Britain). I breathe deeply, but it is true — José Luis has succumbed to a cancer. In the diary I have been happily writing about him in the present tense, but now one of Bolivia's most engaging and brilliant historians has himself joined the past. Scenes flash up: José Luis in the Cochabamba clinic breaking all the rules (and exasperating Miriam) almost immediately after his by-pass operation; a picnic in Wye, Kent, with all the Rocas and John and Wendy Lynch; José Luis egging on Alberto Crespo to tell ghost stories; and — perhaps most vividly and poignantly — this mild-mannered and supremely emollient man delivering an incendiary speech before the statue of Bolívar in London's Belgrave Square following the military coup of July 1980, when he was dismissed as ambassador to the UK. That was the first time I met him and we immediately sealed a trans-generational friendship.[62]

I recall my shock when José Luis told me a few days later that the García Meza dictatorship had apparently put out a contract on his life in London. For some reason, I was amazed that such things could happen 'at home'.[63] However, I knew that only seven years before he had narrowly escaped execution by the Chilean military when detained in Santiago after the Pinochet coup. Because he looked and spoke like most non-indigenous people from the *Oriente*, the officer commanding the firing squad, a Major Darín, refused to believe that he was Bolivian and it was only because José Luis knew the matronymic of Darín's one Bolivian friend (the fascist Federico Nielsen Reyes) that he was believed and spared.[64]

Even from New York, I cannot get to the funeral, so I send flowers in the name of all his many friends in England, the country he loved, not least because during his exile there he undertook much of the research underpinning *Ni con Lima ni con Buenos Aires*. Only later do I learn that he died to the sound of Beatles' tunes arranged and sung by his daughters.

9 April 2009
Olivia Harris dies

This time I learn the awful news on the phone. I am sitting in the spring sunshine outside the Columbia Library, running down the clock before going to Newark airport for my flight home. It is Sinclair. 'Olivia has passed away',

---

62   'Demonstrations of solidarity were not slow in appearing; I received letters and phone calls, and outside the embassy people collected to support my position of denouncing the coup as well as remaining in my place of work. Among the friends from that time, I remember James Dunkerley, a young historian and militant of the Labour party who was completing his doctorate at Oxford on Bolivian themes. He formed part of a large group which accompanied me to Belgrave Square to protest, before the statue of Bolívar, at what was happening in the country to which the Liberator had given his name', *Bolivia, después de la capitalización: una crítica al Gonismo y sus 'reformas'* (La Paz: Plural, 2000), p. 52.

63   'One day I was summoned to the Foreign Office, where an official, Mr Duggan, notified me without circumlocutions and with a grave face: 'Mr Roca, we have called you in to let you know that we have information from a reliable source that they could be preparing to kill you, and the possible assassin will come from Canada. It is the policy of Her Majesty's Government to alert all ex-diplomats to dangers of this type, so that they can take the necessary precautions. Unfortunately, we are not able to guarantee your personal safety in the manner that we would wish to', ibid., p. 55.

64   A version of this anecdote appears in the fine obituary by Marcelo Suárez Ramírez in *El Deber*, Santa Cruz, 25 April 2009.

he says straightaway. I don't believe what I have just heard and deliberately ask him to repeat himself. I am in such shock that I don't immediately break into tears but stumble out into Broadway, as if there will be some solace in that noisy thoroughfare. It is only later in the departure lounge, staring out at the New Jersey industrial landscape profiled by the setting sun, that I start to cry. What Marc Augé calls a 'non-place' is in one sense the best place to realise that I shall never see a darling sister again.

Livy was just 60, so full of life, and so rapidly felled by cancer that an extremely wide range of people will be sorely affected (at her funeral in Southwark Cathedral, there was standing room only). I had just heard that she was ill, sending her and Harry a postcard, but thought that I would see them before it arrived. Now, the person who taught me most about *Pachakuti* has completed her own cycle on the planet far, far too early.

I met Olivia the year before José Luis — at another meeting protesting a military coup. In this case, it was the abortive uprising by Colonel Alberto Natusch Busch in November 1979. She was in a group that was demanding the restoration of the liberal democratic civilian government just overthrown, whereas I was accompanying Bob Sutcliffe in representation of the Workers' Socialist League, which demanded immediate and permanent revolution, the institution of workers' and peasant councils, the opening of the books and whatever else was mandated by the Trotskyist orthodoxy of the day. She was incredibly kind as she quietly tutored me on the real calculi being made by people in the Andean countryside, their wise whys and wherefores — all learned in two hard years of participant observation in the north of Potosí.

I recall taking a taxi with Olivia last year to the Bolivian embassy in Eaton Square, where she presented a copy of *Qaraqara-Charka* to Foreign Minister David Choquehuanca. The building had long since been repossessed by democrats, but it was a particularly uplifting experience to witness a piece of protocol conducted in the soft cadences of Aymara.

Like José Luis, Livy died surrounded by the sound of singing voices. Losing two dear friends in two days is a pretty fierce experience, but the knowledge that they departed life enclosed by sonic beauty provides some balm. At the Southwark funeral, they play '*Gracias a la Vida*' by Violeta Parra, older and more tragic than the Beatles but not dissimilar in her great musical gift of expressing the new revolutionary heart of a generation.

5 December 2009
Evo and the MAS win another election

If the electors didn't read the new Constitution at the start of the year — and few really seemed to have had the stamina to engage with the small-print — then today they were faced with the practical consequences of the new charter in one of the most complicated polls held in Bolivia. In order to keep my ailing psephological powers in trim I turn to *Pronto*, the amiable, well-informed and even-handed blog written by Miguel Centellas.

Basically, everybody in the electorate was eligible to vote for the presidency, and Evo won that very handily, even by his own standards, with 64 per cent of the vote against the 28 per cent scored by Manfred Reyes Villa, whose hard-line opposition must have reduced his attractiveness to the substantial minority, disappointed with the government but not inalterably opposed to it. At this point the 170,000 Bolivians living abroad who were voting for the first time had completed their civic duty. However, all urban and most rural voters in the country could also cast a vote for 'uninominal' parliamentarians along the mixed-member system used in Ireland and Germany. Here again, the MAS had a good day, fortifying its majority in the lower house and securing one in the Senate (where the number of representatives has been increased from three to four per department). With a two-thirds 'supermajority' in both houses, the administration could now force through all legislation, but that assumes that the MAS is somehow possessed of iron discipline and entirely at Evo's beck and call. Even with so many new faces in the legislature, the very looseness of the movement strongly suggests a future of factionalism.

Centellas draws our attention to the fact that has been overlooked in press coverage focused on Evo and the MAS — this poll confirms the collapse of a political party system rooted in the 1940s (MNR) and 1970s (ADN, MIR and their derivations). Not one of those traditional forces even campaigned in the election.[65] This is the other 'logical' result of the process of mobilisation since 2000 that might now be said to have acquired a fully institutionalised resolution. Will the scenario be like that in Venezuela, with a prolonged atomisation of liberal opinion over virtually everything bar repudiation of the *caudillo*? It now seems highly unlikely that the prime vehicle of opposition during the first Morales government — localism pursued in the guise of 'autonomy' — will persist, and certainly not at the levels of conflict witnessed in 2008. Because the other great unspoken story of this election was the total volte-face on that issue, voters endorsing the institution of 'departmental autonomy' by substantial majorities (the lowest was 73 per cent in Oruro) in the highland departments, even outstripping the 2005 levels of support in the *Media Luna*, where there was no vote on this issue. José Luis Roca, a *cruceño* Christian Democrat who urged the MAS to embrace autonomy from the start, would be delighted.

Miguel Centellas is surely right to say that this will 'transform Bolivian politics'. But quite how still remains particularly unclear since the combined effect of new Constitution and the LPP is 'co-equal' autonomy at departmental,

65   www.mcentellas.com/archives/2009/12/bolivias-election-a-quick-postmortem.html#more

regional, municipal and now 'indigenous' levels. It is unlikely that the latter innovation will produce the ethnic domination that conservative scaremongers were denouncing — only seven seats in the lower house are reserved for indigenous representatives, and in the 183 'mixed precincts' where the option exists for electing an indigenous representative, the voters have to declare before casting their ballot whether they prefer to elect an indigenous or a uninominal candidate. That this is an institutional dog's dinner is underlined by the fact that there are no indigenous seats reserved for Chuquisaca or Potosí. Still, that is a modest price to pay for the horse-trading over the Constitution at the end of 2008. No doubt we'll see more innovations and the local elections of April 2010 will open that process, even if they are contended on 'bread and butter issues' (which would make a refreshing change).

The haggling over the Constitution was effectively resolved in October 2008 when Evo accepted that he would not be eligible to stand for a third consecutive term. That deal now seems likely to be overtaken by the scale of this victory, but Evo Morales oscillates between hubris and pragmatism, and nobody in or around the MAS looks remotely like a plausible successor.

22 January 2010
Bolivia is officially 'refounded'

The inauguration of the new government is held again at Tiwanaku, but there are changes from the ceremony of 2006. From his populist-spotting eyrie in Madrid, Carlos Malamud makes much of the designation of Evo Morales as *Apu Mallku* ('supreme leader' will do), and rather labours the Inka absolutism line.[66] For others, the consignment of the traditional symbols of the old republic to a vault in the Banco Central and their replacement by a combination of the tricolor and the *wiphala*, together with the promotion of Túpaq Katari and Bartolina Sisa to iconic parity with Bolívar is long overdue and of a piece with the creation of a 'Plurinational State'. The fact that Alvaro García Linera has unpacked his familiar rap on Andean socialism, dismissed the old republic as 'an illusory state', and embraced 'living well' as an alternative to capitalist egotism all seems unremarkable. But if not exactly a Revolution, this is more than merely another elected administration taking office.

9 February 2010
Félix Patzi gets into trouble

That's Félix Patzi the *enragé* intellectual, co-author of *Ya es otro tiempo el presente*, minister of education in the first MAS government, great baiter of the white middle classes, and now an arrested drunk driver (just at the time when

---

66 'Lugares comunes latinoamericanos: el principe de Tiahuanacu', *Ojos de Papel*, 1 Feb. 2010.

the state was launching a major campaign on that issue). Evo has to dump him as official candidate for the governorship of La Paz in the April elections. Together with the government's overtures to Donald Trump over holding the Miss Universe contest in Santa Cruz — half the cabinet is now female, but not necessarily feminist — this misdemeanour suggests that not everything is going to change under the new Plurinational order.

Patzi is nothing if not resourceful in adversity. He does a good line in repentance to a televised mass meeting at Patacamaya and, in return for its endorsement of his candidature, faces his community punishment of making 1,000 *adobes* like a man. There is surely going to be more of this sort of thing. The World Bank handbook on good governance may have registered the outer lineaments of customary law, but it is way behind the curve on multiple overlapping autonomies. Still, one does feel that a few world bankers might usefully be subjected to such a penalty (and the views from Icelandic voters in their referendum over repayment of debt to the Netherlands and UK suggest that they would probably approve too). Morales, however, knows that this is less *opéra bouffe* than a vital issue of party discipline. No amount of communitarian blandishment can cajole the *hermano presidente* into changing his mind.

13 February 2010
Per ardua ad astra

Bolivia's back in the news again. *The Guardian* reports that the Evo Morales government has created a Space Agency and plans in 2013 to launch a satellite, which will be called Túpaq Katari. Who says cosmology has had its day? *Pachakuti* has always been about space as well as time.

REFERENCES

Official documents and statistical materials

Note: all websites were accessed March–April 2010.

American Embassy, 'Survey of Communism in Bolivia', 29 March 1950, NA 724.001-3-3050.

Asamblea nacional de organizaciones indígenas, originarias, campesinas y de colonizadores de Bolivia, *Propuesta para la nueva Constitución Política del Estado* (Sucre: Asamblea Nacional, 2006).

Comisión Económica para América Latina/El Centro Latinoamericano y Caribeño de Demografía — División de Población, 'Bolivia: Estimaciones y proyecciones de la población de ambos sexos ... 1950–2050', *Boletín demográfico* no. 66 (July 2000).

Consejo Ciudadano para la Reforma Constitucional, *Anteproyecto de Ley de Necesidad de Reforma Constitucional* (La Paz: H. Cámara de Diputados, Programa de las Naciones Unidas para el Desarollo/PRONAGOB-BID, 2001).

Corte Nacional Electoral, *Boletín Estadístico* 3:7 (Nov. 2007), p. 7.

Dirección General de Estadística y Censos, *Censo demográfico 1950* (La Paz: 1955).

European Union Electoral Observation Mission, *Elecciones Generales y Referendos Autonómicos. Informe Final* (2009), at http://ec.europa.eu/external_relations/human_rights/election_observation/bolivia_2009/final_report_es.pdf

Grupo de Desarrollo Rural, *Bolivia: Anuario Estadístico del Sector Rural 1995–1996* (La Paz: 1996).

Instituto Boliviano de Comercio Exterior, 'Bolivia: principales productos exportados al mundo según volumen y valor gestiones 2008–2009 (Datos preliminares)', at www.ibce.org.bo/informacion-mercados/estad_bol.asp

Instituto Nacional de Estadística de Bolivia, *Anuario Estadístico 2000* (La Paz: 2001).

Instituto Nacional de Estadística de Bolivia, *Anuario Estadístico 2008* (La Paz: 2009).

Instituto Nacional de Estadística de Bolivia, cuadro 2.01.01 'Bolivia: población total proyectada, por años calendario y sexo, según edades simples, 2005–2010', at www.ine.gov.bo/indice/visualizador. aspx?ah=PC10410.HTM

Instituto Nacional de Estadística de Bolivia, cuadro 2.01.11, 'Bolivia: población por censos según departamento, área geográfica y sexo, censos de 1950-1976-1992-2001', at www.ine.gov.bo/indice/visualizador. aspx?ah=PC20111.HTM

Instituto Nacional de Estadística de Bolivia, cuadro 2.01.13, 'Bolivia: autoidentificación con pueblos originarios o indígenas de la población de 15 años o más de edad segun sexo, área geografica y grupo de edad, Censo 2001', at www.ine.gov.bo/indice/visualizador.aspx?ah=PC20112. HTM

Instituto Nacional de Estadística de Bolivia, cuadro 2.01.14, 'Bolivia: población de 6 años o más de edad por idioma o lengua que habla segun sexo, área geografica y grupo de edad, Censo 2001', at www.ine.gov.bo/ indice/visualizador.aspx?ah=PC20114.HTM

Instituto Nacional de Estadística de Bolivia, cuadro 2.01.18, 'Bolivia: indicadores Demográficos por Sexo según Quinquenios, 1950–2050', at www.ine.gov.bo/indice/visualizador.aspx?ah=PC20118.HTM

Instituto Nacional de Estadística de Bolivia, cuadro 2.02.01, 'Bolivia: Producto Interno Bruto por año según Departamento, 1988–2006', at www.ine.gov.bo/indice/visualizador.aspx?ah=PC0104010201.HTM

Instituto Nacional de Estadística de Bolivia, cuadro 3.02.01.04, 'Bolivia: nivel de instrucción alcanzado por la población de 19 años y más de edad, por sexo, según área geográfica, 2002–2006', at www.ine.gov.bo/indice/ visualizador.aspx?ah=PC3020104.HTM

Instituto Nacional de Estadística de Bolivia, cuadro 3.06.01.01, 'Bolivia: indicadores de pobreza moderada, según área geográfica, 1999–2007', at www.ine.gov.bo/indice/indice.aspx?d1=0406&d2=6

Instituto Nacional de Estadística de Bolivia, cuadro 3.06.01.03, 'Bolivia: indicadores de distribución del ingreso per cápita mensual [sic], 1999–2007', at www.ine.gov.bo/indice/indice.aspx?d1=0406&d2=6

Instituto Nacional de Estadística de Bolivia, cuadro 4.02.01.03, 'Bolivia: producto interno bruto a precios corrientes, según actividad económica', at www.ine.gov.bo/indice/indice.aspx?d1=0406&d2=6

Instituto Nacional de Estadística de Bolivia, 'Bolivia: indicadores demográficos', at www.ine.gov.bo/indice/indicadores.aspx

Instituto Nacional de Estadística de Bolivia, 'Bolivia: producción nacional de minerales por año', at www.ine.gov.bo/indice/general.aspx?codigo=40106

Instituto Nacional de Estadística de Bolivia, *Censo Nacional de Población y Vivienda 1992, Resultados Finales* (La Paz: 1993).

Instituto Nacional de Estadística de Bolivia, *Encuesta Nacional de Demografía y Salud 2003*, Cuadro 3.01.23, at www.ine.gov.bo/indice/visualizador. aspx?ah=PC30123.HTM

Instituto Nacional de Estadística de Bolivia, 'Resumen de Indicadores por mes publicados anteriormente — Indicadores Demográficos — Marzo 2010', at www.ine.gov.bo/indice/indicadores.aspx

Instituto Nacional de Estadística de Bolivia, 'Resumen de Indicadores por mes publicados anteriormente — Indicadores Sociales', at www.ine.gov. bo/indice/indicadores.aspx

Instituto Nacional de Estadística de Bolivia and El Centro Latinoamericano y Caribeño de Demografía, *Bolivia. Estimaciones y proyecciones de la población 1950–2050* (La Paz: 1995).

Ministerio de Desarrollo Económico, Secretaría Nacional de Agricultura y Ganadería, *El Agro Boliviano: Estadísticas agropecuarios 1990–1995* (La Paz: 1996).

Ministerio de la Presidencia, Unidad de Análisis de Políticas Sociales y Económicas, cuadro 1.5.2, 'Superficie cosechada de productos agrícolas: 1980–2009 (Estructura Porcentual)', at www.udape.gov.bo/

Ministerio de la Presidencia, Unidad de Análisis de Políticas Sociales y Económicas, cuadro 7.3.2, 'Indicadores de educación por nivel según departamento: 1997–2002', at www.udape.gov.bo/

Ministerio de la Presidencia, Unidad de Análisis de Políticas Sociales y Económicas, cuadros 7.9.1a and 7.9.1b, 'Indicadores alineados a las metas del milenio, 2001–2008', at www.udape.gov.bo/

Ministerio de la Presidencia, Unidad de Análisis de Políticas Sociales y Económicas, cuadro 7.9.4, 'Distribución de población por idioma que habla, declaración de auto-pertenencia a algún pueblo indígena, idioma en el que aprendió a hablar y condición étnico lingüística, según municipio', at www.udape.gov.bo/

Oficina Nacional de Inmigración y Propaganda Geográfica, *Censo general de la Población de la República de Bolivia...1900* 2nd edn. 2 vols. (Cochabamba: 1973).

Servicio de Impuesto Nacionales, cuadro 4.1, 'Recaudación por Departamento gestiones 1996–2007', at www.impuestos.gov. bo/Institucional/Cifras2009/4.1%20Recaudaci%C3%B3n%20 Hist%C3B3rica%202009.pdf

United Nations, *Demographic Yearbook, Historical supplement [1948/1997]* (New York: 2000), at http://unstats.un.org/unsd/demographic/products/ dyb/dybhist.htm

United Nations, Comisión Económica para América Latina, *Anuario estadístico de América Latina y el Caribe, 2009* (Santiago de Chile: CEPAL, 2010).

United Nations, Comisión Económica para América Latina, *Panorama Social de America Latina en 2009* (Santiago de Chile: CEPAL, 2009).

United Nations, Comisión Económica para América Latina, *Statistical Yearbook, 2001* (Santiago de Chile: CEPAL, 2002).

United Nations Development Programme, *Human Development Report 2009 Bolivia*, at http://hdrstats.undp.org/en/countries/country_fact_sheets/ ct_fs_BOL.html

World Health Organisation, *Maternal mortality in 2005: estimates developed by WHO, UNICEF, UNFPA, and the World Bank* (Paris: World Health Organisation, 2007).

World Health Organisation / UNICEF, *Review of National Immunization Coverage 1980–2008, Bolivia* (July, 2009), at www.who.int/ immunization_monitoring/data/bol.pdf

Secondary sources

Abercrombie, Thomas, *Pathways of Memory and Power: Ethnography and History among an Andean People* (Madison WI: University of Wisconsin Press, 1998).

Abrahamian, Ervand, '1953 coup in Iran', *Science and Society* 65:2 (Summer 2001).

Albó, Xavier, 'De MNRistas a Kataristas: campesinado, estado y partidos (1953–1983)', *Historia Boliviana* 5:1 (1985), pp. 87–127.

Albó, Xavier, *Pueblos indios en la política* (La Paz: Centro de Investigación y Promoción del Campesinado, 2002).

Albó, Xavier, 'El Alto, La Vorágine de Una Ciudad Única', *Journal of Latin American Anthropology*, 11:2 (2006), pp. 329–50.

Albó, Xavier, 'The "Long Memory" of Ethnicity in Bolivia and some Temporary Oscillations', in John Crabtree and Laurence Whitehead (eds.), *Unresolved Tensions: Bolivia Past and Present* (Pittsburgh: University of Pittsburgh Press, 2008), pp. 13–34.

Albó, Xavier, '25 años de democracia, participación campesino — indígena y cambios reales en la sociedad', in same author (ed.), *25 años construyendo Democracia* (La Paz: Vicepresidencia de la Republica, 2008), pp. 39–58.

Albó, Xavier and Victor Quispe, *Quiénes son indígenas en los gobiernos municipales* (La Paz: Centro de Investigación y Promoción del Campesinado/Plural, 2004).

Albó, Xavier and Franz X. Barrios Suvelza, *Por un Bolivia plurinacional e intercultural con autonomías* (La Paz: Programa de la Naciones Unidas para el Desarollo, 2006).

Albó, Xavier and Carlos Romero, *Autonomías indígenas en la realidad boliviana y su nueva constitución* (La Paz: Vicepresidencia del Estado Plurinacional de Bolivia, 2009).

Albro, Robert, 'The Indigenous in the Plural in Bolivian Oppositional Politics', *Bulletin of Latin American Research* 24:4 (2005), pp. 433–53.

Almaraz Paz, Sergio, *Réquiem para una república* (La Paz: Los amigos del libro, 1985).

Andersen, Lykke E., 'Migración Rural-Urbana en Bolivia: Ventajas y Desventajas', Documento de Trabajo no. 12/02 (La Paz: Instituto de Investigaciones Socio-Económicas, Universidad Católica Boliviana, 2002).

Andersen, Lykke E., 'How unequal is Bolivia really?', in *Monday Morning Development Newsletter from INESAD* (La Paz: Universidad Católica de Bolivia, 11 Feb. 2008), at www.inesad.edu.bo/mmblog/mm_20080211. htm

Andersen, Lykke E., 'Social Mobility in Bolivia is Finally Improving!', Development Research Working Paper Series no. 16/2009 (La Paz: INESAD/Universidad Católica de Bolivia, Dec. 2009).

Arbona, Juan M. and Benjamin Kohl, 'City profile: La Paz-El Alto', *Cities* 21:3 (2004), pp. 255–65.

Archondo, Rafael, 'Comunidad y divergencia de miradas en el Katarismo', *Revista Umbrales* (La Paz: CIDES-UMSA) 7 (July 2000), pp. 120–47.

Averanga Mollinedo, Asthenio, *Aspectos generales de la población Boliviana* 3rd. edn. (La Paz: 1998).

Bakhtin, Mikhail, *Rabelais and his World* (1941; Indiana: 1993).

Barié, Cletus Gregor, *Pueblos indígenas y derechos constitucionales en América Latina: un panorama* 2nd edn. (Mexico City and Quito: Instituto Interamericano Indigenista/Comisión Nacional para el Desarrollo de los Pueblos Indígenas/Editorial Abya-Yala, 2003).

Barragán, Rossana, 'Ciudadania y elecciones, convenciones y debates', in Rossana Barragán and José Luis Roca, *Regiones y poder constituyente en Bolivia: Una historia de pactos y disputas* (La Paz: Programa de la Naciones Unidas para el Desarrollo, 2005).

Barragán, Rossana, 'with the assistance of José Péres Cajías', 'Oppressed or Privileged Regions? Some Historical Reflections on the Use of State Resources', in John Crabtree and Laurence Whitehead (eds.), *Unresolved Tensions: Bolivia Past and Present* (Pittsburgh: University of Pittsburgh Press, 2008), pp. 83–103.

Barragán, Rossana and José Luis Roca, *Regiones y poder constituyente en Bolivia. Una historia de pactos y disputas* (La Paz: 2005).

Barrios Morón, Raúl, *Bolivia y Estados Unidos: Democracia, derechos humanos y narcotráfico (1980–1982)* (La Paz: FLACSO/HISBOL, 1989).

Barrios Suvelza, Franz Xavier, 'The Weakness of Excess: The Bolivian State in an Unbounded Democracy', in John Crabtree and Laurence Whitehead (eds.), *Unresolved Tensions: Bolivia Past and Present* (Pittsburgh: University of Pittsburgh Press, 2008), pp. 125–39.

Bello, Álvaro, *Etnicidad y ciudadanía en América Latina: La acción colectiva de los pueblos indígenas* (Santiago de Chile: Comisión Económica para América Latina, 2004).

Betancur, Ana Cecilia, *Diez temas de reforma constitucional* (Santa Cruz: CEJIS, 2004).

Blaiser, Cole, 'The United States and the Revolution', in James M. Malloy and Richard Thorn (eds.), *Beyond the Revolution: Bolivia since 1952* (Pittsburgh: University of Pittsburgh Press, 1971).

Boelens, Rutgerd, David Getches and Armando Guevara-Gil (eds.), *Out of the Mainstream; Water Rights, Politics and Identity* (London and Washington DC: Earthscan, 2010).

Bolívar, Simón, letter to Colombia, 3 Aug. 1826, in Vicente Lecuna and Harold Bierck (eds.), *Selected Writings of Bolívar* 2 vols. (New York: 1951), vol. 2, p. 627.

Bouysse-Cassagne, Thérèse, Olivia Harris, Tristan Platt and V. Cereceda, *Tres reflexiones sobre el pensamiento andino* (La Paz: Hisbol, 1987).

Burga, Manuel, *Nacimiento de una utopia. Muerte y resurrección de los Incas* (Lima: 1988).

Calderón G., Fernando, 'Oportunidad histórica: cambio politico y Nuevo orden sociocultural' *Nueva Sociedad* 209 (Mayo–Junio 2007).

Canessa, Andrew, 'Forgetting the Revolution and Remembering the War: Memory and Violence in Highland Bolivia', *History Workshop Journal* 68 (Autumn 2009), pp.173–98.

Cárdenas, Víctor Hugo, 'La lucha de un pueblo', in Xavier Albó (ed.) *Raíces de América: El mundo Aymara* (Madrid: Alianza América/UNESCO, 1988).

Cariaga, Juan, *Estabilización y Desarrollo. Importantes Lecciones del Programa Económico de Bolivia* (La Paz: Los Amigos del Libro, 1996).

Chávez, Walter., 'La persecusión de Rocha. ¿Favoreció o perjudicó al MAS?', *El Juguete Rabioso* 21 July 2002.

Chong, Alberto and Florencio López-de-Silanes (eds.), *Privatization in Latin America: Myths and Reality* (Washington DC: World Bank, 2005).

Chumacero R., Juan Pablo (ed.), *Reconfigurando territorios; reforma agraria, control territorial y gobiernos indígenas en Bolivia* (La Paz: Fundación Tierra, 2010).

Coatsworth, John, 'Inequality, Institutions and Economic Growth in Latin America', *Journal of Latin American Studies* 40:3 (Aug. 2008), pp. 545–69.

Contreras, Alex, *La marcha histórica* (Cochabamba: CEDIB, 1994).

Contreras, Manuel, 'Reformas y desafiós de la Educación', in Fernando Campero Prudencio (ed.), *Bolivia en el siglo XX. La formación de la Bolivia Contemporánea* (La Paz: 1999).

Contreras, Manuel, 'A comparative perspective of education reforms in Bolivia: 1950–2000', in Merilee Grindle and Pilar Domingo (eds.), *Proclaiming Revolution: Bolivia in Comparative Perspective* (London and Cambridge MA: Institute of Latin American Studies/David Rockefeller Center for Latin American Studies, 2003), pp.259–86.

Crabtree, John, *Patterns of Protest: Politics and Social Movements in Bolivia* (London: Latin America Bureau, 2005).

Crabtree, John and Laurence Whitehead (eds.), *Unresolved Tensions: Bolivia Past and Present* (Pittsburgh: University of Pittsburgh Press, 2008).

Crandon-Malamud, Libbet, *From the Fat of our Souls: Social Change, Political Process, and Medical Pluralism in Bolivia* (Berkeley: University of California Press, 1991).

Dalton, R. and M. Wattenberg (eds.), *Parties without Partisans. Political change in advanced industrial democracies* (Oxford: Oxford University Press, 2000).

Desmond, Adrian and James Moore, *Darwin's Sacred Cause: Race, Slavery and the Quest for Human Origins* (London: Allen Lane, 2009).

Diamond, Larry, *Developing Democracy. Towards Consolidation* (Baltimore: John Hopkins University Press, 1999).

Dix, Robert, 'Democratisation and the Institutionalisation of Latin American Political Parties', *Comparative Political Studies*, 24:4 (1992), 488–511.

Domingo, Pilar, 'Democracy and New Social Forces in Bolivia', *Social Forces* 83:4 (June 2005), pp. 1,727–45.

Domingo, Pilar (ed.), *Bolivia: fin de un ciclo y nuevas perspectivas políticas (1993–2003)* (Barcelona: Bellaterra, 2006).

Domingo, Pilar, 'Evo Morales, the MAS and a Revolution in the Making', in Jean Grugel and Pía Riggiorozzi (eds.), *Governance after Neoliberalism in Latin America* (New York: Palgrave Macmillan, 2009).

Dunkerley, James, *Rebellion in the Veins. Political Struggle in Bolivia, 1952–1982* (London: Verso, 1984).

Dunkerley, James, 'The Origins of the Bolivian Revolution in the Twentieth Century: Some Reflections', in Merilee Grindle and Pilar Domingo (eds.), *Proclaiming Revolution: Bolivia in Comparative Perspective* (London and Cambridge MA: Institute of Latin American Studie /David Rockefeller Center for Latin American Studies, 2003), pp. 135–63.

Dunkerley, James, *Bolivia: Revolution and the Power of History in the Present* (London: Institute for the Study of the Americas, 2007).

Dunkerley, James, 'Evo Morales, Alvaro García Linera and the Third Bolivian Revolution', in same author, *Bolivia: Revolution and the Power of History in the Present* (London: Institute for the Study of the Americas, 2007), pp. 1–56.

Elwood, William N., *Rhetoric in the War on Drugs. The Triumphs and Tragedies of Public Relations* (Westport CT: Praeger, 1994).

Escobar, Filemón, *De la Revolución al Pachakuti: el aprendizaje de respeto recíproco entre blancos e indianos* (La Paz: Garza Azul, 2008).

Espasandín López, Jesús and Pablo Iglesias Turrión (eds.), *Bolivia en movimiento: Acción colectiva y poder politico* (Madrid: El Viejo Topo, 2007).

Fifer, Valerie, *Bolivia: Land, Location and Politics* (Cambridge: Cambridge University Press, 1972).

Figueroa Cárdenas, Milenka B., '¿Son sensibles los retornos a la educación según la clasificación étnico lingüística de la población que se utilice?', Unidad de Análisis de Políticas Sociales y Económicas, *Revista de Análisis Económico*, 22 (2007).

Foweraker, Joe, Todd Landman and Neil Harvey, *Governing Latin America* (Oxford: Polity, 2003).

Fundación Milenio, *Proyecto de reforma a la Constitución Política del Estado 1991–1992* (La Paz: Fundación Milenio, 1997).

Gamarra, Eduardo, *Entre la coca y la democracia: La cooperación entre Estados Unidos y Bolivia en la lucha contra el narcotráfico* (La Paz : Ildis, 1993).

Gamarra, Eduardo and J. Malloy, 'The patrimonial dynamics of party politics in Bolivia', in S. S. Mainwaring (ed.), *Building Democratic Institutions: Party Systems in Latin America* (Stanford: Stanford University Press, 1995).

García Linera, Álvaro, 'Como lograr la hegemonía indígena-popular en la constituyente?', *Jugete Rabioso*, 12 Dec. 2004, pp. 8–9.

García Linera, Álvaro, R. Gutiérrez, R. Prada and L. Tapia. *El retorno de la Bolivia Plebeya* (La Paz: La muela del diablo, 2000).

Godoy, Ricardo, Mario de Franco and Ruben G. Echeverria, 'A Brief History of Agricultural Research in Bolivia: Potatoes, Maize, Soybeans, and Wheat

Compared', Development Discussion Paper no. 460 (Cambridge MA: Harvard Institute for International Development, July 1993).

Gootenberg, Paul, *Andean Cocaine: the making of a global drug* (Chapel Hill: University of North Carolina Press, 2009).

Gotkowitz, Laura, *A Revolution for our Rights: Indigenous Struggles for Land and Justice in Bolivia, 1880–1952* (Durham NC: Duke University Press, 2007).

Gramsci, A., 'Some aspects of the southern question', in A. Gramsci (Q. Hoare, trans.), *Selections from political writings (1921–1926)* (London: Lawrence and Wishart, 1978).

Grandin, Greg, *The Blood of Guatemala. A History of Race and Nation* (Durham NC: Duke University Press, 2000).

Granier, Jorge Gumucio, *Estados Unidos y el mar boliviano* (Bolivia: Plural, 2005).

Gray Molina, George, 'Popular Participation, Social Service Delivery and Poverty Reduction 1994–2000', paper presented at conference on Citizen Participation in the Context of Fiscal Decentralization: Best Practices in Municipal Administration, Tokyo and Kobe, Japan, 2–6 Sept. 2002.

Gray Molina, George, 'The Offspring of 1952: Poverty, Exclusion and the Promise of Popular Participation', in Merilee Grindle and Pilar Domingo (eds.), *Proclaiming Revolution: Bolivia in Comparative Perspective* (London and Cambridge MA: Institute of Latin American Studie /David Rockefeller Center for Latin American Studies, 2003), pp. 345–63.

Gray Molina, George, (ed.), *El Estado del estado en Bolivia. Informe Nacional sobre Desarrollo Humano 2007* (La Paz: Programa de la Naciones Unidas para el Desarollo, 2007).

Gray Molina, George, 'Bolivia's Long and Winding Road', *Inter-American Dialogue* Working Paper, July 2008.

Gray Molina, George, 'State-Society Relations in Bolivia: The Strength of Weakness', in John Crabtree and Laurence Whitehead (eds.), *Unresolved Tensions: Bolivia Past and Present* (Pittsburgh: University of Pittsburgh Press, 2008), pp. 109–24.

Gray Molina, George, 'Ethnic Politics in Bolivia: "Harmony of Inequalities", 1900–2000', at http://hdr.undp.org/docs/events/global_forum/2005/papers/George_Gray_Molina.pdf

Grindle, Merilee S., *Audacious Reforms: Institutional Invention and Democracy in Latin America* (Baltimore: Johns Hopkins University Press, 2000).

Grindle, Merilee and Pilar Domingo (eds.), *Proclaiming Revolution: Bolivia in Comparative Perspective* (London and Cambridge MA: Institute of Latin American Studies/David Rockefeller Center for Latin American Studies, 2003).

Grebe López, Horst, Fernando Mayorga, Fernando Aguirre Bastos, Franz Xavier Barrios Suvelza, Roger Cortéz Hurtado, Jorge Asbún, María Teresa Zegada and Ignacio Mendoza Pizarro, *Contrapuntos al debate constituyente* (La Paz: Instituto Prisma/Plural, 2007).

Guillermoprieto, Alma, 'A New Bolivia?', *New York Review of Books*, 10 Aug. 2006.

Gustafson, Bret, 'Spectacles of Autonomy and Crisis: Or, What Bulls and Beauty Queens Have to do With Regionalism in Eastern Bolivia', *Journal of Latin American Anthropology* 11:2 (2006), pp. 351–79.

Gutiérrez, Raquel, *Los Ritmos del Pachakuti. Movilización y Levantamiento Indígena-Popular en Bolivia (2000–2005)* (La Paz: 2008).

Hale, Charles, 'Does Multiculturalism Menace? Governance, Cultural Rights and the Politics of Identity in Guatemala', *Journal of Latin American Studies* 34:3 (Aug. 2002), pp. 485–524.

Hale, Charles, 'Rethinking Indigenous Politics in the Era of the *Indio Permitido*', *NACLA Report on the Americas* 38:2 (2004), pp.16–21.

Harris, Olivia, '"The Coming of the White People". Reflections on the Mythologisation of History in Latin America', *Bulletin of Latin American Research*, 14:1 (Jan. 1995), pp. 9–24.

Harten, Sven, 'Social Movements and Democracy in Bolivia. A discursive interpretation' *Cortona Colloquium, 19–22 October 2006* (Cortona, Italy: Feltrinelli Foundation, 2006).

Harten, Sven, *The Rise of Evo Morales and the MAS*, forthcoming (London: Zed, 2010).

Healy, Kevin, 'Political Ascent of Bolivia's Peasant Coca Leaf Producers', *Journal of Interamerican Studies and World Affairs*, 33:1 (Spring, 1991), pp. 88–9.

Hernández Dips, M., 'Elecciones Generales in Bolivia: Evolución negativa de representación', in F. Mayorga, M. Hernández and M. Peralta (eds.), *Foro de Analisis Político Nr.7: Elecciones Generales en Bolivia: Nuevos*

Escenarios, Nuevos Actores y Viejos Problemas (La Paz: Asociación Boliviana de Ciencias Políticas y Konrad Adenauer Stiftung, 2005).

Hill, Christopher, *The World Turned Upside Down. Radical Ideas during the English Revolution* (Harmondsworth: Penguin, 1972).

Hogan, Margaret C., Kyle J. Foreman, Mohsen Naghavi, Stephanie Y. Ahn, Mengru Wang, Susanna M. Makela, Alan D. Lopez, Rafael Lozano and Christopher J. L. Murray, 'Maternal mortality for 181 countries, 1980–2008: a systematic analysis of progress towards Millennium Development Goal', *The Lancet* April 12, 2010.

Howarth, D., *Discourse* (Buckingham and Philadelphia: Open University Press, 2000).

Howarth, D., A.J. Norval and Y. Stavrakakis (eds.), *Discourse Theory and Political Analysis. Identities, hegemonies and social change* (Manchester and New York: Manchester University Press, 2000).

Hudson, Rex A. and Dennis M. Hanratty (eds.), *Bolivia: A Country Study* (Washington DC: GPO for the Library of Congress, 1989).

Huntington, Samuel, *Political Order in Changing Societies* (New Haven: Yale University Press, 1968).

Hutchings, Kimberly, *Time and World Politics: Thinking the Present* (Manchester: Manchester University Press, 2008).

Hutchings, Kimberly, 'Dream or Nightmare? Thinking the Future of World Politics', in Gideon Baker and Jens Bartelson (eds.), *The Future of Political Community* (Abingdon: Routledge, 2009), ch. 1.

Hylton, Forrest, Félix Patzi, Sergio Serulnikov and Sinclair Thomson, *Ya es otro tiempo el presente. Cuatro momentos de insurgencia indígena* (La Paz: Muela del Diablo, 2003).

Hylton, Forrest and Sinclair Thomson *Revolutionary Horizons. Past and Present in Bolivian Politics*, (London and New York: Verso, 2007).

John, S. Sándor, *Bolivia's Radical Tradition: Permanent Revolution in the Andes* (Tucson: University of Arizona Press, 2009).

Kelley, Jonathan and Herbert S. Klein, *Revolution and the Rebirth of Inequality. A Theory Applied to the National Revolution of Bolivia* (Berkeley: University of California Press, 1981).

Klein, Herbert, *A Concise History of Bolivia* (New York: Cambridge University Press, 2003).

Koblinsky, Marjorie A. (ed.), *Reducing Maternal Mortality: Learning from Bolivia, China, Egypt, Honduras, Indonesia, Jamaica, and Zimbabwe* (Washington: World Bank, 2003).

Kohl, Benjamin and Linda Farthing, *Impasse in Bolivia: Neoliberal Hegemony and Popular Resistance* (London: Zed, 2006).

Laclau, Ernesto, 'Populism: What's in a Name', in Francisco Panizza (ed.), *Populism and the Mirror of Democracy* (London: Verso, 2005), pp. 32–49.

Laclau, Ernesto, *On Populist Reason* (London, Verso, 2005).

Laclau, Ernesto and Chantal Mouffe, *Hegemony and Socialist Strategy* (London, Verso, 1985).

Lara, Jesús, *La literatura de los Quechuas* (La Paz: 1985).

Larson, Brooke, *Trials of Nation Making. Liberalism, Race, and Ethnicity in the Andes, 1810–1910* (Cambridge: Cambridge University Press, 2004).

Larson, Brooke and Olivia Harris (eds.) *Ethnicity, Markets, and Migration in the Andes. At the Crossroads of History and Anthropology* (Durham NC: Duke University Press, 1995).

Laserna, Roberto, Eduardo Córdova, Luis Tapia, Fernando Prado, Gonzalo Vargas, Sarela Paz and Álvaro García Linera, *Poder y cambio en Bolivia 2003–2007* (La Paz: Embajada del Reino de los Países Bajos/PIEB, 2009).

Latham, Michael E., *Modernization as Ideology: American Social Science and "Nation Building" in the Kennedy era* (Chapel Hill: University of North Carolina Press, 2000).

Lavaud, Jean-Pierre, *El embrollo boliviano. Turbulencias sociales y desplazamientos políticos (1952–1982)* (La Paz : IEA-CESU-HISBOL,1988).

Layton, Heather Marie and Harry Anthony Patrinos, 'Estimating the Number of Indigenous Peoples in Latin America', in Gilette Hall and Harry Anthony Patrinos (eds.), *Indigenous Peoples, Poverty and Development in Latin America* (Houndmills and New York: Palgrave MacMillan, 2006).

Lazar, Sian, *El Alto, rebel city: self and citizenship in Andean Bolivia* (Durham NC: Duke University Press, 2008).

Lazarte Rojas, Jorge, *Entre los espectros del pasado y las incertidumbres del futuro* (La Paz: Plural, 2005).

Lehman, Kenneth, *Bolivia and the United States: A Limited Partnership* (Athens: University of Georgia Press, 1999).

Lehman, Kenneth, 'Braked but not Broken: The United States and Revolutionaries in Mexico and Bolivia', in Merilee S. Grindle and Pilar Domingo (eds.), *Proclaiming Revolution. Bolivia in Comparative Perspective* (London and Cambridge MA: David Rockefeller Center for Latin American Studies and Institute of Latin American Studies, 2003), pp. 91–113.

Liendo, Roxana, *Participación Popular y el movimiento campesino Aymara* (La Paz: CIPCE/AIPE/Fundación Tierra, 2009).

Lucero, José Antonio, *Struggles of Voice: The Politics of Indigenous Representation in the Andes* (Pittsburgh: University of Pittsburgh Press, 2008).

Luxemburg, Rosa, *The Russian Revolution* (New York: Workers Age Publishers, 1940).

MacCormack, Sabine, *On the Wings of Time. Rome, the Incas, Spain, and Peru* (Princeton: Princeton University Press, 2007).

MacDorman, Marian F. and T. J. Mathews, *Behind International Rankings of Infant Mortality: How the United States Compares with Europe* (Hyattsville MD: Centers for Disease Control and Prevention National Center for Health Statistics, DATA Brief, no. 23, Nov. 2009).

Madrid, Raúl L., 'Indigenous voters and party system fragmentation in Latin America', *Electoral Studies* 24 (2005), pp. 689–707.

Mainwaring, Scott and Timothy Scully, *Building Democratic Institutions. Party Systems in Latin America* (Stanford: Stanford University Press, 1995).

Mair, P., *Party System Change. Approaches and Interpretations* (Oxford: Clarendon Press, 1997).

Malá, Sarká, 'El movimiento "cocaleros" en Bolivia durante los años 80 y 90: sus causas y su desarrollo', *Revista Esbozos* (UFSC, Santa Catarina, Brazil) 20, pp. 101–17.

Malamud, Carlos, 'Lugares comunes latinoamericanos: el principe de Tiahuanacu', *Ojos de Papel*, 1 Feb. 2010.

Malamud Goti, Jaime, *Smoke and Mirrors: The Paradox of the Drug Wars* (Boulder CO: Westview Press, 1992).

Mansilla, H.C.F., *El carácter conservador de la nación boliviana* (Santa Cruz: El País, 2004).

Martí i Puig, Salvador (ed.), *Pueblos indígenas y política en América Latina: El reconocimiento de sus derechos y el impacto de sus demandas a inicios del siglo XXI* (Barcelona: Fundació CIDOB, 2007).

Martínez, Carmen (ed.), *Repensando los movimientos indígenas* (Quito: FLACSO, sede Ecuador/Ministerio de Cultura del Ecuador, 2009).

Martínez, Sebastián, 'Pensions, Poverty and Household Investments in Bolivia', unpublished manuscript, University of California, Berkeley, Department of Economics, 2004, at http://emlab.berkeley.edu/users/webfac/bardhan/e271_f04/martinez.pdf

Marx, Karl and Friedrich Engels, *Selected Works of Karl Marx and Frederick Engels* (London: Lawrence and Wishart, 1968).

Marx, Karl and Friedrich Engels, *On Ireland. Karl Marx and Friedrich Engels* (London: Lawrence and Wishart, 1971).

McPherson, Alan, *Yankee No! Anti-Americanism in U.S.-Latin American Relations* (Cambridge MA: Harvard University Press, 2006).

Medeiros, Carmen, 'Civilizing the Popular? The Law of Popular Participation and the Design of a New Civil Society in 1990s Bolivia', *Critique of Anthropology* 21:4 (2001), pp. 401–25.

Mercado, Alejandro F. and Jorge G. M. Leitón-Quiroga, 'The Dynamics of Poverty in Bolivia', Documento de Trabajo no. 02/09 (La Paz: IISEC/UCB, 2009).

Miranda, Carlos, 'Gas and its Importance to the Bolivian Economy', in John Crabtree and Laurence Whitehead (eds.), *Unresolved Tensions: Bolivia Past and Present* (Pittsburgh: University of Pittsburgh Press, 2008), pp. 177–93.

Molina, Fernando, *Bajo el signo del cambio. Análisis de tres procesos electorales (2002, 2005 y 2006)* (La Paz: Eureka, 2006).

Molina B., Ramiro and Xavier Albó, *Gama étnica y lingüística de la población boliviana* (La Paz: Programa de la Naciones Unidas para el Desarrollo, 2006).

Morales, Evo, *La revolución democrática y cultural. Diez discursos de Evo* (La Paz: Malatesta, Movimiento al Socialismo, 2006).

Morales, Waltraud Queiser, 'Militarising the Drug War in Bolivia', *Third World Quarterly* 12:2 (1992).

Morales, Waltraud Queiser, *A Brief History of Bolivia* (New York: Checkmark Books, 2004).

Movimiento al Socialismo, Instrumento Político por la Soberania de los Pueblos, *Refundar Bolivia para vivir bien: propuesta para la Asamblea Constituyente* (La Paz: MAS/IPSP, 2006).

Müller, Katarina, 'Contested universalism: from Bonosol to Renta Dignidad in Bolivia', *International Journal of Social Welfare* 18 (2009) pp. 163–72.

Muñoz, Jorge A. and Isabel Lavadenz, 'Reforming the Agrarian Reform in Bolivia', Development Discussion Paper no. 589 (Cambridge MA: Harvard Institute for International Development, Harvard University, June 1997).

Muñoz-Pogossian, Betilde, *Electoral Rules and the Transformation of Bolivian Politics: The Rise of Evo Morales* (New York: Palgrave Macmillan, 2008).

Nicolaus, Martin, 'Foreword' to Karl Marx, *Grundrisse: Foundations of the Critique of Political Economy* (Harmondworth: Penguin, 1973).

Panebianco, Angelo, *Political Parties: Organization and Power* (Cambridge: Cambridge University Press, 1988).

Piccato, Pablo, *Public Sphere in Latin America: A map of the historiography*, ms. New York.

Pinto, Darwin and Roberto Nava, *Un tal Evo: biografía no-autorizada* (Santa Cruz: El País, 2007).

Pizzigoni, Caterina, *Testaments of Toluca* (Stanford: Stanford University Press, 2007).

Platt, Tristan, Thérese Bouysse-Cassagne and Olivia Harris, *Qaraqara-Charka. Mallku, Inka y Rey en la provincia de Charcas (siglos xv–xvii)* (La Paz: Plural/Fundación Cultural del Banco Central de Bolivia, 2006).

Postero, Nancy, *Now we are citizens: indigenous politics in postmulticultural Bolivia* (Stanford: Stanford University Press, 2007).

Prada Alcoreza, Raúl, *Análisis sociodemográico Poblaciones nativas* (La Paz: Instituto Nacional de Estadística de Bolivia, 1997).

Prada Alcoreza, Raúl, 'Multitud y contrapoder. Estudios del presente: movimientos sociales contemporáneos', in Raquel Gutiérrez, Álvaro

García Linera, Raúl *Prada* and Luis Tapia (eds.), *Democratizaciones Plebeyas* (La Paz: Muela del Diablo, 2002).

Przeworski, A., *Democracy and the Market. Political and Economic Reforms in Eastern Europe and Latin America* (Cambridge: Cambridge University Press, 1993).

Qayum, Seemin, *Creole Imaginings: Race, Space and Gender in the Making of Republican Bolivia*, PhD, Goldsmiths College, University of London, 2002.

Randall, Vicky and Lars Svåsand, 'Party Institutionalization in New Democracies' *Party Politics* 8:1 (2002), pp. 5–29.

Roca, José Luis, *Bolivia, después de la capitalización: una crítica al Gonismo y sus 'reformas'* (La Paz: Plural, 2000).

Roca, José Luis, *Ni con Lima ni con Buenos Aires. La formación de un estado nacional en Charcas* (La Paz: Plural, 2007).

Roca, José Luis, 'Regionalism Revisited', in John Crabtree and Laurence Whitehead (eds.), *Unresolved Tensions: Bolivia Past and Present* (Pittsburgh: University of Pittsburgh Press, 2008), pp. 65–82.

Rodrik, Dani, 'Goodbye Washington Consensus, Hello Washington Confusion? A Review of the World Bank's *Economic Growth in the 1990s: Learning from a Decade of Reform*', *Journal of Economic Literature* 44 (Dec. 2006), pp. 969–83.

Romero Bonifaz, Carlos, *El proceso constituyente boliviano: El hito de la cuarta marcha de tierras bajas* (Santa Cruz de la Sierra: CEJIS, 2005).

Sachs, Jeffrey, 'The Bolivian Hyperinflation and Stabilization', *American Economic Review* 77:2 (1987) pp. 279–83.

Sachs, Jeffrey D., *The End of Poverty. Economic Possibilities of Our Time* (Harmondsworth: Penguin, 2005).

Sandoval, Godofredo, *et. al.*, *Organizaciones de Base y Desarrollo Local en Bolivia: Estudio de los municipios de Tiahuanaco, Mizque, Villa Serrano y Charagua* (Washington DC: World Bank, Local Level Institutions, Working Paper No. 4, 1998).

Sartori, Giovanni, *Parties and party systems: a framework for analysis* (Cambridge and New York: Cambridge University Press, 1976).

Schultz, Jim and Melissa Crane Draper (eds.), *Dignity and Defiance: Stories from Bolivia's Challenge to Globalisation* (Pontypool: Merlin Press, 2008).

Seemann, Miriam, 'The Bolivian Decentralization Process and the Role of Municipal Associations', Discussion Paper no. 271, Hamburgisches Welt-Wirtschafts-Archiv (HWWA), Hamburg Institute of International Economics, 2004.

Selser, Gregorio, *El cuartelazo de los coca dólares* (Mexico City: Editorial Mex Sur, 1982).

Sivak, Martín, *El dictador elegido. Biografía no autorizada de Hugo Banzer Suárez* (La Paz: Plural, 2001).

Sivak, Martín, *Santa Cruz: Una tesis; El conflicto regional en Bolivia (2003– 2006)* (La Paz: Plural, 2007).

Sivak, Martín, *Jefazo: Retrato íntimo de Evo Morales* (Buenos Aires: Sudamericana, 2008).

Sivak, Martín, *Evo Morales. The extraordinary rise of the first indigenous president of Bolivia* (New York: Palgrave, 2010).

Soria, Carlos, *El Che en Bolivia* 4 vols. (La Paz: CEDOIN, 1996).

Spedding, Alison, *Kawsachun coca: Economía campesina cocalera en los Yungas y el Chapare* (La Paz: PIEB, 2005).

Stavenhagen, Rodolfo, 'Indigenous Peoples and the State in Latin America: An Ongoing Debate', in Rachel Sieder (ed.), *Multiculturalism in Latin America: Indigenous Rights, Diversity and Democracy* (Houndmills and New York: Palgrave Macmillan, 2002).

Stefanoni, Pablo and Hervé do Alto, *Evo Morales, de la coca al palacio. Una oportunidad para la izquierda indígena* (La Paz: Malatesta, 2006).

Suárez, Rubém and Claudia Pescetto, 'Sistemas de protección social para el adulto mayor en América Latina y el Caribe', *Revista Panamericana de Salud Publica* 17:5–6 (2005).

Tapia, Luis, 'Constitution and Constitutional Reform in Bolivia', in John Crabtree and Laurence Whitehead (eds.), *Unresolved Tensions: Bolivia Past and Present* (Pittsburgh: University of Pittsburgh Press, 2008), pp.160–71.

Ticona Alejo, Esteban, *Organización y liderazgo aymara, La experiencia indígena en la politica boliviana 1979–1996* (La Paz: AGRUCO y Universidad de la Cordillera, 2000).

Ticona, Esteban, Gonzalo Rojas and Xavier Albó, *Votos y wiphalas* (La Paz: Fundación Milenio/CIPCA, 1995).

T'inkazos, 'Dossier debate: La media luna: autonomía regional y comités cívicos', *T'inkazos* 16 (2004), pp. 9–64.

Toranzo Roca, Carlos, *Rostros de la democracia: una mirada mestiza* (La Paz: Plural, 2006).

Toranzo Roca, Carlos, 'Let the Mestizos Stand Up and Be Counted', in John Crabtree and Laurence Whitehead (eds.), *Unresolved Tensions: Bolivia Past and Present* (Pittsburgh: University of Pittsburgh Press, 2008), pp. 35–50.

Urenda Díaz, Juan Carlos, *El sueño imperturbable: El proceso asutonómico boliviano* (Santa Cruz de la Sierra: El País, 2009).

Urquiola, Miguel, 'Educación primaria universal', in *Remontando la pobreza. Ocho cimas a la vez* (La Paz: EDOBOL, 2000).

Urquiola, Miguel, *et. al*, *Geography and Development in Bolivia: Migration, Urban and Industrial Concentration, Welfare, and Convergence: 1950–1992* (La Paz: Universidad Católica Bolivia, 1999).

Valencia R., Horacio, *Tendencias del empleo agropecuario y no agropecuario en Bolivia* (La Paz: IDRC-CRDI, Universidad Católica Boliviana, 2009).

Valle de Siles, María Eugenia del, *Testimonios del Cerco de La Paz: el campo contra la ciudad, 1781* (La Paz: Última Hora, 1980).

Van Cott, Donna Lee, *The Friendly Liquidation of the Past: The Politics of Diversity in Latin America* (Pittsburgh: University of Pittsburgh Press, 2000).

Van Cott, Donna Lee, *From Movements to Parties in Latin America: The Evolution of Ethnic Politics* (New York: Cambridge University Press, 2005).

Van Cott, Donna Lee, *Radical Democracy in the Andes* (Cambridge: Cambridge University Press, 2008).

Wachtel, Nathan, *Vision of the Vanquished. The Spanish Conquest of Peru through Indian Eyes* (Hassocks: Harvester Press, 1977).

Ware, A., *Political Parties and Party Systems* (Oxford: Oxford University Press, 1996).

Westad, Odd Arne, *The Global Cold War* (Cambridge: Cambridge University Press, 2005).

Whitehead, Laurence, 'The Bolivian National Revolution: A Comparison', in Merilee Grindle and Pilar Domingo (eds.), *Proclaiming Revolution: Bolivia in Comparative Perspective* (London and Cambridge MA: Institute of Latin American Studies/David Rockefeller Center for Latin American Studies, 2003), pp. 25–53.

Williamson, John, 'What Washington Means by Policy Reform', in same author (ed.), *Latin American Adjustment: How Much has Happened?* (Washington: Institute for International Economics, 1990).

Yashar, Deborah J., *Contesting Citizenship in Latin America: The Rise of Indigenous Movements and the Postliberal Challenge* (New York: Cambridge University Press, 2005).

Zavaleta Mercado, René, 'Las masas en noviembre', in same author (ed.), *Bolivia, hoy* (Mexico City: Siglo Veintiuno, 1983).

Zavaleta Mercado, René, *El poder dual* (La Paz: Los amigos del libro, 1987).

Zavaleta Mercado, René, *La formación de la conciencia nacional* (1967; Cochabamba: Los Amigos del Libro, 1990).

Zavaleta Mercado, René, *50 años de historia de Bolivia* (La Paz : Los amigos del libro, 1998).

Zegada, Maria Teresa, Yuri Tórrez and Gloria Cámara, *Movimientos sociales en tiempos de poder: articulaciones y campos de conflicto en el gobierno del MAS* (La Paz: Centro Cuarto Intermedio/Plural, 2008).

INDEX

INSTITUTE FOR THE STUDY OF THE AMERICAS

The Institute for the Study of the Americas (ISA) promotes, coordinates and provides a focus for research and postgraduate teaching on the Americas – Canada, the USA, Latin America and the Caribbean – in the University of London.

The Institute was officially established in August 2004 as a result of a merger between the Institute of Latin American Studies and the Institute of United States Studies, both of which were formed in 1965.

The Institute publishes in the disciplines of history, politics, economics, sociology, anthropology, geography and environment, development, culture and literature, and on the countries and regions of Latin America, the United States, Canada and the Caribbean.

ISA runs an active programme of events – conferences, seminars, lectures and workshops – in order to facilitate national research on the Americas in the humanities and social sciences. It also offers a range of taught master's and research degrees, allowing wide-ranging multi-disciplinary, multi-country study or a focus on disciplines such as politics or globalisation and development for specific countries or regions.

Full details about the Institute's publications, events, postgraduate courses and other activities are available on the web at www.americas.sas.ac.uk.

Institute for the Study of the Americas
School of Advanced Study, University of London
Senate House, Malet Street, London WC1E 7HU

Tel 020 7862 8870, Fax 020 7862 8886,
americas@sas.ac.uk
www.americas.sas.ac.uk

Recent and forthcoming titles in the ISA series:

Joaquim Nabuco, British Abolitionists and the End of Slavery in Brazil: Correspondence 1880–1905 (2009)
edited with an introduction by Leslie Bethell & José Murilo de Carvalho

Contesting Clio's Craft: New Directions and Debates in Canadian History (2009)
edited by Christopher Dummitt & Michael Dawson

World Crisis Effects on Social Security in Latin America and the Caribbean: Lessons and Policies (2010)
Carmelo Meso-Lago

Quebec and the Heritage of Franco-America (2010)
edited by Iwan Morgan and Philip Davies

Caamaño in London: The Exile of a Latin American Revolutionary (forthcoming)
edited by Fred Halliday

Fractured Politics, Peruvian Democracy Past and Present (forthcoming)
edited by John Crabtree